TRANSFORMATIONAL COACHING:

Bridge Building that Impacts, Connects, and Advances the Ministry and the Marketplace

Dr. Joseph Umidi
Contributor and Senior Editor

TRANSFORMATIONAL COACHING:
Bridge Building that Impacts, Connects,
and Advances the Ministry and the Marketplace

Contributor and Senior Editor: Dr. Joseph Umidi

Author may be contacted at:
P.O. Box 64394
Virginia Beach, VA 23467-4394
www.transformationalCoaching.com
Accelerated Coach Training Website, see
www.ACTProgram.net
In the USA call 888-TLC-2234

Printed in the United States of America

ISBN 1-597811-63-7

www.xulonpress.com

Table of Contents

Section One:
Foundations of Transformational Coaching

Introduction

Formal and informal teaching and training methods are the standardized manner in which we look for information. There is great value in the formal lecture and educational processes that most of us have accessed all of our lives. There is also very helpful and practical information in the numerous informal seminars and workshops available all over the world, including all of the subsidiary products that go with these events. None of us can imagine doing without the formal or informal training methods, and many of us have resigned ourselves to the reality that we will spend a lot of money on both so that we cover the bases that neither can on its own.

However there is one glaring weakness that goes to the core of both of these popular methods. It is simply that in neither of these delivery systems do the speakers, teachers, or presenters need to reveal anything more of themselves than their material dictates. Anyone can become a master presenter or teacher while possessing an elementary level character of heart. It won't make any difference if the presenter is emotionally locked up, spiritually plateaued, morally bankrupt, or relationally dysfunctional; the material and the way it is presented make all the difference. That is the nature of the information game and anyone can play it, even get tenured in it if we are good enough.

Beyond information, when it comes to character formation or reformation, then we have another problem. Both of these concepts deal with the subterranean rivers that run deep in all of us, a place where platform power-point presentations ignore. This is the land of character, core values, heart, and even perspectives that information transactions miss or only skim the surface.

Now this would not be an issue if our parents, extended families, communities, churches, and other key relationships were knowledgeable and intentional about formation issues. Nor would it be an issue if participants in our schools and seminars did not arrive without major deficits in these areas. Nor would it be a problem if our heroes, role models, and success stories modeled the attributes we cannot get in the formal and informal methods. The Enron scandals of our lives have shattered such delusions. However, too many still think that simply adding a book and paper requirement in a course on ethics will allow us to continue with business as usual.

This book is a declaration that the days of business as usual are over for those of us who want the real deal. In addition to the formal and informal, we are now demanding the non-formal approach of authentic relationships in our lives—relationships that penetrate to the core of who we are and what we are to become. These relationships are known by various terms as spiritual fathers and mothers, mentors and coaches, but all exhibiting one thing in common: to be truly effective, to move beyond informing to forming, reforming, and even transforming, they require something that the other two methods do not. That requirement is a powerful connection at a heart-to-heart level with a person who is willing to be real and not religious, personal and not merely professional, authentic but not authoritative.

The world around us is all about image. The impression is often more important than the reality. "Fake it till you make it." This concept is deadly for anyone who hungers for authentic spirituality. The reality is that God looks at the heart (1 Samuel 16:7) and many times ignores the external. God will promote integrity which is the measure of difference between the transforming internal work and the informing external behavior. That integrity of life, or character, cannot be hidden when we are up close and personal with another in the non-formal process. And here is the open secret; transformation will happen only in this relational context.

The process of character formation is defined by the Greek word *paideia* which is translated as "training" or "formation" in the Bible. (2 Timothy 3:15, 16). Formation involves transformation (*morphe*) which is a change in the inner man or essence. (Romans 12:2; Galatians 4:19) It is the continual change in the life of a teacher, mentor, coach, or even a parent, that calls forth a continual change in the life of a student, mentoree, client, or even a teenager. Those who will have the most transformational impact in our lives will themselves need to be in transformational relationships that are life giving. We cannot export what we have not imported.

So then, who needs a transformational coach? Those who want to go to the foundations and who are not at peace with building something in others that may stand only a small degree of testing. Or those who will not be satisfied merely achieving a success goal instead of the test of a life finished well and legacy for others to aspire to. It is for those who perceive that a life lived by core values is a life worth living. It is for those who want to export to the world a person, a process, a people movement that transforms more than informs.

Transformation is more than the latest buzz word. Coaching is more than the latest cliché. Put them together and you will find a powerful, penetrating process that will go to the heart and foundation of a person and an organization.

It works for non-profits and for-profits, for churches and conglomerates. It will last because it is cross-cultural and cross-generational. It is a bridge builder in ways that other delivery systems have failed us.

This book begins with foundations. The prophet Haggai double emphasized to foundation builders to "Consider now from this day forward...from the day that the foundation of the LORD's temple was laid—consider it" (Haggai 2:18-19). Before we rush to see how we can use the technique of coaching for the latest trend in church growth or corporate profits, we will do well to give thought to the foundations. We are building a worldwide coaching movement to last, and this section lays a foundation for transformational coaching that will be standing when the dust settles.

CHAPTER ONE

Bridges Over Troubled Waters— Awakening and Connecting Hearts through Transformational Coaching

By Dr. Joseph Umidi

My heart was troubled. I knew that the last couple years of my life were not as compelling and engaging as I expected. It seemed like I had settled for something far less than what I had envisioned I would be living and doing. I began to sense that my life message of "finishing well" was not going to be fulfilled. I became aware of a growing internal restlessness.

As the assigned driver for the guest speaker at a local event, I was asked to pick him up and drive him from the restaurant to the designated meeting place. Knowing the trip was a short 25 minutes, I wondered what kind of person he was, and prepared myself to be his tour guide of the history and geography of our area by rehearsing in my mind historical facts and timelines.

What happened on that car ride was far more than a transaction of information; it was a 25-minute transformation of my heart. Something was awakened within me and I sensed a bridge being made. It was a bridge over the troubled waters of my career; a bridge that connected my future to the hopes and dreams of my past; a bridge that opened up access to roadways I had not envisioned.

I deemed the bridge an experience of the power and dynamic of transformational coaching—the power to cross over areas that seem troubled, stormy, and agitated. That bridge is not a program or a platform. It is not something we can acquire, like an education or a degree. That bridge is a relationship that releases a breakthrough into our destiny, one conversation at a time.

The word coaching was not even on my radar screen at the time of that significant encounter. I remember when I first began to research coaching during my sabbatical as a graduate school professor that most of the references brought me back to the sports arena. It was as if the word could only bring images of whistles, half-time motivations, discipline, and inspiration to be a winner. The famous coaches who challenged teams and individuals out of mediocrity...they got results, they made a difference, they required and inspired...but did they transform?

I have discovered over the past few years of coaching and coach training that a transformational coach does not have a whistle. She does not have advice. He does not require half-time challenges or yelling in your face intimidation. Rather, transformational coaches find a way for you to tap into that internal river of motivation deep inside, a river that does not run dry.

So, how do you recognize a transformational coach?

Transformational Coaching

A Transformational Conversation

As you read this book, you may be asking yourself the questions that many ask: What is coaching? Is it a fad? How long will it last? What is the difference between different kinds of coaching? Defining transformational coaching as, first of all, a transformational conversation means that transformational coaching transforms the way we interact with one another.

> *"I've discovered that my conversations are not about my relationships; my conversations are my relationships. This has given me a whole new passion for my stewardship of every dialogue I engage in throughout my day."*
>
> *(Executive in TLC training)*

So, what is transformational coaching? Transformational coaching is, first of all, a transformational conversation. What took place in that 25-minute conversation with the gentleman I served as chauffeur was a conversation that brought a breakthrough in my life and started a process of several months of reflection making the kind of changes in my life that reconnected me through the troubled waters of my heart to a place of fulfilling what I believe is my destiny and legacy. Today, several years later, we have one of the largest movements of coach training in the world, in multiple languages, all from a perspective that is thoroughly biblical and that honors the living God and the spiritual reality in each individual's life.

With over 600 trained coaches (at the time of this writing) in all parts of society, many stories are coming in of transformation, sustainable change, and dynamic impact. What is amazing to me to realize is that out of one awakened heart, through one 25-minute conversation, has come a movement of awakening and transformation, one conversation at a time.

> *"I've been through counseling and all kinds of training in business and in church, but I've never*

*had anything like this before...that combines the
business world and the church with what is really
going on inside me....I'm just growing so much."
(Entrepreneur and owner of five companies who
is taking TLC training)*

I recently met the Israeli ambassador to the United States and was amazed at the quality of the conversation that he initiated in just a few minutes. More than politically correct clichés he engaged me at core levels of dialogue in a compelling exchange of ideas. I left the room stimulated, challenged, and hungry to engage others in the same manner that he engaged me.

Leaders who can consistently transform the depth and quality of conversations will represent their professions and ministries in the same manner that skilled ambassadors represent their nations. The goal of TLC is to transformationally train 10,000 coaches over the next 10 years who can impact leaders from all professions, one conversation at a time. Every organization deserves to have someone in-house who knows how to raise the level of conversations among the workers, staff, and volunteers. Our TLC coaches are "transformational ambassadors" whose mission is to improve the culture or climate of organizations by improving the quality of the conversations that happen at the conference table or at the water cooler.

TLC offers one-day "Extra-Ordinary Conversation" seminars that are highly interactive "real-play" rather than "role-play".1 Parents and teens, employers and employees, leaders and staff, have been impacted in many nations and have reported a fresh "awakening" to the role of conversation in their key relationships. Those who add on the "plus" of coaching after this breakthrough event have reported sustainable change in this foundational area of their lives. If there are schools for ambassadors in the diplomatic core of the nations, I am convinced that every one of them places top priority on turning everyday encounters into extra-ordinary exchanges.

> *"Thank you for creating a powerful experience and a safe environment for me to discover that my manner of conversing was part of the problem that affected the entire company. Even though I was laughing throughout the day, I was deeply touched to realize that I have a way to be part of the solution to turning our group around."*
> *(Vice President of a corporation who attended an "Extra-Ordinary Conversation" seminar with her colleagues)*

A Transformational Seeing

All of us experience the ups and downs of life, but how we look at and process those experiences determines how our lives will benefit from that experience. I have known this personally in two major ways. My son has had five major back operations and has lived with chronic pain for over twelve years. I have seen how devastating this has been to his dreams and his hopes. A very athletic person who thrived on physical activity and really enjoyed working with his hands, he has been unable to do the things that once brought him great joy.

The second major way I have personally experienced this is in the life of his daughter, my granddaughter, who was diagnosed with a rare spinal disease, SMA, at age two. Now as a teenager she is limited most of the time to a wheelchair. She is a vibrant young girl who dreams of attempting to dance and dramatically express herself, and she has had to watch life go by from a chair, not knowing how it happened or how it would end. Within the past year she has also been diagnosed with diabetes.

In both of these situations, I have discovered that whenever my granddaughter or my son had the kind of conversations that transformed the way they looked at their circumstances, something powerful happened to their perspective on their lives. Those transforming conversations would touch their hearts and awaken them to find a way to get beyond the troubling circumstances and bridge themselves to opportunities to feel fulfilled, and to bring fulfillment to others. This is truly amazing—to understand that our power in transformational coaching is what I often call *perspective power*, defined as the ability to understand what is our calling and our destiny in the midst of disappointing and difficult circumstances.

That is the key toward living a transformed life despite the circumstances. This key separates transformational coaching from simply helping people to be more successful in their achievements. What is really happening is that those who are coached transformationally gain a clearer perceptive in their understanding and redefining of success and achievement, and of their unique role in bringing that about. Both my son and my granddaughter have a perspective power that continues to astonish those around them.

Over the years we have consistently recorded feedback from coach trainees on what have been some of the most transformational parts of the training process. Consistently at the top of the list are the exercises that take a look at past experiences to see, with the help of a transformed coach, where there still may be some veins of unexplored gold in those events— nuggets of life, purpose and perspective that have been passed over. To the amazement of many there has come a larger, more integrated interpretation of those past events that was not even imagined at the time the events happened. Predictably, there was no one trained in their work or ministry relationships who knew how to take them there without giving them platitudes or warmed over advice from their own storage sheds of past stories. Many of us are sitting on personal gold mines that a coach can enable us to reclaim for the fulfillment of our calling and destiny.

With a new perspective on the past has come the possibility of a new perspective on the present. It seems as if transformational coaching finds the key logs that have jammed the movement down river, and once they are freed then everything starts to flow. Consistent creativity to look at present challenges from a new perspective is one of the lasting joys that our coaches are reporting from their clients.

> *"All of a sudden it was as if a light bulb went on in my mind. I saw the downsizing and loss of my job in a whole new light. Now I have new categories to process what my company is going through now. It has given me so much more confidence!"*
> *(Mid-career manager of a bank after taking a coach training track from TLC)*

Life coaching has become the most popular form of coaching today and TLC has designed a unique approach in our Life Focus training track and Life Purpose seminars and their coaching "plus." At the end of either of these transformational processes, participants converge past and present perspectives into "on target living" for the future. What is rewarding beyond measure is to sense the laser-like focus and renewed passion for life as clients and learners take charge of their future in bold ways. For the first time they enjoy saying "no" to those things that have kept them from saying "yes" to their unique design and purposes.

A Transformational Source

When we think about the ways we look at life and the perspective power that is required to courageously appreciate all of it, we have to look in deeper places for deeper answers. Many of us have looked in all the wrong places for answers, but a transformational conversation also transforms the place we look for answers.

Some of you who are reading this perhaps have tried church or religion, and you have been disappointed. In too many cases curious seekers have discovered that looking to the church or looking to the church's representatives for the answers had been the wrong places, even if some of these representatives call themselves coaches! Transformation comes from the inside out, not the outside in.

The hidden pearl behind that awakened desire in each of us has been that it is God Himself who is drawing us to communicate with Him transformationally. He is the source of an awakened heart in us toward Him to experience real and lasting change. True transformation comes from hearing His voice and then finding our voice and destiny despite any circumstances beyond our control. His voice resonates in our hearts and confirms in us that He is the right source to look for the right answers for each of us.

An orchestra knows that they cannot be absent for the pre-performance "tuning" in which all of the instruments find their pitch and tone according to the standard set by the leader. It is only when they hear that pitch from the concert-master that they can find their own unique voice that will resonate with themselves, their colleagues, and the audience that they are serving. Transformational coaches help clients rediscover a Voice greater than their own that puts them in touch with the source of transformation in and through them.

The voice of God is promised to those who would seek after Him. He has made it clear that man does not live by bread alone, but by every word that is ("*continually proceeding*") out of the mouth of God (Luke 4:4). In the powerful passage in the gospels, Jesus Christ said, "My sheep hear my voice" (John 10:27a) ...hear His voice. What a powerful thing—that we can actually sense intuitively the voice of our Creator and Designer, calling us to a perspective on our own circumstances, calling us to a fulfillment of our destiny that resonates with our own voice in a way that brings such energy and enthusiasm and living hope. I am thankful for the people who have helped me understand my own voice, coached me to knowing what I wanted to do, but I am certainly glad I did not stop there. Coaching that is short of transformational only puts us in touch with ourselves, many times a self that is on the throne, a self that we can too easily idolize, a self that can become an imposing taskmaster itself.2 But thank God for transformational coaches who understand that God's voice fulfills our voices, and God's heart awakens our hearts to a fulfillment that is not only eternal, but makes this side of Heaven so much more significant.

TLC is a worldwide movement that serves people from all faiths and from no faith background. Our transformational coaches are trained to respect and release people from all cultures and faith traditions. They do so not as a company policy or even as a rote technique, but as a result of an enlarged heart they have experienced for the image of God that is seen in everyone. Transformational coaches have been transformed themselves to view and respond to people outside their own limiting past perspectives and to see each person in an unconditionally loving and affirming way. The value of life-long learning and spiritual pilgrimage into calling and destiny enables coaches to partner with clients to take the next steps in their personal journey.

One year after I had that 25 minute extra-ordinary conversation (five years ago as of the writing of this book); I met the man who had brought that breakthrough in my life. My first questions to him were "How did that happen? How come I didn't get defensive or change the topic like I usually skillfully do when I don't want strangers to get too close?" His response was an example of a transformational source when he said: *"I decided before I even met you that day that I unconditionally loved you and believed the best for you. I couldn't wait to let you experience that."*

It was then that I realized that it is not how clever a question or any other technique that coaching can give you that transforms. Rather it is the ability to have a heart posture towards another that is genuinely and authentically for them. Really, it is the heart of the Father for all his created children, a heart that is the source of transformation.

It would be conveniently marketable if we could produce coaches in slam-dunk seminars who could approach people in this transformational manner. It doesn't work that way. The transformational process requires time plus a quality level of relational equity with a coach who gives timely and specific feedback to form this heart that will transform our conversations. All of our coaches were hesitant when faced with the 9-12 month certification process in their initial investigation of us. None of them have said upon completion that the depth of transformation could have happened in the "quick fix" marketing packages offered by many in the coaching industry today.

A Transformational Hearing

Coaching then not only transforms the place we look and the way we look, it also transforms what we listen to. We are listening to that which ties together the loose ends of purpose and legacy; what has been resonating within but rarely expressed. For many of us this inner monologue has been going on for years. At different points in our childhood and throughout our development, we begin to see this is not something new, but something that has been ongoing, something that is part of our story. The problem is that we have not had a transformational coach to help us to recognize it.

I know one researcher who was startled he asked CEOs of Fortune 500 corporations "When did you first become aware that what you are doing today was something that you had dreamed or reflected about before?" He discovered that 80 percent said fourth grade!3 Now they did not necessarily sense that they would be CEO of a particular company, but that they would be in leadership or overseeing something, or in other words, they began to have glimpses, they began to have ideas, they began to have awakenings. Most began to pursue those destiny clues without the benefit of a coach, and many went in circles for years until they came into the place of focus that they have today.

What if every high school graduate had six months of life purpose coaching before they graduated? What if every detention center inmate had it before they were released back to the community? What if all military personnel had it after deployment or retirement? What if every missionary had it coming off the field for furlough? What we are getting at here is that we have become dull of hearing and without an intentional, proactive approach to help us hear fully, we are only getting brief blips on the sonar screens of our lives.

The prophet Amos predicted a famine in the land, in particular, of hearing the Word of God (Amos 8:11). God's Word to us may be all around us, but the issue is that we need a transformational process to hear it at a new level for ourselves. So in an age of Ipods and cell phones, we have much hearing but little transformational listening.

In our training process we ask the question, "What are we listening to that really makes the conversation transformational?" Most of us are stuck at level one—what does that mean to me? How does this impact me? What difference does this make to me? We are on task and on mission with ourselves and listen to others according to how it hinders or helps us achieve our goals. In fact, we limit ourselves to hearing others through the filter of our particular design.4

Transformational hearing is focused on listening to God's dream in each of us. That dream is always expressed through the Designer's plan in the specific way He wired us to process His dream through our lives. That means that we also need to listen to the way others express themselves as the clues to how they are motivated and designed for that expression. TLC offers a two-day workshop in activating gifting/design that moves people off the block of discovery of personal design to interacting with others according to their design. That workshop is followed up with the "plus" of either personal coaching or coach training in this key area of understanding and responding to others in life giving ways.

> *"That workshop was like a landmine going off in our leadership—in a good way. It blew such a hole in our paradigm that everybody is looking around and saying, "Gosh, we've got to fill that hole with a new way of relating!"*
> *(Canadian denominational executive leader)*

Once we are hearing others according to how they need to express themselves, then we can help them match God's dreams in them with God's design in them. Transformational hearing can be likened to a 21st century expression of ancient dream interpretation as described in the life of Joseph, a patriarch in the Bible. Joseph was promoted from slave to second in command of Egypt because of his dream interpreting ability. Today, transformational coaches are being promoted to levels of access and influence because they have the ability to help others get in touch with God's unheard, unrecognized, and underutilized dream in them.

> *"I had become so hardened to dreaming since I was so disappointed about the gap between my expectations and how things always seemed to work*

out. Now through this coaching process, I have iden-
tified my daydreams from my Designers life dreams.
I feel like a child again."
    (TLC participant in the Life Focus workshop) ·

These dreams always surpass the daydreams and the
self-centered dreams that we all have substituted for the
ones that really resonate within us. God-sized dreams
connect to the very things that He designed in the make-up
our lives, from circumstances beyond our control to those
things in which we feel inner fulfillment and have brought
such great fruitfulness to the lives of others. When we hear
those core dreams in another, we can be their advocates to
call them forth in the stewardship of their own lives. Once
we have helped them to hear and see it, they will own it with
a persevering passion!

A Transformational Asking

Conversations that are transformational transform even
how we ask questions. We can learn to prepare, rehearse,
and ask significant questions that catalyze a powerful
conversation wherever we are. But the real adventure comes
from listening to the responses to these questions and then
asking spontaneous questions from what we are transformationally hearing. This can be likened to a dance team that is
so skilled that they seem to flow like liquid in response to
each other's movements. It is creative, intuitive, adventurous, curious, and courageous. It separates superficial coaching from transformational coaching.

One of my students came across a doctoral research
paper that dealt exclusively with the questions asked by
Jesus Christ in the Bible. When we study the types of questions that he asked we find that they were very powerful.
What made them a more effective means of impacting and
simple transformation rather than by telling or advising?

Most people who think about this and who read the Bible can remember His famous question, "Who do men say that I, the Son of Man, am?" (Matthew 16:13b). That is a powerful question, especially because Jesus Christ asked it in a specific place at a specific time. That place was called Caesarea Philippi, a crossroads of the Roman Empire where many came to inquire about the pantheon of gods that was all set up in little shrines along the roadways. As people walked along this major thoroughfare, pilgrims, travelers, and business people would constantly be asking, "Who do people say that this one is or this god or that one?" By making that inquiry, that question, at that specific place, Jesus Christ was training leaders to ask the questions that the predominant culture was already asking, already reflecting, already passionate about seeking solutions for. He knew how to dance with the music of His day.

Think about the five questions that this man asked me— the man that I picked up in the restaurant who spoke words that did not make me defensive, but in reality opened up a perspective that I had not either seen or pursued before. In his penetrating questions I sensed his heart connecting to my core-value issues that made me stop flying my life on auto-pilot, stop responding to conversations simply with a reaction or a clever idea. Instead, I took control of the steering wheel myself, and I began to speak from my heart, first to him, then to myself, then beyond that to others as I reflected during the following three months on the impact of that extra-ordinary conversation. Those transforming questions became a bridge over troubled waters for me and others, a bridge of transformational coaching beginning with a transformational conversation.

A Transformational Relating

The secret weapon of transformational coaching is that it is a transparent relationship—an organic, life-giving, empowering relationship. Today you can go to the internet and hire a coach and have a coach-client relationship. It can be helpful, productive, and very unique to someone who is only used to supervising, consulting, or even mentoring. But what will make it transformational is the quality of authentic friendship and partnership that embraces the kind of transformational processes that has been revealed in this chapter.

In the accounts of the gospels, when Jesus was on earth, something quite interesting is discovered. As He is making disciples, the Bible records only about 45-minutes worth of teaching content that Jesus spoke. If you eliminate all the duplications, it would take only that long to read all of the teaching content. However, much of the other things that are recorded about the life of Christ were intentional experiences He put His disciples through so that they would experience two things: first, to be touched at the heart or the core value level; and, second, to have a transformational conversation around that experience that would change their lives. But in order to do that, something had to happen in the very relationship of Jesus with the disciples. That is why a very powerful statement is recorded when He said, "No longer do I call you servants, but now I call you friends." Friends, authentic companions, kingdom partners, transformational learning community—this is the key.

A transformationally-related friend is one who sticks with you through thick and thin, who believes in you when you do not even believe in yourself. It is someone who empowers and releases you to finish your race well, to cross the finish line, to not give up or throw in the towel. It is someone who is with you, enabling you to complete the task and to make the change and to get through the difficult transitions in life. A real friend is one who calls forth your true identity.

Transformational coaches understand that one of the biggest battles in the hearts of people today is to be secure in who they really are, who they are designed to be. So many people are insecure about their gender identity, about their generational or cultural identity, about how they fit or who accepts them, how they feel about themselves, and more. Yet all of those things can be loosed off of us when a true coach calls forth our identity—helping us to name it, and then enabling us to be free to live by it. The Bible passage with Jesus and Lazarus is quite amazing when Jesus speaks to the dead Lazarus wrapped in grave clothes and says, "Lazarus, come forth" (John 11:43b). In that instant, we see a man coming out of his sepulcher, standing in his grave clothes, and then the words from Jesus, "Loose him and let him go" (John 11:44b).

A transformational coach calls forth the heart to become alive and awakened to the reality of our true identity, and then allows the coaching process to unbind us and let us live that out in a way that causes the breakthrough. Yet more than a breakthrough moment, coaching insures the possibility of a breakthrough movement that results in a sustainable change for freedom and for a sense of adventure as we live out our purposes on earth. All this is done because a coach models how God has used people to bring about this freedom, this identity and this change in their own lives. And so a transformational coach is one who does not try to export what has not already been imported, but is a person who has experienced themselves the power of transformational conversations, transformational friendships, transparent relationships, and now has the ability to know how to bring that about, how to replicate that in the lives of others. Good transformational coaches are people who bring about great things in the lives of others.

Reflection and Discussion Questions
Chapter One: Bridges Over Troubled Waters—
Awakening and Connecting Hearts through
Transformational Coaching

1. Who in your life sparks transformational conversations? What is it about those conversations that are different than ordinary conversations? What difference would it make in your career calling if you were able to initiate this exchange in others?

2. What is the correlation between a growing intimacy with the Voice of God and a growing ability to be in touch with our own Voice? How might that enable us to help others do the same? How is this process distinctly transformational as compared to other styles of coaching?

3. When did you first have awareness that what you are doing today, or are aspiring to do, was something you had dreamed of or reflected upon earlier? What if you had a transformational coach to help you identify whose Voice that was and enable you to be more "straight line" true to following it than the meandering path you may have taken? What if you were one of those coaches helping others find their path at a much earlier age or stage?

4. What would happen if you began to craft questions prior to your meetings with others that were more intentional and powerful in targeting the heart? What would it be like if you became known as a person who left a signifi-cant imprint on others whenever you engaged them in brief conversations? How might transformational coach training help facilitate this even if you never became a professional coach?

5. Famous violinist Isaac Rubin relates that as he grew up his father would turn to him regularly at meal times and say, "Did you ask any good questions today?" What questions did Jesus ask that you may need to reflect upon more deeply to see the difference that it made in the lives of others? What would happen if you began to accumu-late a notebook of all the good questions you hear throughout a normal week in your life as a life long pursuit of this lost art?

CHAPTER TWO

A Transformational Learning Philosophy for Coach Training

By Tony Stoltzfus

TLC training programs are based on a proven set of values and principles that we've found consistently produce transformational learning. Four key training values are listed below, and then later described in depth along with thirteen important training principles that flow from these values:

1. **Character and Competence:** *Training that produces significant, lasting behavioral change will ground new skills in changes to underlying values and beliefs.*
2. **Adult Learning Methodology:** *Effectiveness in training practicing leaders comes from an understanding of how adult leaders learn.*
3. **Relevant Format:** *Training presented in a way that is relevant, applicable and accessible for practicing leaders.*
4. **Relational Context:** *Transformational learning is maximized in a community of authentic, accountable relationships.*

Values form the bedrock foundation of TLC training, the core philosophy behind what we are imparting. Values are consistent and unchanging. Methodologies are the means we use to communicate coaching values, skills, and concepts.

Value 1: Character and Competence
Training that produces significant, lasting behavioral change will ground new skills in changes to underlying values and beliefs.

> *To transform others, first be transformed.*
> *Values are forever.*
> *Training over time produces habits.*
> *Trust the process.*

The TLC process is designed to work at character and competence (being issues and skills) simultaneously. Training in skills is the more familiar—we present a concept, model it, debrief, ask trainees to give it a try, and then provide additional opportunities for practice. For instance, to learn to ask open questions, we describe what they are (questions that can't be answered "yes" or "no") in an input session, demonstrate what they look like in a role play, discuss what happened, and then give trainees opportunities to practice the skill with feedback. Skill development is learning to do something in a certain way to become more effective. The process is fairly utilitarian.

The character component takes things to a deeper level. Skills can be practiced as techniques—expedient ways to get something done—or they can flow out of an underlying set of beliefs and values that provide a compelling reason to implement them. A skill grounded on explicit values is used longer, more consistently, and more effectively than when it is done simply as a technique.

For instance, a coach can learn to ask open questions

because they do a good job at getting the client to talk and explore. In other words, open questions are a technique that gets a certain kind of result. But a coach can also learn to ask open questions because he or she becomes so convinced of the value of the individual being coached and the importance of that person's insights that asking about them becomes a passionate, instinctive response. This type of deep value shift causes the coaching behavior to become part of the way the coach lives, not just part of the way they coach. Every conversation—with a spouse, boss, co-worker, child, or peer —will be affected by this significant values change. Coaching becomes a lifestyle and not just a technique.

Transformational learning is learning that changes who you are, not just what you do. A transformational learning program is one that consistently catalyzes changes in being (values, beliefs, character habits) in the trainees.

Transformation is usually highly experiential and tends to be catalyzed by relationships and life circumstances, so it is somewhat unpredictable. Most of the examples of transformation in TLC's history had to do with life circumstances and the coach training program intersecting to form a turning point in the person's life. For instance, one trainee had a major breakthrough when her partner dropped out halfway through the initial Formation Track, and she realized she needed to confront another individual for the first time in her life. This kind of learning event can't be planned; the coach simply has to respond to what life brings. In a sense, transformational learning program sets the table and then waits to see where the teachable moment occurs.

The TLC training process is designed to create teachable moments in the process of learning certain skills. For some trainees, a particular session might be a breakthrough moment. But for others, the transformation may take place two months later when a spouse gives an honest appraisal of the trainee's listening skills. For another it may happen six months later when she listens to the tape of her first appointment and realizes how often she interrupts and completes her client's sentences. All the while we are waiting for and leveraging those coaching moments when life circumstances provide the chance for the flash of lightning that is a transformational learning experience.

Character and Competence Principles

Principle 1: To Transform Others, First Be Transformed

Four practical principles help translate the character and competence value into reality in the TLC program. The first is, "To Transform Others, First Be Transformed." It is hard to coach transformation if you aren't personally familiar with what it looks like. A coach who has been transformed through coaching will be passionate about coaching transformation in others. Since personal transformation is so important to effective transformational coaching, the TLC program spends a lot of effort setting the table for these experiences to happen.

Much of the time spent in the initial TLC Formation track on relationship and accountability is working toward this goal. For instance, in the accountability plan exercise, trainees are working at the skill of asking accountability questions, but at the same time they are experiencing how accountability helps them change in their own life—which may lead to a breakthrough insight. Another example is the feedback exercise where trainees learn skills like how to receive feedback or how to write effective feedback questions. The experience of getting personal feedback from friends and colleagues can open the door to transformation, either seeing how beneficial feedback is or by having one of your own blind spots exposed!

Principle 2: Values Are Forever

The second principle, 'Values are Forever', ("diamonds are forever" marketing commercials) means that values change tends to be lasting change. When a trainee embraces a value like Transformation Happens Experientially, it forms a life-long foundation for moving away from using advice-giving and lecturing to produce change, and toward using a relational coaching process. But since the change happens at the core values level, it also ripples out through the remainder of the coach's life. A trainee in a pastoral role who embraces this value may decide to add testimonies to every service, because he sees the power of stories and experiences in a new light. Or a mother who grabs on to this value may suddenly stop saying, "Pick up your room!" for the 500th time and let the child experience life with no clean laundry as a means to catalyze change. When values change, everything changes.

The exercises in the TLC manual are keyed to our core values, because we want trainees to embrace a value set and not just a skill set. By the end of the Formation Track, a trainee should be able to articulate a number of values that have deeply impacted their lives.

Principle 3: Training Over Time Produces Habits

Changes in being involve changes in life patterns. You can learn a skill in a day, but habits are formed over months and years. For instance, a coach trainee can realize in a momentary flash of insight that advice-giving doesn't work. The trainee can see the value of the coaching approach, embrace a new paradigm for working with others, and even make a decision to change at the behavioral level. But if a person came to that same trainee the same day with a real problem, the trainee would probably still end up giving advice instead of coaching! How is it that we can know what the right thing to do is, and still not be able to do it?

It's because we have habits. The fact is, most of us are in the habit of advice-giving, and that habit isn't going to change overnight; we're going to have to work on it.

This is why TLC training is a year-long process. TLC training forces trainees to engage a skill every week instead of just at series of weekend events or in a one-week intensive. Habits are formed by the repeated application of a skill or discipline over time, with six weeks to three months being the minimal amount of time needed to really get a new pattern ingrained in a lasting way. TLC takes a long time because old habits die hard, and forming new ones takes time.

This is also the reason TLC tracks are arranged in parallel threads instead of sequentially (covering one topic completely before moving on to the next). For instance, we could cover everything having to do with accountability in the Formation Track in two weeks. But by stretching it out over the entire 13-week track, trainees get 13 weeks to practice accountability, build it into their schedule, and develop it as a habit. In a workshop or training event you could talk about accountability, but you couldn't really have people practice it in any realistic way.

Principle 4: Trust the Process

The "Training Over Time" principle flows over into another principle of character development we call "Trust the Process." What this means to a trainer is that the whole TLC environment is designed to catalyze character change, produce teachable moments, and provide a safe place where accelerated growth can occur. The training process itself changes people in the same way that being in a greenhouse changes a plant. Because the greenhouse plant gets just the right amount of soil, fertilizer, sun, and water, it grows bigger and faster than the outdoor version without any intervention on the part of the greenhouse owner.

God will meet your trainees in this process even if you don't feel like you are doing anything special, because the TLC process is an environment where there are plenty of great opportunities to engage our spiritual lives in a real rather than a religious manner. Trainers who have been around for a while develop a faith that the coach training process itself is a powerful force for change, and that given time trainees will often get to where they need to go without an intervention from the coach.

Value 2: Adult Learning Methodology
Effectiveness in training practicing leaders comes from an understanding of how adult leaders learn.

Effective adult learning is experiential and interactive.
Reflection, feedback, and debriefing maximize retained insight.
Practice makes perfect.

TLC aims to train leaders in skills and character qualities that will be immediately and widely applicable in real world situations. Our target is not to create people who understand coaching theory at a cognitive level, but people who can go out and coach effectively in real situations.

Real-world performance is best generated by real-world training. Leaders who've practiced a skill on people they know and seen real results are more confident in their abilities and more motivated to continue to practice those skills. That's one of the prime purposes of the peer relationship established in the TLC coach training: to provide a place where trainees can practice on each other. That's also why when we role-play, we ask people to come up with real scenarios from their own lives. It's more life-like, provides a richer training experience, and often the prospective coach gets to experience seeing a "client" have a genuine break-through.

Adult learning research confirms this approach. Adults learn best when they:

- Are solving their own real problems instead of merely collecting information.
- Have the opportunity for immediate application.
- Are self-motivated, self-directed, and personally responsible for the outcome.
- Build on what they already know.

In TLC we've tried to design our training to leverage these principles as much as possible. When we debrief on an exercise with a trainee, usually the first question is, "What was significant *for you* in this exercise?" We want to tune in to what the trainee thinks is important and applicable, not to our agenda as trainers. Application exercises (where an exercise first done with a peer or coach is done again with a friend or fellow leader) push trainees to apply what they've learned in real life. The entire TLC program is designed to make the trainee responsible, and allows for plenty of scheduling flexibility, so that trainees are self-motivated and self-directed.

Adult Learning Principles

Principle 5: Effective Adult Learning Is Experiential and Interactive

Several key principles flow out of our value for using adult learning methodologies.

The first is that effective adult learning is experiential and interactive. Because they focus on real-world problem solving and immediate application, adult learners flourish in engaging, experiential settings. Training that focuses on theory alone forces learners to figure out how to bridge the gap between theory and actual practice (the part they are most interested in). Training that includes practice, integration, and application supplies this bridge ready-made, making training more interesting and the skills much more likely to be actually used. In TLC, coaching and peer appointments, application exercises, and workshops are all experiential, interactive settings.

Principle 6: Practice Makes Perfect

> *"Without some form of exercise, participants will forget one quarter of what they learned in six hours, one third in 24 hours, and 90% in six weeks."*
> *(Gary Kroehnert, <u>Basic Training for Trainers</u>)*

Repetition is a great way to produce both habits and retention. When we experience something, our brains make memories by creating patterns of physical connections between brain cells. Each time we repeat the experience, or even think back over it and remember what happened, that pattern of connections is strengthened. The more we practice, the more we retain.

Practice also bridges the gap between theory and application. I remember the first time I built a major piece of furniture—it was an engagement present for my wife. I had worked as a furniture designer for years; I had designed this table; and because I broke down projects into steps to price them I knew every operation that it would take to build the table. What I didn't know were all the little tricks and tips for how to run the equipment. I asked a ton of questions, had the craftsmen double-check my machine set-ups to make sure I wouldn't hurt myself, and actually let them do several of the tricky operations. I came out with a nice table, but I never could get the top flat; it has a noticeable dip in it to this day. I knew all about the theory of building a table, but when it came right down to it I couldn't have built that one on my own.

Trainees may hear about a skill in an input session, but until they've done it successfully several times, most of them will lack the confidence to try it in a real-life situation. That's why many exercises are repeated more than once, or done in different ways or different contexts. We're building people's confidence in their skills, so that when a real opportunity to coach comes along it seems easy. The other benefit of providing practice opportunities (especially when they include feedback from a trainer) is that the trainee can make mistakes in a safe environment where no one gets hurt. For these reasons, over 50% of total time in TLC workshop and teleclass sessions is devoted to trainee practice.

Principle 7: Reflection, Feedback and Debriefing Maximize Retained Insight.

Almost any training exercise can be improved with the addition of reflection, feedback, and debriefing. All of these practices add repetition to the learning process; the learner has to go back and think through the training experience again, strengthening the memory pattern for that event and enhancing their ability to recall what was learned.

Feedback and debriefing are used to enhance training sessions. For instance, the Formation and Implementation Track workshops include role plays where trainees try out certain coaching skills and then debrief afterward. This targeted feedback helps ensure that the skill is being practiced correctly (it's very hard to unlearn something once you've learned to do it wrong!), provides affirmation to reinforce what is done well, and helps the trainee identify areas for improvement. Debriefing can also be used to give the trainee a window into their trainer's mind. If you have a "coaching moment" with one of your trainees5, take a few minutes afterward to debrief. Letting the trainee see what you were thinking, how you decided to ask a particular question, or even a place where you didn't know what to do can be very enlightening!

Reflection is the key to translating personal transformation into a form that can be replicated in others. By thinking about what happened and distilling biblical principles out of it, learning can be passed on to others or applied to new situations. While some individuals are naturally reflective, others rarely stop long enough to ponder on what they've done. The reflection exercises in the Formation Track are designed to help trainees learn to reflect as a habit and a life pattern.

A powerful habit you can cultivate as a trainer is to get your trainees to reflect on every new learning experience. When a client gets a breakthrough, I often ask, "Think it through: how did that happen? What principle can you distill from this event?" Or I'll suggest that they journal about the circumstances that led up to the insight. If you know something good happened to you, you can give a testimony about it. If you know how it happened, you can replicate it in others.

Value 3: Relevant Format
Train in a way that is relevant, applicable, and accessible for practicing leaders.

Train for replication.
Emphasize integration and application of all new skills.
Maximize flexibility.

Even a great training program can fail if it isn't accessible to the leaders who need it. With 180 training hours over 40 weeks, TLC coach training is a demanding program. For leaders to see it through they need to see how it can be used in their world to solve their problem, and they need help fitting it into their already-busy schedules. TLC is committed to making coach training relevant, applicable, and accessible to those who are in actual leadership roles, not just to students or those on sabbatical.

Relevance comes from two places. First, we've chosen to emphasize the things leaders need but don't receive in a formal education: conversational skills, relationship building, destiny discovery, leadership development, conflict skills, etc. Most leaders quickly see the relevance of what they are learning, because these are skills they use every day but often have received little help in. Second, relevance comes from making connections between what is being learned in a coach training and what is going on in the trainee's life. The "Think Like a Coach" questions in the coach's notes are an example of this—they push the trainee to think through how a coaching concept would apply in their own world.

We are also committed to making training accessible to leaders with real jobs and responsibilities. Using the phone as a training venue (both for coaching appointments and teleclasses) removes many geographic and time limitations. The schedule flexibility that comes from one-on-one coaching instead of large group sessions also helps make our training accessible. If trainees have jobs, vacations, ministry trips, or prior commitments, we want our trainers to make a good-faith effort to work around the "givens" of life.

Relevance Principles

Principle 8: Train for Replication

The first question practicing leaders ask about a leadership training program is, "How can I use this?" And what they are often thinking is, "How can I turn right around and take these materials and use them with others?" Leaders don't want to just learn something; they want to learn something they can use. Part of the reason the TLC manual is designed in an exercise format is to answer this question with a resounding "Yes!" Our licensing program allows TLC coaches to turn around and copy any of the printed pages in the manual for coaching their own clients. This means coaches graduate from TLC with over 150 exercises and handouts they can immediately use.

We also emphasize replication through reflection, distilling principles, debriefing, and tying training back to core values. We don't want trainees to only experience TLC! We want them to experience it and understand what they experienced and how it was brought about, so they can replicate their experience with others.

Principle 9: Emphasize Integration and Application of All New Skills.

In the TLC program, every new concept is followed up with opportunities to discuss, integrate, practice, and apply that skill. At first, some trainees may try to get out of the integration phase by skipping the application exercises. That's evidence of the old, "If I've heard it, I've learned it," paradigm. The coach's appointment notes contain check-up questions to make sure trainees are doing these important exercises.

Principle 10: Maximize Flexibility

Practicing leaders (and especially top-caliber ones) have busy schedules. The TLC program is designed to work around real-life schedules while still delivering quality, intensive training. It is possible for a leader to have a ten-day vacation or overseas ministry trip and still not miss out on any of the training, because peer and coaching appointment schedules can simply be adjusted around the trip.

We've also tried to design a portion of the program so

that it can be done as part of an existing ministry or job role. For instance, the *Getting Feedback* exercise can be done "on the clock" at work, because it is designed to improve job performance and working relationships on your leadership team while you are learning to coach. Up to one quarter of program time is these "two-fers" that leverage commitments already in the trainee's schedule

Value 4: Relational Context
Transformational learning is maximized in a community of authentic, accountable relationships.

Build in authenticity and accountability.
Story and modeling have power to transform.
Provide individualized training for each person.

In the last week of the Formation Track I'll often ask, "What difference did it make to go through this with a peer? What would it have been like to go through this course on your own?" A comment I often hear is, "I never would have even finished this without my peer!" Distance learning programs often have high drop-out rates, but the relationships in the TLC program keep people on course and help them finish what they started. We're just more motivated and have better follow-through when we're in a learning community (a group that has banded together formally to learn or grow in a planned way together).

Accountability is an important component of the learning community. Members are accountable to each other to complete agreed-upon action steps (like the exercises in the certification schedule) because they recognize that without accountability it is too easy to let things slide and get much less out of the training experience than they could. Accountability is a support structure that helps us get done what we want to do.

Authenticity is another key to making learning communities work. When members are transparent, trust is built, and the community becomes a safe place to share hopes and concerns or practice a new skill without fear of rejection. When a coaching relationship has a high degree of transparency, trainees start talking about what is really close to their hearts, and the potential for transformational learning skyrockets.

Relational Context Principles

Principle 11: Build in Authenticity and Accountability.
Coaching is all about taking responsibility for your life, and accountability is about making yourself responsible. It may seem difficult to uphold this at the beginning of a coaching relationship when you don't even know the person, but if you are clear about your expectations most people will embrace them and be grateful for them.

The coach trainer is also the key to quickly establishing authenticity in the learning community. Trainers oversee the process of covenant that makes the learning community real in the first place. Then they model authenticity by "going first," sharing personal stories that catalyze openness in the trainees. Trainers also model how to supply the healthy accountability that keeps the process on track. The ability to *trust the process* to produce change is largely dependent on the trainer's ability to create an authentic, accountable learning community.

Principle 12: Story and Modeling Have Power to Transform.
We are so used to telling stories all the time in all kinds of places that we tend not to think of storytelling as a skill, but stories are a powerful part of the transformational learning process. Stories are real, they are self-disclosing (so they

create authenticity), and they create bonds between us that open us up to learn vicariously from each other. When we are telling a story we are uncovering who we are. Many of TLC's input sessions include powerful stories as a tool to connect listeners emotionally and spiritually to the content being presented.

Modeling is closely akin to storytelling. Instead of telling a story to illustrate a skill, value, or principle, with modeling you demonstrate it. Part of the power of modeling is that it gives the trainee the chance to see the thing done right; but even more powerful is having the trainee see that you live what you teach. Any training becomes more powerful and transformational when the trainees realize that the trainer is living out the skill and being effective with it. Then learning becomes not just a rote process, but a conscious imitation of a trainer who is respected for his or her skill and integrity. Modeling makes the learning process about lifestyle, not just about technique.

Principle 13: Provide Individualized Training for Each Person.

Individualized training is important, because people are individuals. A 55-year-old apostolic leader needs different things from TLC training than a 26-year-old youth pastor does. A full-time student will have different insights and issues than a leader with a full time job.

There are a number of ways that we've designed flexibility into TLC to account for differences in life stage, personality type, age, and other areas. For instance, reflection exercises are spread throughout TLC tracks instead of concentrated in one area, so that people who find reflection tough aren't overwhelmed all at once. We've also tried not to specify a format for reflection: while introverts will enjoy sitting down alone for an hour and writing out their thoughts, extraverts may find it much more life-giving to talk through what they are thinking while another person takes notes, or dictate into a handheld recorder. People who aren't writers may want to journal in bullet lists or incomplete sentences—for things like this, it doesn't matter *how* they reflect, as long as they are reflecting!

Another way training is adapted to individual needs is that we try to match people with compatible coaches and peers. Younger trainees will tend to get younger peers and younger coaches (unless they request otherwise, which they are free to do) who have similar concerns and experiences.

The heart of our individualization is that most TLC training happens in one-on-one relationships instead of large groups

Reflection and Discussion Questions
Chapter Two: A Transformational Learning
Philosophy for Coach Training

1. Think about some of your most significant learning events. How many of these happened when a speaker or book intersected with a past or present experience you had and brought an ignition to the way you are "wired" that sparked your heart or mind? What if you had a coach who could help this happen in you more frequently? What if you were able to do that for others because of a transformational training in your life?

2. After reading this chapter, explain why the transformational process for coach training cannot happen in a weekend seminar event. What would happen if you're normal daily experiences were actually the curriculum for your transformation by having a coach help you see the unique and powerful principles that are within those experiences?

3. Think back to those training or teaching events you have attended where you had an opportunity to debrief with the presenter on why they did this and not that, etc. How did this timely specific feedback (TSF) deepen your learning and forward your action? What if you were able to design training opportunities that included this because of your own coach training that transformed you

in this way? What difference might that make in your organization?

4. What training have you given or received that was easy to replicate in others; i.e. they were able to pass on the same to others at close to the same level that you had done? What made this so easy to replicate? How does the TLC training philosophy make coaching more than a skill for a few people but a value and methodology that can be replicated in a movement throughout our churches and organizations around the world?

5. Where are you already getting an individualized approach to training that is tailor made for your needs? What makes it so different from what you have received in traditional approaches? Where do you sense your organization is going in the area of personalized training for leaders and employees? How does coaching address that trend?

Bridges Over Ruined Roads— Coaching as a Bridge for Personal and Leadership Transformation

By Dr. Joseph Umidi

Ruined Roads

Those who travel frequently know that the roads are in disrepair in many of our cities, villages, and towns. It is easy to see that we need some kind of reconstruction projects to make roadways less congested and find new ways to facilitate commerce and travel between our homes and workplaces. Unfortunately, with tight budgets and high taxes, many bridges and roadways have to operate in their present condition longer than planned. Time is running out to repair the bridges and roads that connect our communities together.

Just as roadways are in critical need of repair, so are the needs evident for restoring and repairing ways in which people communicate into one another's lives. With the increase of security threats, gated communities, and telemarketing restrictions, more of us seek refuge and isolation in front of our home theatres with surround sound. While communication has emphasized the use of technology; the time has come for repairing the content of that communication, the dialogues that bridge our lives together as families and partners.

One of the favorite expressions of historians is in the "fullness of time." It describes, in the biblical sense, how God brought forth his son to the earth in a time when all of the necessary components for his coming were fully prepared. The Roman Empire existed in one of the greatest historical times for well-prepared roadways ever seen. Roman provinces were connected by intricate systems of roadways and the ability to converse, commerce, and traverse back and forth. Historians attribute to the Roman roadways the "just in time" development for the early missionaries, disciples, and apostles to bring the ministry and message of transformational reconciliation to the cultures of their day.

That exciting, very pregnant time in history is matched again today when we see the development of a new way to communicate, a new way to connect with one another. More than the latest in the Internet, technology, or fiber optics, coaching is really a modern version of the Roman's roadway. This new language from the heart and a new ability to communicate to the core values of another is resonating in a very big way today in culture after culture and between generations.

The communication need for today is to build bridges over the ruined roads; to find a new way to access one another; and to bridge over ancient territorial and cultural divisions. People can thereby experience the joy of unity in the diversity of pluralistic cultures and oneness in heart and spirit with the people from those cultures. Transformational coaching bridges God's passion and interests in the hearts of those who want something much better than parochial and narrow ways of thinking, even when packaged in religious language.

Building Bridges

Transformational coaching bridges can and must be traversed by those who understand the transformational process and those who would raise up leadership for the next decade and beyond—leaders who will finish well, leaders who will lead well, and leaders who will leave a legacy of transformed lives because of the way they communicate the heart of God and their own hearts to those they are raising up. A true story that illustrates this is of a leadership training college in Canada that innovatively decided to match 175 of its students with seasoned and wise mentors with whom the students would communicate once a month. This communication would enable them to traverse the ruined roads of the traditional educational system and find a personalized way for these students to get on-time help in the areas where they most needed it, rather than simply jumping through academic hoops. It was a bold move!

After a year of this innovative program they questioned the students and evaluated their level of success. They were shocked to find that over 90 percent of the students said it did not work, it was not productive and it was not helpful. When they closely examined the reasons for their discouragement, they discovered that most of the students were spoke with a common theme.

"They did not want to listen to us or communicate to us in a way that we could understand. They did not want to traverse a bridge into our own lives and hearts to see what we struggle with. They simply had an agenda of giving us their advice, giving us their exhortations and ideas. It seemed as if we were simply another place for them to exhort and to advise without really understanding and helping us understand how we could best deal with our issues in a way that was life giving."

Soon after reading my article in a national magazine on coaching6, this organization called me to come speak on a Saturday. They put me before these mentors with the topic of my seminar that day called, "Extraordinary Conversations: How We Can Enable Conversations to be Transformational". My first topic for the seminar was; "The number one killer of authentic relationships: giving advice prematurely!"

Somewhere during that first lecture a few of the people got up and walked out of the room, but those who stayed experienced a mini-transformation, coming to the realization that even though their hearts were right in desiring to help these emerging leaders, their techniques were an outdated, almost archaic way to communicate to this generation. The method that had worked so well for them had now become a highway that was littered with potholes and in need of repair.

By the end of the day I was so proud of these older men and women because they caught the vision that they could rebuild the bridges and try again to communicate in a transformational way. The great news is that these precious leaders did bridge one generation to another and enable these emerging leaders to have spiritual fathers and mothers that would help them into their own future. That day became a bridge to a common ground between these mixed generations— common ground based on a common experience of transformation. Those common experiences now have produced a common language and that has enabled them to have a common ground of understanding.

Bridging into Transformational Process for Leadership Development

In the rapidly expanding worldwide youth culture that is taking the reins of leadership from a shrinking older generation, there is a priority list of what to emphasize for bridge-building. At the top of the list is to bridge into the latent desire in others for a more personalized approach towards formation, development, and training. When we look at the sports world, the entertainment world, the marketing world, and the executive world, we see the continual use of one-on-one coaching and one-on-one training. Without this critical part of the formation and training process, people feel that they are getting a "one size fits all" approach that does not quite fit them.

More and more people today, in every culture, are recognizing that they have a unique dream and a unique design that they want to discover and express. There is a sense of a "masterpiece creation" in them that wants to get out and be made known to others. And so, many people from many cultures are looking for personal touches, one-on-one. Those who are bridging to them are minimizing the polished platform presentations and maximizing a one-on-one approach that enables them to know that here is something tailor-made for them.

We have one leader couple, a husband and wife, who received coach training and then led a Bible study in their corporate offices in a transformational process. The husband, who did not have a Bible school or seminary degree, simply read over one passage of Scripture all week long and kept asking himself questions until he found the right questions that were tailor- made for his group. At the weekly Bible study the husband would read the Bible text and then simply ask his prepared powerful questions to those in the group. The questions were timely to the issues on the attendees' hearts and were transformational in the ability to elicit not just yes or no responses, but open hearted responses.

While the participants answered, his wife would listen. She was also trained transformationally to listen at a core level—not just to what it meant to the listener, not just to what it meant to the speaker, but what it meant to their hearts, core values, sense of purpose, life calling and destiny.

The combination of the two, the husband who prepared powerful questions and the wife who prepared powerful listening, brought a transformational approach to leadership formation and development. During each weekly meeting they were able to discern those people who were ripe and ready to move forward in their spiritual development. The rest of the week they would visit those in whom they sensed there was an urgency to respond to; those that were desperate; those that were open to change and willing to go further. They were able to help those people make progress in their spiritual development. All of this resulted in the group growing and multiplying, and their own leadership base grew beyond any other in that corporation. It was a transformational approach that was exponential in its results.

As you think about your own leadership development, your own use of bridging to people's hearts in ways that connect and ways that enable an ability to interact with others in the issues of life with authentic conversations, ask yourself the following question:

"How can I achieve my training goals by doing less telling and more asking?"

To personalize this, simply draw a straight line on this page. On the far left of the line write the words "love to tell," and the far right, "love to listen." As you put a pencil mark along that bar closest to what you really love to do, many will discover that you have been trained towards an addiction to telling!

It is time for us to be free from our addiction, be recovered from this propensity to constantly talk and give advice, and develop the ability to listen, beginning with those we are training. Transformational coaching is bridging leadership development over the worn out rocky roads of traditional talking-head methodologies into an effective paradigm of leadership formation and multiplication. The end result will be a transformational coaching movement that will fuel a rapid development and deployment of transformed leaders.

John Wimber, the founder of the Vineyard Churches, impacted much of the training strategy of churches from various streams because he emphasized a clinical aspect of training. He always tied extensive teaching times to this particular phrase, "Well, now let's practice it." That application moved learners from the information to the transformation mode. The increasing desire for transformation no longer can be satisfied with the old formula of seminars, books, or tapes. There needs to be a relational connection to a person who will walk alongside us to empower us to "practice it"—a trigger that will release through you the ability to live out your life on purpose.

Those of us who have led church and business organizations over the years have discovered that if we are going to bring about value transfer or value change, we are going to have to have more than policy papers or sermon series. What is needed is experiences connected to people that we have allowed to speak into our lives and question us powerfully; so that we can relate to these experiences with feedback. Someone said that feedback is the breakfast of champions, and many of us leaders today have not been trained this way. We have been trained with lectures, classes, sermons, seminars, workshops, and consulting but we have not actually been able to have TSF – "Timely Specific Feedback" based on strategic experiences that enable us to penetrate below the surface of our training to the foundational level where our heart and values lie.

We need to understand that though information is critical and knowledge is necessary, though we will need sermons and seminars, the greatest impact in leadership training in the future will be when whatever is told is interpreted by the present experiences we are having. And that interpretation is not someone telling us the interpretation, but someone coaching us to have our own revelation or illumination of what that experience means to us. This is where transformation takes place—in the everyday experiences in our lives in which we can identify and embrace God at work shaping and forming us from the inside out.

How can we redesign our training practices to be more relational, to include personal demonstration of what is being taught, and to be sure that the kind of coaching dynamics are there to bring about the needed transformation? How can we incorporate a clinical approach to our training time that involves our learners in real-time learning, and how can I move toward transformational experiences rather than informational transfers from my notebook into my students' notebooks? All of these questions are designed to help us move ourselves into the transformational future— a future that is not limited to old paradigms and ways of training and releasing. This is a future based on life-changing awakenings of hearts and consciences that results in marketplace and ministry groups that are transformed by a sensitized awakening of what it means to live out our lives on purpose, individually and corporately. This is when the bridges will have been built—bridges over ruined roads, bridges over troubled waters, bridges that build transformation into the lives of others.

The fully accredited graduate school where I have been teaching for the past twenty years is typical of the overkill of the "telling" model of leadership training. After sitting in lectures each week for two to three years, students are then expected to have a culminating experience with a field mentor with whom the dialogue enables the student to process what they value and then assess what they have integrated from those lectures. It is a great opportunity that is really a missed opportunity because it comes at the wrong time. Dialogues with trained coaches and mentors for students that will have the greatest impact will be up front and throughout their training programs as well as at the end.

In 2000 we offered Transformational Leadership Coach (TLC) training as an unadvertised graduate credit elective to a few select faculty, administrators, and students. This was the same methodology as our non-academic coach training system with added graduate level work required. The emphasis of this training is the integration of the coaching paradigm as a transformational process for leadership development. We wondered whether this would be well received in a setting that had staked its reputation on the quality of the "telling" and the latest technology to do it in a cutting edge manner.

> *"The coaching method of learning puts the typical seminary educational method to shame...I feel like I am coming away with more practical knowledge than any other class."*   *(Master's student)*

> *"I have probably gotten more out of these classes than 98% of my other ones."*
>   *(Master's student)*

> *"You bring some things (at TLC) in terms of professionally developed curriculum that nothing else I've seen comes close to."*
>   *(Professional Trainer)*

Five years later, the evidence has been overwhelming that this is just what has been missing in the lives of both faculty and students. Without any promotion or recruiting, except word of mouth by satisfied customers, TLC courses have become the most popular electives across the entire campus. These classes on transformational coach training have drawn more students and faculty from across the different departments than any other class in the history of the school. Graduate students come from the Business, Leadership, Education, Psychology, Communication, and Divinity Schools in both the master's and doctoral levels. In hundreds of student evaluations and feedback sessions the overwhelming response is that this has been the missing process and dynamic for their leadership development.

This bridge of transformational coaching is now being requested by several other schools to become a way to traverse over the ancient pathways of academic lecturing to a transformational path of developing leaders from the inside out. It works both in and out of academic settings because it is designed to work on what leaders want and need to deal with to be authentic and culturally current in their careers today.

This TLC model is also working in Brazil, El Salvador, Norway, Singapore, Hong Kong, Indonesia, Korea, Russia, Canada, Jamaica, with certified coach trainers and translations in these nations as well as here in the United States. With the goal of 10,000 certified TLC coaches throughout the world over the next ten years, TLC is on track to become the coach training industry leader from a transformational and spiritual perspective.

Bridging into Transformational Creativity for Leadership Development

Coaching and Creativity
Many people today are hungering for a creativity that has eluded them for years. A recent survey revealed that 85% of people are not fulfilled in their jobs, including 50% of CEO's.7 Most are bored and are not getting out of bed each morning with a passion for their life on the job. Their creative juices have dried up and they are on auto-pilot just going through the routine of a day. The same old beaten cow

path has become worn and weary, and they need a bridge to a new pathway to look at their development and fulfillment in the workplace where they spend most of their lives. They need a transformational coach who doesn't simply help them do their job better, but to view their life at work more creatively.

In a recent study at California's Stanford University, researchers came to the conclusion that the number one inhibitor of consistent creativity, the primary thing that holds back creative expression in people, is a judgmental attitude.8 Most are judging themselves, judging others, and being fearful of being judged. The product of this is an inhibited creative expression in an individual and in an organization. People can't be themselves on the job and so are looking for more time to be themselves off the job.

The dream of the TLC staff, worldwide TLC partners, and our army of TLC certified coaches is that every culture, organization, church, or business will enable people to experience personal coaches who believe in them, who stand by them, and who will not judge them. Through our Accelerated Coach Training (ACT) we are bringing coaching training to organizations so that select people within their own organization can be trained in as little as 21 weeks provide coaching as needed, in-house.9 Not only is this powerful for an individual, but in a corporate sense this becomes one of the most creative advantages for that organization. It releases the leadership to look at things from new perspectives and to begin to sense the larger reason why they exist, with the ability to express that in ways that energize and renew the vision and purpose of workers and employers alike. When the workplace becomes a creative place, it will exhibit a renewed passion for life, work relationships, and productivity.

"This accelerated coach training has already

impacted our staff and department in tangible ways. There is more laughter and positive attitude in our staff and workers than I have seen here in years. It seems that people are really enjoying being here as compared to a few short months ago."

(Staff Director of a large church that became ACT trained)

Research has also shown that consistent creativity does not come from tired people. When we look at the historical patterns of great breakthroughs in science, we usually see hardworking men and women at the laboratory or at the workbench who put in heroic hours looking for a solution. Yet many times the creative breakthrough came when they got away from the work environment and were playing tennis or taking a swim or perhaps even taking a shower, and then it all came together—the divine ah ha!

It all began to make sense when they had removed themselves from the work environment. Why? The reason is simple but profound. They actually were able to enter into a disengaged mode, a place of rest and restoration. Then and only then were they able to experience the creative flow that was locked up when they were so focused only on producing and on the work itself. Those that are coaching transformationally enable people to examine why they are so driven, why they cannot feel a sense of accomplishment unless they hit the ground running from the moment they get up. An organization that embraces coaching is one that embraces creativity and will become a place that most people want to get out of bed for each day.

Creativity and Coaching Intuition:
A Prophetic Approach

Many people today begin the coaching process desiring to achieve something—write a book or reach a goal—but somewhere along the line they begin to sense the intuitive power in a transformational coach and it creates a longing in them to get in touch with their own sense of intuition. Intuition is hard to define, but it is the ability to intuit, discern, to have a sense of an inner knowing, the ability to read between the lines or sense the heart of an issue. The role of intuition has been reserved in many ways for the creative artist and for those who are inspired poets, writers, or musicians.

But now more and more people are tired of the 9 to 5 and the emphasis on the scientific rational approaches and logical patterns. They are looking for things that touch them at a level where they have not been touched before and to experience more of that in the workplace. They are awakened to the desire to be more discerning, to be more intuitive in their experiences and expression of life in their marriages, in their families, in their careers, in their hobbies. Work cultures that help people embrace and celebrate this quality of life will become more conducive to creativity and more attractive for top people than just those who look at the bottom line of profit and loss margins. This is the agenda of the emerging "post-modern" generation that is entering the workforce today.

What is different from the old language of "modern" to the new language of "post-modern"? The bumper-to-bumper, well-traveled road of modern language deals with information exchange, classical apologetics, linear and logical thinking, objectivity and impersonal analysis, fill-in-the-blanks, and multiple choices. The bridge to the wide open less- traveled road of post modern language deals with understanding, relational experience and connection, real-life emotion, and metaphors that can readily morph into the prophetic. These conversations can become prophetic—not because they predict the future, but because they highlight what is on the heart and agenda of God for that individual. The new era has shifted language from logic to illumination, mind to heart and spirit, proposition to intuition, literate to prophetic, impersonal to personal, individual to community.10

Transformational coaching speaks to the heart more than the head. Speaking to the heart may mean a number of things. It could mean speaking to the dream destiny that is in the heart and aspirations of each person. Jesus did this by "calling forth" that destiny, or true identity, before He led them into their life purpose. That is why we must first "call by name" before we "lead them out" (John 10:3). Prophetic heart to heart conversations, not just messages, are founded on this cornerstone.

Though the coaching industry has magnified the value of intuition, the biblical approach to transformational coaching has the uncommon advantage of understanding the role of the Spirit of God in prophetic communication. Most of the controversy around the use of the charismatic gifts has been over their role in church meetings, with few people realizing that they have real value outside the "stained glass" and into the "plain glass" of the workplace. Transformational coaching acts as a bridge to bring this power dimension to people who will never darken the door of a church meeting.

Just as dedicated missionaries spend years in preparation to speak the language of the people they are called to serve, so transformational coaches are preparing themselves to impact post moderns, one prophetic conversation at a time. The core of Transformational Leadership Coaching (www.transformationalcoaching.com) is to train new language missiologists in a one year-plus process of speaking this dialect. A compelling case for this dialect can be found in the author John Eldredge, who claims that the power of metaphor and myth are keys to speaking to the thoughts and intentions of the heart.11 In powerful ways for post-moderns, metaphors can act as a prophetic bypassing of the natural logic mind to speak directly to the heart; just as the parables of Jesus did in His day. The disciplines of deep subterranean listening coupled with powerful penetrating questioning and catalyzed by relevant metaphors, will become the cross-cultural tool kits for post modern transformational coaches.

One of my favorite verses for post modern pilgrims is the answer by the blind candidate for the healing question of Jesus, "I see men like trees walking" (Mark 8:24). The metaphor is both other-worldly and this-worldly. It is a "covert" language that puts together opposite pairs in a controlled contradiction. It exemplifies the post modern pleasure at simply putting things together than don't go together (as is commonly done in modernity).

Because I am committing myself to stay in touch with the culture I am coaching others to reach, I am preparing myself transformationally to experience and communicate this "speaking in metaphors." Beginning in late 2005 I will take post moderns on a one week a year "eco-tour" where they can dialogue with me on the sunset of each day first on their awakened heart to creation ("I see men as trees"); second, on their awakened heart to the Creator, the one who will completely open what has kept their eyes from recognizing Him (Luke 24:16) and then see everyone clearly (Mark 8:25). The metaphor has become the bridge over worn out modern roadways and must be crossed by both the seeker and the sent one.

Prophetic conversations for post modern coaching are organic. It is part of our everyday life itself as compared to an institutional or programmed meeting event. It is more on the road of the grocery line than the ministry line at a church altar. It connects the everyday to the Day the Lord has made. It bridges the mundane and the magnificent. It "metaphors" what the Bible calls a "word of wisdom" or "word of knowledge" in the dynamic of the coaching relationship, and even mixes in a sense of humor!

Bridging into Transformational Excellence for Leadership Development

Coaching and Excellence

Too many people have the wrong definition of excellence. Excellence is wrongly defined not just how well you do, but how well you do compared to how well others have done. This roadway is littered with the debris of losers and "has beens" who are deemed irrelevant because they are not on someone's "top ten list" or are not in the media front pages. But that is not a transformational definition. The transformational definition of excellence is much more in line with a biblical view of excellence. In the Bible, excellence is not how you do compared to others, but how you do in relationship to what is invested in you, endowed in you, from the creator, Himself. It is time for a bridge over this destructive road to one that is more "win/win" rather than "win/lose."

In the biblical parable of the talents (Matthew 25:14-30), one person is given one talent, one is give two talents, and one is given five talents. The one talent person buried the talent, yet the others invested it and brought forth an increase. One take-away of this story is that we can be a one or two or five-talent person and have excellence by fulfilling what we are called to do and what we are capable of doing with what we have. That means that a five talent person who only does three or four of his or her talents may look excellent because they have done more than the one or two talent person, but in the eyes of the Creator who knows what they have been endowed with, they have squandered; they have not fully invested, they have taken the easy road and, as a result, they have missed personal excellence to the degree of what they were capable of doing.

Transformational coaching is not just a methodology, but a theology rooted in the character of God Himself. God is the author and creator of excellence, and a proper view of His character is one that brings a transformational view of excellence to the workplace. A transformational coach calls forth creativity and excellence in people—not to define that excellence by how well they do compared to others, but to recognize that excellence in terms of what they are given and how they invest it. There are too many people who do not have a spirit of excellence in the workplace because they are looking at what others are doing. A coach who is worth his or her hire will challenge that employee that "For everyone to whom much is given, from him much will be required" (Luke 12:48).

> *"This process (TLC training) is inspiring me by reinforcing what God has already been putting in my heart in terms of using these next 20+ years to invest in younger men. This material is giving me an excellent framework on which to express what was in my heart."*　　　　　　　*(College Chaplain)*

Excellence is advanced in the very ways that coaching is strong: asking rather than telling, affirming, acknowledging, and calling forth. These are phrases that are new to many people, but coaching seems to have brought them to the surface today. The ability for a transformational coach to acknowledge a client means to affirm who that person had to be in order to accomplish whatever change was achieved. That ability is not just to identify where someone is, but how far they have had to come to get there; not just what they have done, but what it took for them to do that in the context of that particular culture or background.

> *"I have never come across anything like TLC training. Some other types of training programs cover these principles, but where else do you get to*

sit down and talk one on one with a coach. This is having an immediate impact on my life, and I am getting more out of this relationship than I have in any other training program."   *(Manager)*

"My productivity has gone up to a level it has not been at for 20 years because I focused on the values that I want to live by and the goals that are attached to those values."   *(Business Leader)*

"This training program is far beyond what I have been through before. It is not just the material, it is the way leaders and the coaches themselves have helped me to reinvent why I am even in this process and understand at a deeper level. I have been transformed."   *(Pastor)*

"I was extremely skeptical, but I believe I grew more as a person by working out my fears and allowing this process to work itself out in me. I am changed and I am going to change others because of this."   *(Executive)*

**Reflection and Discussion Questions
Chapter Three: Bridges Over Ruined Roads—
Coaching as a Bridge for Personal and
Leadership Transformation**

1. What did the true story of the students and their mentors tell you about a key to what has been called the "generation gap"? How might coach training be used to bridge that gap in your ministry or career context? Who do you know that models the ability to close that gap and why are they able to do so?

2. What did the true story of the couple who led a Bible study tell you about how you might utilize this team approach in your training process? Have you experienced the power of being matched with a teammate because of an intentional process of gifting or temperament matching to maximize the impact of your unique design combined together? How might coach training in gifting/design give you confidence in doing this for others?

3. Where are you along the continuum of "love to tell" and "love to listen"? As a peer to give you support, encouragement, and accountability each week as you seek to move more towards a listening/asking mode. Notice the

difference responses you will begin to receive from those closest to you.

4. If you have any responsibilities for training others or if you have any opportunities to give feedback to the training programs in your organization how might you incorporate a "clinical" and coaching approach to what you are already doing? How might those changes bring about more transformation in the lives of the participants?

5. How would you describe the role of "Intuition" from a biblical perspective? How does coaching enhance it development in our lives and how may coach training bring that out more in your life?

CHAPTER FOUR

Bridge Building— How Transformation Happens

By Tony Stoltzfus

What is Transformation?

The appointment between Janice and her coach was way off track and straying further by the moment. While in many ways Janice was a mature "mother of the faith," who held down a position of responsibility in a large non-profit organization, she did not seem able to rein in her need to talk. The exercise she was working on called for her to deliver a "One-Minute Message"—60 seconds of focused sharing around a principle she'd learned from experience. Twenty-seven minutes after she started talking, Janice finally wound down with a sheepish question: "How long was that? I talked too long again, didn't I?"

"After five minutes I was squirming," her coach remembers. "At ten minutes I was getting upset, at 15 I was checking out, and at 20 all I could say was, 'Help, Lord!'" The silence following Janice's question was a crucial moment. Taking a deep breath, the coach told her how long she had talked, but then went on to affirm the invaluable lessons she had learned in her 65 years and suggested they work together to help her better communicate them. While Janice had known for a long time that her over-talking put people off, this was the first time anyone had ever both been honest with her and also offered to help. She jumped at the chance to make a change.

Janice continues to be transformed by that moment two years later. It eventually led her to revisit and reinterpret a painful divorce 40 years before that constricted her view of life, to recast her relationships at work (which are much improved), and even to do simple things like introducing people and then stepping back to let *them* do the talking. Janice is quite simply a different person today—and it's a lot more fun to carry on a conversation with her!

Transformation is *deep, lasting, significant change*—the kind that Janice experienced with her coach. It happens when we experience a seismic shift on the inside, in the areas of our being that define us most deeply:

- **Our Beliefs:** the values, worldview, strongholds, and priorities that are remade when we get new perspective.
- **Our Identity:** the gifts, calling, life purpose, and life stages that shape our understanding of who we are as we discover them.
- **Our Personhood:** the sense of security, acceptance, fears, and self-confidence that develop through relating to others.
- **Our Character:** the habits of behavior that we cultivate through discipline.

For instance, transformation may involve finding an acceptance through a significant relationship that launches us into a whole new realm of self-confidence, freeing us to do things we never thought we could. Or we finally overcome the obstacles that kept us from establishing regular devotional habits, and our newfound ability to embrace discipline spills over into a whole bunch of other areas of life. Or we discover what we were made to be and the direction of our life changes as we realign our choices with our new sense of identity. All these are examples of how changes in who we *are* create lasting transformation in how we *act*.

Being and Doing

Often our attempts at self-improvement stop short of working at this being level, targeting skills or outward behaviors alone and producing results that fall short of our expectations. For instance, I may set out to become a more encouraging person by making sure I give my spouse at least one compliment every day. That's a great goal, and doubtless would improve my marriage if I attained it. But what would happen if I went to a deeper level? What if instead of disciplining myself to make daily compliments, I changed my whole outlook on life? What if I began to grapple with the reasons why I'm critical—that I'm unhappy with my life and wish I was somewhere else, or that the joy has gone out of my marriage, or that I'm so wedded to my work that I don't have the energy for my relationships?

Our actions flow naturally out of who we are. According to Jesus, a good tree (being) bears good fruit (doing). Out of the abundance of the heart (being) the mouth speaks (doing). The key of knowledge (Luke 11:52) is *being* something, not just knowing or talking about it. So in order to permanently transform the way we act instead of just making external adjustments, we first must change who we are. Then the behavioral changes we want come naturally. When the romance returns to my marriage and I love being with my spouse, complimenting her is a natural reflex instead of a difficult discipline.

Seeing this kind of change is one of the most satisfying

parts of transformational coaching. I love to hear a client say (like one did not long ago), "I've grown more in the last five months than I did in the previous five years." The same is true in all of Christian leadership: we want to see transformed lives, transformed organizations, and ultimately to transform our communities and our world. If we can create an environment where people are consistently transformed the way Janice was in her coaching encounter, life in the Kingdom will start to get pretty exciting.

So let's take a look at how transformation happens.

The Dominate Change Paradigm

The methods we use to work at change provide clues to our understanding of how change works. If we examine those methods, we begin to see a model for producing life change that is often used in secular as well as Christian circles. In this model, if change is needed, we teach on it. We write books, present information, hold classes, and give a seminar, conference or lecture.

A lot of time is devoted to crafting a compelling presentation of the truth. Graphics, handouts and PowerPoint slides are added, along with jokes and stories to maintain people's attention. However, comparatively little thought is given to what happens after the presentation is finished. Debriefing, opportunities to practice new skills, personal encouragement, accountability, or structured support systems are not often part of the plan. These things may be absent simply because they take a lot of time and effort to develop. Or it may be that we just don't know how to create a structure to reinforce a choice once it is made. But the fact that our focus is so consistently on presenting truth so that people choose to change as opposed to following up afterward reveals our unspoken assumptions about how change works.

This understanding of change is based on two key beliefs:

- Right information produces right action.
- We initiate change.

The first statement means we believe that if people know what the right thing to do is, they will do it. So when we want to see change, we focus on presenting the truth in a compelling way so people will choose to live it out. Right information leads to right choices that yield right actions. Follow-up is treated as unnecessary; because the unspoken belief is that the choice is enough to make the change. If we really believed that a follow-up support structure was a vital factor in transformation, we would provide one. The fact that we don't means we're assuming that right information produces right actions.

The second statement means that the ability to receive the truth and choose it is independent of the hearer's life situation. The first belief assumes that effective choices to change can be made without attention to follow-up after the choice. The second belief says that the ability of hearers to make choices is independent of any prior preparation in their life. Since when and whether we change is basically a question of will and initiative, any presentation of truth that offers a choice can produce change. So as the writer, speaker, or presenter, I can choose whatever change agenda appeals to me, present it to my audience, and they will be impacted by it regardless of what's going on in their lives. Essentially, what this belief system does is strip change out of the context of real life, and reduces it to something that can be jump-started by the right kind of event, right words, or the right presentation.

Together these assumptions lead naturally toward using large group events or mass marketing initiatives almost exclusively to produce change. If transformation required an individualized approach, or we believed it grew out of what was uniquely going on in each person's life, we'd work at it on an individual basis. But if change is a function of choice and information, 100 or 1000 or 10,000 people can be addressed as easily as one, simply by increasing the audience for the presentation. In a large group approach, the growth area to be addressed is chosen by the leader or teacher based on his or her assessment of the needs of the group. It isn't necessary to approach each person's needs individually, because any person can make any change at any time. Right information produces right action, and we initiate the change process independent of the life-context of the hearer.

Most formal training methods largely follow this paradigm; they involve a teacher dispensing information to a large group in a pedagogical setting. Follow-up, support, relationship, accountability, coaching, or opportunities for practice with feedback are usually lacking, as is customization of the training program to individual needs. The desired outcome is that as many people as possible make a choice to act on the truth that it is presented, because it is assumed that change will follow choice.

These same beliefs can also play out in the way we work with people one-on-one. If you ask another individual for help with a personal problem, most likely you will get an answer like..." "You should talk to Bob—he's got some great resources for this..." "That reminds me of something I experienced a few years back..." Advice-giving assumes that you are coming to me for an answer, and if I can give you that answer then things will get better. In other words, the right information will result in positive change. Occasionally a conversation like this will end with a promise to pray for the need, or to check back, or even sometimes in an agreement to be accountable. But for most of us, the normative experience is probably that we get information but not follow-up.

When we start talking about advice-giving, the flaw in this change paradigm becomes more obvious. How many of us really want someone to give us a bunch of unsolicited advice? In small group settings I've often asked what people want when they share a need, and the unanimous answer is, "We don't want advice!" We want support, we want to feel heard, we need encouragement, we may desire prayer or accountability, but the last thing we're looking for is to be told what to do. But turn around in that same group ten minutes later and share a need, and you're almost guaranteed to get some advice! The instinct to give it is pretty deeply ingrained in us.

So in summary, when we think about helping others change, our instinct is to try to present the truth in a compelling way to catalyze a choice, but we rarely think about how that truth fits into the prior context of the person's life, or how we will follow-up to make sure the change sticks.

Does This Model Work?

Many positive benefits can and do come out of informational training, and sometimes the counsel of others can be very valuable. But does the "right information produces right action" approach consistently catalyze *transformation*?

I've been querying leaders for a number of years about what actually *has* transformed their lives, and the results are remarkably consistent. When I ask a group to jot down "two things that transformed your life, after which you were never the same," participants *almost never* report an instance involving a seminar, conference, class, or informational training event. Conversely, almost every individual selects one of the following two types of experiences as most transformational: 1) overcoming a difficult set of circumstances, or 2) a significant relationship. Christian leaders virtually always point to experiences and relationships as most transforming, and rarely to the kind of formal training events that we customarily set up to produce change.

The story of Janice's transformation is a good example of the kinds of experiences they cite as being transformational. It wasn't a training event that transformed her life, but a difficult real-life experience (her failed one-minute message) happening within the context of a significant relationship with her coach that set in motion the process of transformation.

What does this mean? Transformation seems to require a significant experiential or relational component to take place. When you scratch the surface of the transformational experiences individuals report, usually you'll find that there was an informational component. But the information came in and addressed a pre-existing condition in the person's life (negating our second assumption) while the experience was the primary element in the change and information was secondary (negating the first assumption).

Informational training divorced from experience and relationship does not tend to produce transformation. Information alone produces cognition ("head-knowledge") much more readily than transformation. In other words, while having the right ideas is important, they tend to impact us in the midst of experiences and relationships that prepare us to receive the truth and push us in an ongoing way to walk out that truth. *Information alone does not produce transformation.*

A Transformational Change Paradigm

Transformational coaching is based on a different paradigm. It starts with two very different assumptions:

- Transformation happens primarily through experiences and relationships.
- God initiates change.

These assumptions lead to a distinctly different method of working at transformation. Since God initiates change through real-life experiences and relationships, what is *already going on in* the client's life is the growth focus. A training event does not need to be created—*the client's life is the training event*, and what God has already begun to do in the client's life is the change agenda. The job of the coach, then, is not to choose a change agenda, but to allow the client to choose it based on what God is doing in his or her life. God must initiate the change by creating an experiential context that opens the individual up to change at a deeper level than usual. The coach simply helps the client identify these teachable moments instead of coming with an agenda.

And once that change agenda is determined, the coach's role is not to present information or provide answers, but to provide a support structure to help the client realize the change. The choice alone is not enough—without follow-up, encouragement, and accountability the client is likely to make a great choice but then fail to fully walk it out.

This coaching process is completely individualized—there is no script or program of predetermined steps to follow. God's activity in life circumstances defines the agenda and provides motivation for change, while coaching supplies a relational support system that maximizes the client's ability to engage God and grow no matter what the situation. And sometimes within this broader change context the coach *will* speak a powerful word of truth that connects the client with reality, alters perspective, or helps the client connect with God's purposes.

Doing It the Way Jesus Did

These ideas about change aren't new—they were practiced by Jesus himself. After giving the parable of the sower, Jesus made an interesting comment about why he used parables. His disciples, the people who had a relationship with him and who were experiencing life with him, were to have the privilege of understanding how the Kingdom works. But for those who only heard the truth *without the experience of a relationship* with Jesus, the truth was given in parables so they wouldn't understand it (Matthew13:10-17). In other words, Jesus refused to dispense information to the crowds outside of the context of experience and relationship. Jesus was not repudiating public ministry (on the contrary, he did a lot of it!), but he was giving us a picture of its limitations. Information alone does not produce transformation, but truth in the context of relationship and experience is trans-formational.

The gospels give repeated examples of how Jesus' belief in experiential learning influenced his ministry. For instance, he did not choose to address his disciples' hidden hunger to be the top dog by sitting down with them one day and doing a little teaching on pride. Instead, he waited for a teachable moment. On that day on the highway, when the heated words of their argument over who was the greatest still hung in the air, he seized the moment and asked a seemingly-innocent question: "What were you talking about on the road?" Silence. In that awkward experience, Jesus *shows instead of tells* the truth by leading a child into the middle of their circle, giving them a graphic picture of the contrast between pride and humility. Jesus' invitation to become like children instead of like big shots is a timeless truth, but the depth of its impact on the disciples is inextricably tied to the context.

Jesus understood that our ability to even hear (let alone choose) the truth depends on God's preparing us to receive it. So he was constantly on the lookout for those unpre-dictable teachable moments when life experience made his disciples particularly open to being transformed. For instance, the disciples' astonishment over their great catch of fish made them receptive to hearing their call to be fishers of men. Jesus confirmed his power over death by having them feel the nail prints and place their hands in the wound at his side. These were powerful, life-changing moments that they never forgot. Instead of a mere memory of *words* of truth, the disciples recalled a full-blooded *experience* of it – sights, sounds, emotions, smells and touch.

A look at the results of this approach confirms the wisdom of Jesus' choice to build intimate relationships with a small circle of disciples and entrust his legacy to them. Eleven of the twelve had lives that were transformed, became key leaders of Jesus' movement, and had an almost immeasurable impact that continues to reverberate down through the centuries. Contrast this with the outcome of his healing encounters, where (for instance) ten were healed but only one came back to even thank him (let alone become a leader in his movement), or with his public ministry, where he spoke to tens of thousands but only had a total congregation of 120 committed followers at his death. These events were important evangelistic and pre-evangelistic encounters, which also laid the groundwork for the apostles' later evangelistic success. But Jesus' legacy was passed on by those he built relationship with and walked with for three years. *Although Jesus' public ministry touched several thousand times more people, the relationships he cultivated with his disciples arguably produced more long-term impact.*

Change in the Business World

Studies from the business world also support the idea that lasting change is more dependent on experiences and relationships than information. One large study found that out of the billions of dollars spent on corporate training programs (seminars, e-learning, classes, etc.), only about 10% of those who attend show any measurable, lasting change in their actual work behavior. In other words, 90% of the people went away from the event and promptly went back to the same old way of doing things.

By contrast, two studies (Oliver et. al. 1997, and Strayer and Rossett, 1994) found that following up formal training with a coaching relationship had dramatic results. The first showed that executive coaching increased performance four times as much as training alone. The second study, at a well-known realty organization, used a coaching program to cut the time needed for a new associate to get his or her first listing to less than half the industry average. The first month's commissions for those in the coaching program were three times greater than of those who went through the same training but had no coaching follow-up. In other words, tying training back into a life-context (instead of offering stand-alone training divorced from life) was considerably more effective at producing change.

Putting it All Together

It's clear that deep, lasting, significant changes happens best in the context of experience and relationship. Let's look at a real example of how this works in the form of an actual coaching conversation.

Randy is a senior apostolic church leader who does counseling, writing, and travels internationally to speak and to work at leadership development. He'd just been through a difficult transitional time in his life—he and his wife had both switched jobs, his wife's mother had endured a long illness and eventually died in a situation that had been exacerbated by family difficulties. In our coaching appointment that morning we were using a life purpose tool to look at what his values were and what he wanted in different areas of life. The conversation was rolling along smoothly until we came to the hobbies and recreation category. While Randy is an enthusiastic, verbal person who is usually not at a lack for words, he was struggling to identify what fit in that area of his life.

"Well, what do you like to do for fun?" I asked, trying to

help him think things through. Randy wasn't sure how to answer. Fun wasn't really an important part of his life. He rarely took time out from working to just play. The conversation soon turned to rest and recreation, and there wasn't much to say in that area either.

Then something hit me. When people are having trouble in their financial life, the question I ask is, "Do you tithe?" because tithing is the discipline that God gave to help us keep our financial life in balance. The thought occurred to me that when a person can't rest and work is consuming his life, the question I should ask is, "Do you take a Sabbath?" That's the discipline we've been given to keep our work and rest in balance. It seemed like a perfect teachable moment, so I took the plunge and inquired: 'When was the last time you took a Sabbath?"

There was a lengthy silence. Finally, Randy replied, "Probably 1998." It had been over five years since he'd taken a day just to rest. By then our appointment was nearly over, so after chatting for another minute or two on the subject, I requested that as an action step Randy look up Exodus 31:13 and think about its content.

That evening Randy looked up the verse: "Surely My Sabbaths you shall keep...that you may know that I am the LORD who sanctifies you" (Exodus 31:13-14). "I couldn't sleep that night," Randy remembers. "I was up 'til three in the morning studying what the Bible said about rest. The idea that rest was connected with God's way of sanctifying me was a completely new idea. My wife had been trying to convince me for years that I needed to take time off, but I never did. Before I went to bed I e-mailed my coach and told him what a 'Eureka!' moment that was."

As he reflects back now, Randy says, "The idea of rest keeps coming up everywhere in my life now—I was just preparing to preach on the Sabbath the other day. Since then I've noticed a phenomenal difference in my productivity...

and in my clarity of thought and creativity. I had been struggling to finish reading a book for months, and after I started taking a day a week to do nothing, I was able to finish it in about a week and a half.

"You think you are going to get under conviction in some meeting where there is preaching and teaching going on, and here we were just having a conversation. There has only been one other time in my life where I've been under that level of conviction—I would have thought it would have come through someone getting on my case and saying, 'You need to change! You ought to get some rest!' But instead it happened in a natural, casual conversation."

Debriefing

This situation is a great example of a teachable moment. Randy had heard many times from his wife about his need for rest, but the added pressures of a transitional time provided a deeper motivation to rethink his life patterns than he had before. The act of staring at an empty blank under *Hobbies and Recreation* and not being able to think of anything to write was a pivotal moment, a process that God had begun came to the point of decision.

The coach sensed that this was an important moment, so he asked a direct, challenging question that pushed Randy to engage the situation at the transformational level. The transparent relationship Randy had with his coach allowed him to explore changing his ideas about rest without becoming defensive or trying to conceal what his life really looked like. Notice too that the truth that was brought to bear on the situation wasn't something told to Randy, but something Randy became motivated to discover on his own in the scriptures—a great example of coaching!

This story illustrates the key elements in the coaching approach to transformation: a *set of circumstances* God used to initiate change in a certain area, a key *experience* that got

Randy's attention, and an important *relationship* that formed the context for being transformed. Truth or information was presented not in a sterile, classroom situation, but in the context of life, and in that context the truth had tremendous power to set Randy free.

Reflection and Discussion Questions
Chapter Four: Bridge Building—
How Transformation Happens

1. If our actions flow naturally out of who we are at a core level, how does transformational coaching get at that core in ways that other methods may not? How we respond under pressure may be an indication of what lies just below the surface of our learned responses. What areas of your life would you like to see addressed for transformation?

2. Where have you grown frustrated, weary, or even hopeless that certain areas of your life will just not experience sustainable change? How might the dominate change paradigm in traditional approaches contribute to your present attitude about change? How might the transformational paradigm give you results where others methods have failed?

3. How does the concept that "God initiates change" fit into our common view of New Year resolutions and other self-help tendencies? How would you be confident that it is God initiating change in some arena of your life? How might a transformational coach have helped you see this

more clearly in past times when you did not recognize God's role in the change process?

4. Take one core value or competency that Jesus Christ tried to instill in His disciples such as "servant hood" Can you find the transformational ways that He used to help them really get it? What does this say about the methods we use in our organizations?

5. If transformational coaching was a foundational part of your leadership's personal lives and a key part of your leadership development strategy in your organization what differences might you expect to see in the outcomes? What might happen if you wrote an outline of a proposal to your organization that incorporated this transformational process? What if they approved it and then asked you to make it happen!

Section Two:
Coaching for Church and
Ministry Transformation

Introduction

Within the next ten years we will see an explosion of churches that will spring up in places we once thought were unheard of, taking shape in ways we presently could not imagine. At a time of some of the greatest spiritual hunger our cultures have ever seen, many of the churches people will visit may not offer or model a level of spirituality that will be compelling to them and will fall short of their expectations. This is sad, even devastating to those who have been preparing God's people for an end-time harvest of historical proportions. Our normal church life, including that found in a large portion of the 365,000 churches in the U.S., may be teetering on a foundation that needs to be rebuilt to deal with a fundamental weakness at the core. What is it?

Most anyone will mentally respond to the question, "What is the foundation of the Christian Church?" with the answer, "Jesus Christ." What is not realized, however, is that this foundation is expressed in His Body, the Church, in the way they express that life relationally. In fact, He said it was the one way they would know who we are...by the love (quality of our relationships and therefore the quality of our conversations) that we have for one another.

The foundation of this relational community is the Trinity itself. According to the foundations of Christian doctrine, God lives in a divine community of three in one: Father, Son, and Holy Spirit. We need more of God in our midst to meet the more-of-God expectation in the hearts of those around us. So if God is going to be attracted to His representatives on earth, if He desires to demonstrate His manifest presence in a church and not only His omnipresence in the earth, then the church is going to have to move more to the relational dynamic that is happening right now in the Godhead. "...Be done on earth as it is in heaven" (Matthew 6:10b).

Think about it. In the beginning in Jerusalem, Christianity was a lifestyle. There were no fine buildings, no hierarchy separating clergy from laity, no theological seminaries, no Christian colleges, no Sunday schools, no choirs—only small groups having big relationships; only small prayer meetings having big results; only small households having big city-wide transformation. When Christianity came to be accepted in Rome in 360 AD it became an institution. When Christianity came to be accepted in Europe it became a culture. Now in America, Christianity has become an enterprise in many places. Somehow the relational part keeps getting left out.

"But God..." scripture frequently says. But God has shown up just in time for the coming harvest by turning the hearts of the fathers (leaders, spiritual fathers, coaches, earthly fathers) to the children (followers, spiritual children, coach clients, earthly children). Finally, people are starting to pay heart-to-heart attention to one another. That is the big part; getting us off the launching pad where 80% of the rocket fuel is expended. For the American enterprise church, that launching pad is the heart issue. Even wanting to have our horizontal relationships with others is the barometer of the quality of our vertical relationship with our Creator. The next part, transformational coaching relationships, is the easy part. We only need to give 20%.

Transformational Leadership Coaching is coaching values and methodology from the perspective of how God relates to us. It is all about the Father's heart of seeing us as sons and daughters, not as slaves or servants. "No longer do I call you servants…but I have called you friends…" (John 15:15a). It is all about the reality of a family that has unconditional love for one another rather than an orphanage that has children trying to earn a family to adopt them. That is what makes it transformational. Because a coach has experienced an authentic life-changing relationship from another coach, and has been trained to replicate that in others, she or he is qualified to bring a renewal of relational credibility, one conversation at a time.

The church needs transformational coaches. They will create a relational DNA that will be seen and heard by those who are looking for the real thing. It will be seen in the way speakers are more transparent, the way staff relationships are more authentic, the way parents and leaders call forth destiny in another's heart rather than call down fire on another's head. Transformational coaching is not about better time management for greater productivity, but better life and organizational focus for greater creative destiny.

Within the next ten years people will expect nothing less than to have a real person be real with them, to help them really live their lives to make a real difference. They will want a one-on-one personal trainer or coach; someone who can help them design their own spiritual growth plan that takes into account what God already did and is presently doing in their life before they ever visit a church. They will not be disappointed when they discover that the churches that God is attracted to are the ones who have leaders who are expressing God's heart in a methodology that helps them get it. People will come when they know that God is coming, too. People will stay when they know that after the program lights are turned off the real lifestyle of the church goes into action. God will hang around and make His presence known when He sees happening in our town what is happening in His throne.

CHAPTER FIVE

Critical Issues for Coaching in the Church and Ministry World

By Dr. Joseph Umidi

The global marketplace has embraced one-on-one coaching models for personal and organizational development that are rapidly replacing hierarchical supervision, consulting, and even traditional mentoring. At the same time the post-millennial and post-modern youth around the world are looking for leaders and role models that they can authentically connect to at a heart level. This is a *"kairos"* time for the Church. The bride of Christ has the value base and heart motivation to become the most powerful source of highly relational and authentic transformational coaching to both its members and its surrounding community in the next decade and beyond.

Scriptures describe a heart posture of the Father to his sons and daughters, the ministry and methodology of Jesus, and the examples of the apostles in both transformational and coaching terms. Though the word "coaching" is not clearly used, there are key concepts and expressions that unveil the dynamic of what is described as coaching today. When understood from a biblical and theological framework, it can be seen that transformational coaching has its roots in the character and Kingdom of God and should be reclaimed as a key value and methodology of the Church.

Transformational Coaching is an Extraordinary Conversation

> *"Did not our heart burn within us while He talked with us on the road..." (Luke 24:32)*

Since the Kingdom of God can be identified by right relationships with God and others, the way to measure those relationships can be seen in the quality of our conversations. In many ways "the conversation is the relationship".12 Instead of giving advice from the perspective of the teacher or mentor, the coach enables the client to transform the way they look at their life by assisting them in their own perspective—one of engaging God and getting His heart and word for themselves.

This is the core of the biblical view of **incarnation** (Philippians 1:1): Jesus Christ left His "frame of reference" around the throne and glory of God the Father to enter into the world of those He came to serve. Coaching is the service of a coach leaving their own perspective or frame of reference to enter into the world of the client he or she is serving. Transformational coaching goes another step beyond most coaching by engaging, with the client, the perspective of what God is presently doing in the client's life situation.

Coaching involves listening and asking questions rather than simply telling and giving advice from the perspective of the speaker. Transformational coaches listen because the person they are conversing with is created in God's image and therefore has infinite value just as they are right now. They are worth paying attention to in an individualized manner. More than simply a technique, this attention overflows from a heart in the coach that has personally experienced transformation from another who has related to them in an extraordinary conversation.

Transformational coaches ask powerful questions because the person they are coaching has such tremendous God-given capacity to live the life they have been given to live. They give responsibility to the person to make and own the decisions for their own development because the transformational coach sees the power and privilege God has given them of carrying it.

Transformational Coaching is a Transparent Relationship

> "[The good shepherd] calls His own sheep by name and leads them out." (John 10:3)

A coach can become your biggest advocate and supporter, someone who knows you well enough to call out the best in you. A transformational coach helps you know your true identity and destiny in Christ and calls you by that, even when you do not see it yourself.

Jesus calls us by name before leading us out. To call by name in biblical times meant much more than one's generic name identity. It meant the hopes and aspirations of the parents in giving that name as a legacy or destiny of that particular family line and individual. Emerging leaders who experience the transparent relationship of an under-shepherd who knows, affirms, and forwards their deepest hopes and God-given aspirations will be led out into the calling of God for their generation. This authentic, transparent, life-giving coaching relationship is a critical component of a theology of transformation. It only happens one conversation at a time.

Before we ever knew God, He believed that we were worth saving and loved us even before He changed us (Ephesians 2:1-6). Transformational coaching is the discipline of loving and believing in what God is doing and will do in a client until the coach is duplicating the character of God toward that person as part of his or her life.

> *The heart of a transformational coach is*
> *the heart of God: loving before changing,*
> *accepting before fixing, believing with*
> *unconditional love instead of judging*
> *according to religious conditions.*

Transformational Coaching is a Sustainable Leadership and Personal Development

> *"...for the equipping of the saints for the work of the ministry..." (Ephesians 4:12)*

When we take a closer look at Jesus the Trainer instead of only Jesus the Teacher, we find that Jesus emphasized transformation over information and even adjusted His equipping to meet the individual needs of learners. (John 21:22, "If I will that he remain till I come, what is that to you? You follow me.")

It has become too easy to simply read what the gospels say but miss the point that what is said has an experiential, relational context—the essence of transformational coaching. Much of the key leadership and personal development for the disciples happened in coaching-type exchanges with Jesus after the sermons and teachings. (Matthew 13:34-36) Without them they would not have had the opportunity to process things at a core value level.

In fact, the entire content that scriptures record of Jesus' teaching, after eliminating the duplications, can be read in less than an hour. Many of the other things scripture records are the intentional placing of His disciples in situations that would reveal their hearts and values and provide Jesus with a transformational coaching opportunity.(Luke 9:51-56)

Present Challenges That Coaching in Church and Ministry Must Face

Church Leadership Culture

Let's face it! We may be thankful for the ability to trace our theologies to the early patriarchs and matriarchs, but the ecclesiology of how we structure church needs some updating. The hierarchical structures of many churches and denominations have been modeled according to the prevailing cultural patterns of their times. Just about any style of leadership can find a Bible verse to support it, but it may not model the transformational values that are in the very heart of God towards His people. Even the popular military commander or CEO styles found in churches today fall short of how the contemporary church needs to be relevant to the culture it is serving. Most have not seen an emerging model of leader as coach in the manner described in this text and may be threatened by a spiritual authority that is defined more by relational credibility than one's position or title.13

In addition, some leaders will not initially appreciate the value of transformational coaching since they may mistakenly associate it with the purely secular version in the marketplace. Prejudice may cause some church leaders to minimize a methodology that is sweeping the business community but remains relatively unknown in the typical church.14

This religious tradition challenge can be met by finding a key church that has the respect of many in an area or region and demonstrate how a new kind of leader as coach is effective. A strategy can be designed to have one day "Extraordinary Conversation" seminars that provide both a "taste and see" experience of coaching and the soundness and biblical mandate for relational versus positional authority, thereby setting the stage for the introduction of coaching into the church leader's lives. TLC is presently seeking these "gateway" churches that are willing to both experience and model this relational aspect of authentic ministry leadership.

Coaching Images and Definitions

Educational challenges begin with the need for clear definitions to counteract the images that "coaching" will bring to people's minds in different cultures. Beginning with the misconnection of the athletic coach who yells and blows whistles at the team to the very lack of such a word in some cultures, there will be a need to make a clear association to a biblical imagery that conveys the process of coaching itself, such as "Barnabas ministry."

This educational challenge can be met by questionnaire and discussion feedback on the appropriate terminology, definition, and biblical metaphor for transformational coaching according to the target nations or local culture where the church and ministry organizations are operating. TLC has encountered this challenge in Brazil and Indonesia, and, even in the U.S. churches. However, in each of these situations these churches had members in the corporate world that were familiar with the coaching terminology in their own companies. They were more informed than their local church leadership as to what was resonating in the hearts and minds of people in the marketplace sector. Unfortunately, in the realm of coaching, the church had become the tail and not the head; they were reactive rather than proactive.15

Past Association with Toxic Relationship Movements

Spiritual challenges include the past misuses of relational models of discipleship and authority that have been abusive and left a toxic residue of fear of anything that might make participants vulnerable. Since most will not have experienced for themselves the power of transformational coaching, the association may be made with past negative or non-productive experiences. This has become the unfortunate residue of the "Shepherding Movement," and too many people have been living out of this fear instead of the fear of God that reveals we really do need one another in ways the institutional church has not expressed.16

This challenge can be met by designing a brochure, policy paper, DVD teaching, or audio-file that preemptively deals with past abuses of relational discipleship and how coaching safeguards participants from similar pitfalls. Key testimonies of how respected leaders have been transformed without the pressure to "conform" to someone's toxic leadership style will be distributed in the early stages of a coaching awareness campaign. We can be strategic in anticipating the diversionary devices of the devil to snuff out the fire of true transformational relationships and can demonstrate a more excellent way according to 1 Corinthians chapter 13.

Quick Fix to Use Coaching Terminology without Real Coaching Transformation

Social challenges include the proliferation of people, churches, or books using the new word "coach" as a catch all for many things. The same old wineskins will be labeled with a new buzz-word label. Some will call themselves coaches without specific training in both the safeguards and boundaries of coaching and the heart and methodology that makes coaching transformational. An underdeveloped appreciation for the training process of transformational coaching will tempt some to jump on the bandwagon without embracing the process that will ensure its success. Many will make money on being first to get marketplace awareness without marketplace credibility. They will certainly over promise and under-deliver, resulting in inoculating many from the real issue of transformation.

The social challenges can be met by establishing the value of "coach trainer certification" that will insure high standards, on-going learning, support, encouragement and accountability, and credibility in the marketplace to those who will increasingly be asked, "By what authority are You doing these things? And who gave You this authority?" (Matthew 21:23).17 Transformational coaching must be both personally transformational and professionally credible (in its standards of conduct and oversight) if it is to be sustainable over time. We will not start an exciting "moment" of coaching unless we have the system in place to finish with a "movement" of coaching that will impact the three generations of 2 Timothy 2:2.

Lack of Awareness of the Value of the Cost of Coaching

Economic challenges include the higher cost of one-on-one people development as compared to the seminar or classroom approach. This cost involves the time, travel, and communication from a distance for individuals who will model the coaching process in a highly relational manner. Many of these coaches will have themselves invested considerable time and resources to be trained to do this effectively and will need to steward that in a manner that can serve leaders in churches with minimal resources, non-profits, and ministry leaders in developing nations.

The economic challenges can be met by establishing a scholarship fund for matching or covering costs needed to initially launch the coach awareness and coach training in those organizations without resources. This will be funded from grants and public/private partnerships for the first year until each of these groups can run their own in-house coach training and resulting movement with minimal oversight. TLC has also initiated a core volunteer force of coaches who are willing to raise their own financial support to go to places without cost to the host organization and bring the coaching paradigm into existing organizations. It is our humble vision that this group will become known as a "transformation corps" as compared to past attempts that left the historical footprint known as the "peace corps."

Short Circuit by Taking Shortcuts

Character challenges include the desire for many to take shortcuts and simply copy materials on coaching without embracing the process of transformation. This propensity exists all over the world, but in some places the very words "copyright" only mean the "right to copy." The procedure to counteract this involves being coached and learning how to coach others. This will involve more than a seminar or manual, but a transformational process that takes the time for reflecting and debriefing along the way.

This "easy road" character challenge can be met by establishing a high standard in the beginning that protects the integrity of the process and insures that transformation is happening according to specific competencies that can be measured along the way. Those coaching organizations who choose to "lower the bar" in the beginning stages of a coaching movement mistakenly assume that they can raise the bar later. TLC has chosen to start with standards that will ensure transformational change and always "give grace" to those who struggle without lowering the standards. Proven methods of success in this endeavor will be relied on so as not to re-create the wheel for each church, ministry situation, or nation.

Overemphasis on Teaching

Many churches have been following the Great "Omission" rather than the Great "Commission." Most quote Matthew 28:18 as to go into the world to teach everything Jesus taught rather than to teach them to "obey, apply, put into practice," everything Jesus taught. The end result is a multiplication of mini Bible schools and seminaries in churches without a relational process to walk out these truths in their everyday lives. Even Sunday school classes and training seminars tend to default to primarily preaching events, perhaps with an addition of questions and answers. It is amazing how far we have moved from the methodology of the Master Teacher and assumed we would get the same results.

Benefits and weaknesses of formal (preaching and lecturing), informal (seminars and workshops), and non-formal (coaching) will need to be balanced and embraced to bring transformational coaching into the churches and ministries in our cultures. The formal approach communicates quickly to mass audiences, but creates more spectators than participants. The informal approach gives the quick steps to success, but avoids the critical value formation that will undergird those steps when we meet opposition and resistance. The non-formal approach provides a tailor-made, personalized process, but is subject to the idiosyncrasies of those who are up close and personal in our lives.

The "telling/preaching/teaching" overemphasis challenge can be met by encouraging small early adaptors in key churches to prototype a balanced approach of the "formal/informal/non-formal" methodology in coach training and see the fruit that it bears. Mini-manuals will be given on how and why to maintain this balance and testimonies recorded and published on the impact of this "Jesus approach" on the lives of the participants.

Lonely Leaders Whose Lives Preach That Coaching is for the Immature
The rise of the apostolic movement without the heart of spiritual fathering has also contributed to a modern day non-denominational top-down hierarchical approach in which godly men and women do not model having coaches in their own lives. The non-spoken message is that leaders can

arrive at a spiritual place where the need for others speaking into our lives is not necessary. Followers aspire to be like their leaders and may view the emerging role of transformational coaching as a sign of weakness rather than "iron sharpening iron" strength.

The hierarchical overemphasis challenge in some of the modern apostolic movements in the nations can be met by bathing the transformational coaching message and methods in the refreshing waters of the Father's heart theology and ecclesiology. Models of coaches as spiritual fathers and mothers who release this Father's heart will be seen as the standard and heroes of the movement in the future. The goal will be to create a desire among those trapped in pecking order religious systems to want to be part of a movement that has redefined success according to Jesus' view as compared to man's view.

Making Coaching a Part of a Supervisor's Portfolio

Church systems that simply add the coach title or methods to existing supervisors' or leaders' job descriptions may find that the only benefits of coaching for them may be in higher productivity and performance motivated by fear rather than the lasting benefits of transformation motivated by growth. The power of transformational coaching will be reserved for those relationships that allow for authenticity without fear of job loss or lack of favor for possible promotion. In the short term this will mean providing coaches who are not direct reports to those whose very careers depend on good recommendations by a supervisor.

The short-cut "jump on the bandwagon" and "call anyone a coach" challenge can be met by a consistent communication of a theology of transformation that requires being changed at the heart level over a period of time, with a relational peer and coach, that does what standard management models have not been able to produce. The most powerful way to bring this to pass is to allow key "influencers" to experience true transformation in the coaching process and become the spark to ignite the kindling in the hearts of others who trust them, even when they do not understand them.

Opportunities for Development of Transformational Coaching as a Renewal of the Church

Transformational coaching may well have "come into existence for such a time as this" (Esther 4:14). The convergence of an emerging youth culture that is desperately seeking meaning in relationships with an increasing desire in existing church leaders to see fulfillment of "turn the hearts of the fathers to the children" (Malachi 4:6) is met at the doorway of transformational coaching. Many who were not mentored and do not know how to mentor others can find this fulfillment through the way transformational coaching bypasses the need for great wisdom or years of experience to pass on to others, since the answers are not in the coach but in the client's heart that is connecting with the heart of God.

The increased move of God to bridge the church to the home, education, media and entertainment, communication, government, and business and finance spheres is spanned by the new "Romans Road" of transformational coaching. Just as in Jesus' day, the roadways were just in time for the fullness of time to reveal Christ and spread the Gospel, so today coaching is becoming the timely highway to travel to the hearts of men in each of these spheres in our nations. Many will be awakened and experience transformational beginnings through disciples who are themselves transformed and coaching them in extraordinary conversations.

Transformational coaching will take place to serve parents, marriages, marketplace leaders, and every area as the church recaptures relational credibility with gatekeepers in each of these disciplines. Known only for those who are interested in being "spiritual," churches will become known for being holistic in a new way. Ambassadors of Christ will be sought after because they will be competent in the increased emphasis on emotional and relational intelligence fields. Ministries of reconciliation will be led by disciples who have been transformed and can bring transformation in critical conversations, conciliations, and negotiations. Like Joseph and Daniel of old, transformed leaders will know how to operate in the "wisdom" that must complement the favor of God on them. That wisdom will be seen in the heart and methodology that is found in transformational coaching, even when the relationships and conversations do not involve a coaching relationship.

For some, coaching practices will become a bi-vocational income to supplement church planting and other ministry start-ups. Many of these will find an eager market looking to them to be part of the explosion of coaching companies and ministries who will want men and women of character and competence. In every profession and career, people will want a personal coach and will be willing to pay for it.

Models From the Past in Church History

Many of the renewal streams in church history carry elements of the values and methodologies of transformational coaching. The spiritual directors of the monastic movement utilized powerful questions and reflection to help those desperate for God to find him when the church was not able to help. The reformers recovered the priesthood of all believers only to miss the structures that would release this new reality. The rise of communities like the Moravians brought powerful transformation as a one-hundred-year prayer and missionary sending force impacted even the likes of John Wesley on the deck of a storm-lashed ship.

The house church, small group, and cell church movement over the years has modeled many of the transformational values in a community context.18 Equipping the saints has evolved to the place of understanding God's majestic design in each of his creations. Ministries that have gone beyond gift identification in Romans 12 to gift implementation have moved to empowering members and leaders to fulfill their ministries and callings. This is the day where many of the elements in transformational coaching have been seen before, but rarely in the unique way that this ministry combines and delivers them to the church and community.

Summary

The church at large is the one place in which transformation must be most visible. Transformational coaching is a key toward multiplying this transformation process in the lives of leaders in a way that will have immediate results as well as long term sustainability. With the addition of this element to transformation, leaders will be highly likely to model a new kind of leadership relevant to our emerging generation, transform their own staff and leaders into a transformational learning community, and finish their course in life and calling well.

If leaders ignore the role that coaching will have in their communities and in the commerce of their cultures they will abdicate the opportunity to steward this rapidly advancing means of transformation. As a result they will also default on their responsibility to protect their people from the agenda inherent in much of the secular version of the coaching movement. This will undermine the Kingdom of God and the Lordship of Christ approach to transformational coaching that is the birthright of the people of God.

If the efforts of this transformational coaching are successful, we can expect the worldwide Christian community to become the bridges of transformation to those outside the Kingdom of God. Multiple thousands will come to Christ as a result of a Christian coach who knows how to facilitate the transformation process in their lives.19 Young people will find their spiritual fathers and mothers through the authentic relationship and extraordinary conversations of a transformational coach. Leaders and workers in all the culture-shaping professions of government, education, media, market place, etc., will be transformed by an army of transformational coaches who, like Joseph and Daniel before them, will find promotion and favor from God as they flesh out what it means in today's world to be an ambassador of reconciliation.

The modern day Romans Road is being built. It is a highway to the presence of God. Those who know the power of transformational coaching will remove the stones of hindrance for many to travel.

To God be the glory!

Reflection and Discussion Questions
Chapter Five: Critical Issues for Coaching
in the Church and Ministry World

1. TLC is the only coach training organization in the world that has developed a biblical and theological basis for its values and methodology. What difference does that make for those in church and ministry? Why does the Church need this biblical foundation to embrace the worldwide coaching movement today?

2. Examine the leadership style and structure of your church or organization. In what ways does it simply duplicate the predominate leadership style of the culture's heroes (military, business, etc.) as compared to the biblical patterns of progressive revelation into the New Testament styles of leadership? In what ways does it move toward the coaching model of a leader as a coach?

3. It takes a high level of emotional security for spiritual leaders to move toward a coaching style of leadership. It takes an increased level of maturity for followers to receive a coaching style of leadership. What issues do you see in yourself that make it a challenge to be a leader

or receive a leader who functions in a coaching style of leadership?

4. Think back on developmental moments in your life that truly stand out as transformational. What was it about them that you remember? Over 80% of those we asked responded that it was a relational impartation or conversational transformation that kindled much more than an information exchange in a lecture or sermon. What does this say about the role of coaching in church and ministry to reach and release the next generation of workers and leaders in the Kingdom of God?

5. Thinking of coaching as a key part of the Kingdom of God "ambassador" skills, how might coach training be a normative part of every church's training program? How might it be a normative part of parenting skills training? What other ways do you see coaching as filling a void in our culture today?

CHAPTER SIX

A New Breed of Leaders— How Coaching is Transforming the Way Leaders Lead

By Bobby Hill & Andrew Arroyo

Throughout history, mankind has engaged in "selective breeding." Selective breeding is the process of taking two or more breeds of plant or animal, and, through a process of intentional, repetitive mating, producing a new breed. As a result, many plants and animals ranging from roses to poodles now exist in varied kinds.

In observing some of the spiritual leaders appearing in our day—occupying sectors ranging from ministry to business to government—one might ask, "Has God been doing some selective breeding of his own? Has God been creating a new breed of spiritual leader?"

I answer, yes! God is raising up a new breed of leader, a new spiritual generation that is defined less by chronological age than by hallmark spiritual qualities. What kind of leader is this new breed? What values and philosophies does he/she exhibit? How does he/she act? What are their hallmark spiritual qualities? After looking more closely at what is required to become a new breed of leader, my goal in this chapter is to unpack ten key spiritual qualities, and to explore something of the intricate coach-client partnership that helps a leader become the new breed. Who knows, maybe you will discover that God is selectively breeding you, too, and that a transformational leadership coach might be just what you need to make the changes stick!

The Human Will and the Role of Coaching

I believe the emergence of a new breed of leader is more than incidental, but instead, uncovers a spiritual movement. There has been a noticeable evolution of leadership values and paradigms for several years, particularly in the United States throughout the 20th century. More than any past movement, I predict this latest movement will impact the way many leaders lead and the way leadership is taught. (The great irony is, of course, that many of the new ways of leadership are actually very old!)

But there is a hitch. It is one thing to breed a new species of flower or dog, but quite another to create a new kind of leader. God does his part by releasing a new leadership dispensation into the earth and supplying the power of his Spirit to energize and accelerate the work (Genesis 1:1-3; Acts 2:1-4; Colossians 1:29). It is then up to each leader to attend to the Spirit's work and to partner with him by literally "willing into being" the required changes in his own life. The leader who makes the changes transforms himself into the new breed of leader I mentioned above.

Notice, I used the phrase "willing into being." Human agency plays a key role in the selective breeding of spiritual leadership. Yes, unlike in the breeding of animal species, the breeding of new leaders involves the will of the very leaders being bred. We are participants in the process. Leadership transformation follows much the same rule as salvation, which, in the words of renewal theologian J. Rodman Williams, is "God all the way through man all the way."[20]

This is where transformation can become difficult. For, while "The spirit indeed is willing, but the flesh is weak"

(Matthew26:41b). "For the good that I will to do, I do not do; but the evil I will not to do, that I practice" (Romans 7:19). So many of the spiritual mutations required to transition from old to new breed often fail for lack of our own will to see those changes through.

It is here that transformational coaching steps in. While the coach cannot do the leader's work for him, the coach can come alongside the leader to motivate and strengthen his willpower to go to the next level. The right coach can assist the client (the sincere leader) to develop and maintain the hallmark spiritual qualities that define the new breed of leader.

Join me now in looking at ten of those spiritual qualities. I encourage you to read these not through an academic lens, but through a personal one. That is, allow the Spirit freedom to change your breed even as you read!

Ten Qualities of the New Breed of Leader

1. Character is first and foremost

The new breed of leader knows that advancement and fruitfulness require character, and that character requires a heart that seeks first after God. This leader understands that character and integrity must hold a high priority—not be an afterthought. As Booker T. Washington stated, "Character is power!" Without that kind of power, leaders become toxic and dangerous to themselves and their followers.

A Character Crisis

A lack of character among professing Christian leaders over the past few decades has damaged the gospel's influence worldwide. From Jimmy Swaggart and Jim Bakker to the scandal among certain Catholic priests, public failures have undermined the credibility of spiritual leadership and the Church, not to mention spiritual leadership at-large. This is to say nothing of the damage caused by private failures that never receive press, but undoubtedly outnumber the public ones.

I agree with Dr. Howard Hendricks when he estimates, "the number one problem of spiritual leaders in America is the lack of character." We all have seen the damage done to churches when pastors fall prey to the enemy's temptations, and we all know of believing leaders in other sectors of society who have fallen to the same. The media is replete with corporate icons, sport heroes, and Hollywood darlings who have compromised their integrity and are now facing criminal or civil charges in court.

Ability vs. Character

Spiritual leaders should have a higher standard. Why? Because Jesus set the bar for us. Have you ever noticed that 75% of the prerequisites for church leaders in 1 Timothy 3 and 4 and Titus 2 focus on character, not ability? The leader of the past made the mistake of selecting leaders based on talent and ability while minimizing character issues. Sometimes we were able to get away with it, but it often burned us in the end.

Not so with the new breed. The new breed of leader approaches the character issue differently. It is a priority. Integrity trumps image, because the new leader is less concerned with popular approval ratings and more with God's pleasure and long-term fruitfulness.

A Heart Check

In my coaching relationships, character issues are common subjects of discussion. Sexual temptation, honesty, financial integrity, arrogance, and inappropriate staff relations are the kind of issues spiritual leaders face regularly. And, as indicated earlier, it is not just the public ones that need attention. Private character issues need addressing as well.

For example, during a recent telephone coaching session, I asked the client about his personal life. I probed into where the Holy Spirit was bringing conviction. "Can you describe any particular area the Spirit has been pointing out which needs your attention," I asked. After a prolonged thoughtful silence, he responded, "I have been feeling uneasy about promising to pray for people's needs and never getting around to it." "You mean that people approach you as their pastor, requesting prayer, and you give the typical pastoral response, 'I will be praying for you,'" I clarified. "You have developed the habit of lying in order to placate them, but you rarely follow through. Is that accurate?"

In the end, the pastor agreed that this long-standing practice of making empty promises was dishonest. It revealed a character issue. Since he is among the new breed of leader who seeks to make character a priority, he took advantage of our coaching relationship and received the conviction rather than becoming defensive. Today he is back on track.

If we are not handling the small foxes that come to steal the grapes, we will never be on guard for the broader threats against our churches and organizations. For the new breed of leader, coaching provides an excellent means of processing character.

2. Accountability is sought and honored

The new breed of leader makes an accurate appraisal of his blind spots and seeks accountability to prevent being blindsided. For this breed, accountability is more than a box to check off on a to-do list; it is a non-negotiable incarnational value.

In many ways, accountability is a prerequisite to character; and like the leader in the previous example, the new breed of leader seeks out accountability. The main problem with accountability in the past has been that everyone said, "I have it," but few really did. In actual fact, few have cared enough to delve into what it really means and how to make it effective.

Thankfully, we are witnessing a different trend among the new breed of leader that involves putting measures into place that gives accountability teeth, as it were. Two such measures are outside lines of accountability and layered accountability. Both are unconventional, if not controversial, and both involve coaching.

Outside Accountability

Business and ministry leaders alike have grown dissatisfied with the form and function of accountability within the established hierarchies of their organizations. Such hierarchies have become more concerned with production than people, especially where authority has become authoritarian. Many of the new breed feel unable to share personal matters for fear of uncaring or punitive pre-judgment. So they have turned to outside forms of accountability.

In our home region, localized clusters of pastors have sprung up in many cities. These are men (and in some cases, women), representing a rainbow of denominations and races, but who are so thirsty for accountability that they make coming together a priority. Fellowship, sharing, and prayer are the typical agenda of these informal gatherings— which, in effect, amount to peer-to-peer coaching.

Business leaders seek outside accountability as well. Increasingly executive coaches are resourced who are outside of the formal corporate hierarchy. This type of relationship allows the executive to feel less troubled when sharing personal information and less intimidated in their quest to bring genuine change to areas of their life. For those willing to invest the time, money, and effort, the payoffs of outside accountability are phenomenal in terms of personal and professional growth.

Layered Accountability

Layering is another way the new breed of leader ensures that accountability is comprehensive and three-dimensional. Former leaders had perhaps one or two lines of accountability, usually coming from a formal chain of command and a spouse. This left them open to misdirection and group and cultural blind spots. New leaders open multiple channels delivering real-time feedback, in order to improve the chances of staying on the straight and narrow.

One practice of layering we are seeing is that of building circles of accountability. Each circle contains a few voices, with those in the closest daily working relationship having more regular and immediate impact, while those in the outer circles comprise voices with which the leader interacts whenever needed. Weekly, monthly, quarterly, annually, or on special occasions, the leader gets feedback from the various circles at the appropriate times. Typically the coach falls into the monthly and/or specialized feedback circles.

Of course, the danger with layered accountability is having too many voices. In making the shift from old to new breed, we have known some leaders who have put in so many voices that the new accountability crippled them. You do not want paralysis due to over-analysis. Accountability should exist for the leader and not the other way around. It is not so much having the accountability that provides the protection, but using the accountability that the leader has. The new breed of leader layers accountability relationships, but makes sure also to keep them meaningful and functional, not like the older model of accountability by organizational flowchart only.

3. Servanthood is valued and embraced

The new breed of leader recognizes Jehovah God as King of Kings, and seeks to lead in the Kingdom as a servant-subject. He practices dutiful service, following Jesus' teaching that says, "when you have done all those things which you are commanded, say, 'We are unprofitable servants. We have done what was our duty to do'" (Luke 17:10).

Looking back on past breeds of leaders—and even on those alive now who persist in that paradigm—I am saddened at how many leaders shed the servant disposition as soon as they amass a large enough following. The new breed views servanthood as a total life process of becoming what we wish to be *and* what we wish to see. Years ago, Robert K. Greenleaf elegantly, and we might say prophetically, defined this leader: "Servant leaders become the change they wish to see in the world."21 The servant leader is a lean officer on the field, not plump royalty tucked away safely in his castle!

I acknowledge this is a radical position. If we are to be servant leaders, we must reject staged moments of service that lead to self-serving photo opportunities. Instead, we must get our hands dirty as a servant of all (Mark 10:45), and we must mean it. The world needs more leaders like this, and God is working to breed as many as are willing. Are you willing?

360 Degrees

There is that word again: "willing." Each leader must be willing to shift from superstardom to servanthood. Then the natural question of how we know we are servants arises. How can you measure your servant status? The danger of rating ourselves is that we tend to think we are better than we really are. New breed leaders use coaches both to keep their will strong, and to offset the danger of unrealistic self-scoring.

To illustrate, one CEO requires his coach to ask him about his community service since their last talk. Notice, the coach is not asking some general question like, "Are you a servant?" The coach is asking a data-based question that is not easy to skirt: "Have you served the community since we last talked? How? When?" Additionally, the coach has built a 360-degree feedback system the CEO's employees use to grade his leadership, and it contains a section that asks whether and to what degree they perceive him to be a servant.22 This CEO epitomizes the difference between merely doing service and striving for servanthood.

For Coaches, Too

The quality of servanthood is a must-have for every spiritual leader because every leader is an influencer. We must ask ourselves, "What sort of influence am I exerting?" If we are servants, then we are more likely to generate the development of more servants. If not, the old breed will continue to live.

The example of the CEO is inspiring in this regard. Not only is the CEO a servant-leader, but he/she is a servant-coach. Everyone in their organization looks to them for feedback, and as a new generation leader that can take them in the right path. This follows the maxim, "Physician, heal thyself!" We who would be of the new breed should attend to ourselves, whether we are coach, client, or both.

4. Ministry is Kingdom-minded and Christ-centered

The new breed of leader understands that his/her efforts are one part of the whole. They practice with the big picture in view. They value and appreciate the work which others in their city or territory are doing for the Lord's Kingdom. This lifestyle reflects a clear "Christocentric" mindset and commitment, which is rare since many leaders are building kingdoms for themselves.

Kingdom-Building or Empire-Building?

Two mindsets exist: Kingdom-building and empire-building. The Psalmist wrote, "Unless the Lord builds the house, they labor in vain who build it" (Psalm 127:1). This implies that many labor to build the house themselves without God's direct involvement, an action that is not only sad but dangerous because of the mindset it reflects.

The mindset from which any leader proceeds is an outgrowth of those inner motives that are behind our outward leadership. The show often masks what stands behind the curtain. It is really easy to get confused and develop a blind spot to the fact that we are building something to or for our own purposes, plans, or glory. We must lead with hearts set on bringing glory to the Lord alone, not investing energy in building empires for our own sake.

The new breed of leader is selfless and nameless when it comes to building the house and receiving glory for results. God is set on having leaders with this quality. He desires to shape leaders who adopt a mindset that sees their leadership activity ultimately as a small part of the overall kingdom activity, be it in a church or other organization. For ministry leaders, you are not the only one in town. For business leaders, you are not the only one gifted in your market. There are many other men and women contributing a significant giftedness to the overall task of redeeming our community and extending the influence of God's Kingdom. They are co-builders, not competitors.

An Important Realization

Pastors especially suffer from seeing one another as competitors rather than co-builders. I recall when I was pastoring my first church in Austin, Texas. God had blessed our young church with growth, and in my youthful zeal at age 23 I was trying to build the largest church in town. From time to time I would hear the news of someone coming to our city to pioneer a new church. I remember the sinking feeling in my gut when I would ponder the prospects of someone moving onto my turf. Never would I have admitted it at the time, but I was upset at those I perceived to be competitors.

Thank God that with maturity came the realization that my mindset was wrong! Some of this realization I owe to my personal coach. He pointed out to me in one conversation that he discerned an impure motive in my heart. After first denying it, I later saw it. After repenting and praying together, I walked with a renewed level of humility and Kingdom focus, living out the values that I had been preaching to others. Frequently, my coach would check up on me in this area to remind me of the blind spot and ask for an update.

A Man Called Peter

One of the most admired spiritual leaders in American history was Peter Marshall. He pastored New York Avenue Presbyterian Church in the 1940's and served as Chaplain to the United States Senate. During the 1940's, New York Avenue was one of the largest and most influential churches in the nation. It was commonly referred to as "the Church of Presidents." Eight presidents have worshipped there including Abraham Lincoln. It was one of the first mega churches in America—more than a thousand people attended services in the 1940's, which was a rarity then.

At one point during his pastorate, Peter Marshall experienced an extended period of illness that kept him out of the pulpit for many weeks. He was concerned that it would have a negative effect and was surprised that it didn't. A friend asked Peter Marshall what he learned during his time on the sidelines. Without any hesitation he said, "Do you really want to know? I learned that the Kingdom of God goes on without Peter Marshall."

Did you hear the humility in that statement? Peter Marshall was acknowledging that the Kingdom of God is a lot bigger than one person or one church. He was a new breed of leader who was excited about what God was doing in his church and excited about what God was doing in other churches in his city.

Complication

Of course, some people will follow us for the wrong reasons or with wrong motives. And sometimes those we lead complicate this issue by fanning our wrong motives into flames by favoring our leadership and being critical of other leaders. The new breed of leader knows that followers are all too willing to crown king the next leader they perceive to outshine the others. They learn to spot and diffuse a political agenda before it has a chance to subvert their Kingdom mindset. In response, the leader echoes Paul's declaration that, "I planted, Apollos watered, but God gave the increase...For we are God's fellow workers; you are God's field, you are God's building" (1 Corinthians 3:6, 9). Paul spoke like the new breed of leader he was!

5. Learning posture is teachable and lifelong

The new breed of leader has a life-long, uncommon hunger and thirst for knowledge and wisdom. The gospel writer was describing this clearly when he penned, "And Jesus grew in wisdom and stature, and in favor with God and men" (Luke 2:52). This is the standard for our time as well.

Ahead of the Curve

The one who can articulate problems and solutions most clearly is the one who emerges as the leader. In our day, the many problems we face require creative, God-inspired solutions. Leaders who are committed to learning all they can, filling their barns with knowledge, wisdom, and understanding, are the ones the Holy Spirit will call on to articulate cutting-edge solutions when needed. We cannot afford to rest on yesterday's news; we must be ahead of the curve by maintaining a steady pace of learning.

Too many people wait for revelation to be handed to them. Particularly in Pentecostal or charismatic circles, the hope is that a syllabus or secret answer key will mysteriously appear on our desk one morning, containing all the answers or, at least, a hidden path to finding them. The movement of leaders who partner with God in lifelong learning rather than leaders hoping for wisdom by a moment of impartation is one of the brightest hopes for our future.

How We Learn

Much learning takes place through reading. Proving true that readers are leaders, this new breed is reading several titles at one time or another. If we were Paul, we too would say to Timothy, "When you come [bring]…the books, especially the parchments" (2 Tim.4:13)!

As good as books are, the best learning takes place through life experiences.23 This is where coaching really shines, if conducted correctly. While the primary purpose of the coach-client relationship does not revolve around instruction, the new breed of leader astutely draws water from the coach's stream of wisdom with a listening ear to the powerful questions that he/she is asking.

6. Cultural relevance is essential and intentional

The new breed of leader strives to make timeless truths applicable to a changing audience. He realizes that staying current with the culture requires discernment. The Bible describes the sons of Isaachar as this kind of leader, "And of the children of Isaachar who had understanding of the times, to know what Israel ought to do" (1 Chronicles 12:32).

This new leader is on the watch for trends that forecast the next wave of need. They have developed a keen awareness of surrounding spiritual activity—whether it's the Spirit of God or satanic activity. They habitually take the pulse of their context to monitor cultural shifts.

Cultural Exegesis

Most traditionally trained church leaders are skilled at

biblical exegesis, but the new breed of leader places equal importance on cultural exegesis. (In the Greek, exegesis means "to interpret.") All contemporary Christians must interpret and analyze the times, but especially the new breed of leaders.

Mark Batterson, Senior Pastor of National Community Church in Washington D.C. has said, "Irrelevance is Irreverence." We agree! Another pastor, Rob Bell, is forging the pathway for other discerning leaders. At 33 years old, his "Doubt Night" at Mars Hill Bible Church in Grandville, Michigan promises an evening of brutal honesty and searching for young adults. On those nights Bell fields questions about anything related to Christianity and life—often about deeply personal issues ranging from suicide to addiction. With remarkable speed, Mars Hill claims to have grown to 10,000 weekly attendees since inception in 1999 with a small group. These churches are not anomalies. The rise of young pastors like Mr. Bell, Mr. Batterson and others of their generation represent a new breed of leaders who are purposely exegeting and responding to today's culture.

Staying Current

We must stay current. I recently crossed the age 50 barrier, and I am more cognizant of this than ever. To keep myself current, I have committed myself to a ministry where relating to and leading "twenty somethings" is not an option but an integral part of our vision. A few years ago, I purposed to identify several young, emerging leaders who were conversant with the culture to serve me as cultural coaches. I have found it extremely beneficial to bounce ideas and plans off these younger counterparts. Every time they question me on a project or idea, I am reminded of how out of touch I can be. We do not need to be younger than 30 to be current!

New breed leaders stay current, and use models of

ministry befitting to their audience. Recently we heard Ted Haggard state that he asks all of his pastoral leaders to keep current by reading popular magazines and newspapers. "I ask them to keep a newspaper in one hand and a Bible in the other." When in Athens, Paul was greatly disturbed by the prevalence of idols, but he made his way into the market-place and eventually into the seat of Greek philosophy, the Areopagus, to share his life-giving message. As Mark Driscoll notes, Paul's use of the phrase "in him (Zeus) we live, move, and have our being" would be like our quoting today the latest sports or entertainment stars comments in a Sunday sermon. "Paul recognized that all things are pointers to the truth, and that life is a puzzle of grace with pieces strewn everywhere." The new breed of leader recognizes this truth as well.

7. Relationships are authentic and healthy

The new breed of leader cultivates interpersonal connec-tions designed to be natural and meaningful, and from which spring strong teams to do the work of God. He prac-tices true friendship and works diligently to maintain a high degree of health in his relationships: "...the soul of Jonathan was knit to the soul of David, and Jonathan loved him as his own soul" (1 Samuel 18:1b).

This new breed of leader understands the importance of relationship. As Drs. Les and Leslie Parrot observe, "No man is an island! We need camaraderie, affection, love. These are not options in life, or sentimental trimmings; they are a part of our species' survival kit. We need to belong." Leaders are no exception, and yet a misguided philosophy remains among many that today's leaders should isolate themselves and never allow their followers to know their personal struggles.

Unfortunately, that type of leadership fosters anything but trust and respect. We are continually finding that the strength of our bonds with the people we lead grows stronger when they know our weaknesses. Followers feel more like opening up their own hearts to us, because of the authenticity we choose to model before them.

Two Ingredients

Quality relationships require two ingredients: Authenticity and organic growth. First, they should be authentic. Shallow and superficial relationships are worth very little. Every leader needs those people in their lives to whom they can open up and share their deepest needs, hurts, and joys. Authenticity leads to trust, and trust in a relationship is essential to promote the deeper sharing of one's life with others. A healthy leader develops relationships of this sort. Toward the end of his ministry, Charles Spurgeon wrote, "Friendship is the sweetest joy of life." Spurgeon was a new breed of leader in an old breed day.

Second, relationships should be organic. Organic means natural, not artificial or contrived. Leaders, by the very nature of their roles, can experience relationships being imposed on them. Generally, these are neither productive nor life-giving. The best relationships are those which God orders and which seem to happen naturally. Scripture compares such relationships to joints in a body. Hundreds of joints exist in the human body—some in closer proximity than others. It is the same with our relationships.

The new breed of leader cultivates relationships at different levels of intimacy. He follows Jesus' model. Jesus had his 500 acquaintances, his 120 close associates, his 70 disciples, and his inner circle of 12 eventual apostles. It is also clear that He shared a deeper relationship with 3 of the 12 than the others. Proverbs 18:24 holds liberating truth for the new breed of leader: "A man of many companions may come to ruin, but there is a friend who sticks closer than a brother." NIV

Leads to Healthy Teams

Another facet of relational quality is that the new breed of leader does not work alone, but appreciates the increased effectiveness of teamwork. They identify others who complement their own giftedness and build a team. They recognize that the day of solo or autocratic leadership is over. Team relationships are vital to accomplishing organizational goals and maximizing impact.

This is where a key payoff of healthy relationships is realized. Healthy relationships lead to healthy teams. New breed leaders work in teams, but not teams of strangers. They are largely comprised of people from existing healthy relationships. These are relationships free from resentment, positioning, jealousy, and strife. This leader wastes little time investing in unhealthy relationships, but instead practices Ephesians 4:31-32: "Let all bitterness, wrath, anger, clamor, and evil speaking be put away from you, with all malice. And be kind to one another, tenderhearted, forgiving one another, just as God in Christ forgave you."

For those leaders who desire to move from the old to the new breed with respect to teams but do not know how, coaching can help integrate this relational value into a leader's behavior. I discovered that a pastor I was coaching was not enjoying the benefits of team ministry. The church was stuck in a traditional wineskin of solo leaders running each department or committee. We set out a game plan and he began to implement a team paradigm. He shared with his key leaders how basic to vital ministry are face-to-face relationships where we can shape vision and ideas with each other, where we are free to disagree with one another, and where we respect, love, and serve one another.

Month by month we dialogued about his progress. Now, his church is experiencing a new vibrancy among its members and new enthusiasm for doing ministry together. Doing ministry as a team is not only fruitful but fun as well!

8. Risk-taking is faith-based and strategic

The new breed of leader plows new ground. He is like an ox, treading along under the yoke of the Lord, breaking up fallow lands and planting for new growth.

In times past the work of plowing new ground seemed reserved for a fearless few. In our day, God is breeding vast armies of visionary leaders! We are in what some have called the day of the saints, meaning that a mantle of newness is descending upon the body of Christ at-large. "Your troops will be willing on your day of battle..." (Psalm 110:3, NIV). People who never fancied themselves as leaders are awakening with dreams and visions of what could be, and are quietly yoking themselves to ideas and plans that yesterday would have seemed too risky.

Faith-based

It is in the risks of our lives that faith shines. Life that only follows in the safe shadows requires little faith. While comfort is a virtue and blessing, we are concerned for those leaders whose plans and ideas permit too much comfort, because their faith suffers. It is refreshing to hear of stories where leaders are stepping out, basing their decisions on faith rather than merely what they see.

Evangelist Reinhard Bonnke began his ministry in faith, and continues to this day in the same. For years he would travel days throughout the African continent, only to speak to a handful of people—none of whom would respond to the gospel. Each journey required faith that, as Bonnke says so frequently, "Africa shall be saved." Now he holds crusades with millions in attendance. He stands ready to take giant risky leaps founded on genuine faith in God. He is a new breed of leader.

Strategic

Faith does not mean foolishness or presumption. The

new breed of leader has made their share of mistakes of placing faith in the wrong initiative, only to experience failure. Yet they have recovered from those experiences not just older, but wiser and more strategic.

God desires strategic thinkers. He wants leaders who apply principles of stewardship to their faith by *investing* it rather than merely *using* it. We can use our faith to go here, there, and ultimately everywhere, or we can invest our faith to go where God wants us.

9. Passion is contagious and Spirit-controlled

The new breed of leader emulates fervency mixed with restraint. They emulate the fire of Apollos (Acts 18:25) while demonstrating conformity to Proverbs 19:2: "...it is not good for a soul to be without knowledge, And he sins who hastens with his feet." Leaders who achieve this complex balance are rare but growing as God matures the new breed.

Contagious Passion

If we were to liken a leader to a ship, passion would be the sail. The sail is needed to move the ship. Without passion, the ship either stays at the dock or drifts aimlessly— neither of which is a good thing! Passion catches the wind of the Spirit, and transfers that energy to the rest of the ship to make it move.

This generation is waiting to see more leaders with more passion. Too many leaders start out with passion, but do not finish well. I remember once overhearing a conversation between some leaders from a large church in the region. We were at a restaurant and they were talking loudly, so tuning them out was difficult. They were recalling the good old days, when they and other church leaders would take to the streets and minister to whomever God would send across their paths. Now those days were over. Why? Surely they could have come up with multitudes of excuses. The under-lying truth is that they had simply lost passion.

The loss of passion explains a great deal of the muck that mires our organizations. Government leaders give in to the bureaucratic system because they lose passion, whereas in their early days they were radical enough to sit through downpours to protest a cause. Entrepreneurs who once worked from dawn to dusk—and then sat up late dreaming how to get their next big idea to market—trade that life for a steady, lifeless job, all because they have lost their passion.

The new breed of leader maintains passion rain or shine so as not to get stuck in that rut. At the same time, they exer-cise Spirit-control so the passion burns in the right direction.

Spirit-control

The danger of passion is that it becomes all-consuming. Not just a little consuming, but *all*-consuming. Passion, like fire, will burn wherever and whatever it can, and what it burns it destroys. All new breed leaders have a few classic firsthand stories of times we ourselves allowed passion to cross the safety line. While seeming sane at the time, we have launched projects, reacted to threats, and undertaken a host of other actions with misplaced passion that became destructive.

One gentleman I coached once let his passion for help-ing people in need drag his family into deep debt. Although the facts stared him in the face, he ignored them. He simply did not move into the situation with sound reason. Month after month as the bills piled up, at many points he should have put an end to the charitable giving that had long since become a charitable expense he could not afford. Yet his passion so blinded him that he just knew financial break-through would soon come. It never did. Finally, circum-stances got him free from the entanglement and his family is slowly climbing out of debt.

This brother's ticket to freedom from this prison was a

peer coach. To this day he is in a coaching relationship that keeps him accountable to keep his passion for social ills and people in need from dragging down his family into the very category they are trying to reach!

10. Empowerment is endearing and enduring

The new breed of leader shuns the traditional turf protection which many spiritual leaders practice. They understand that effective leaders empower people to reach their full potential.

Empowerment is a term used in a variety of contexts, but for our application it means the act of equipping, supporting, and mobilizing people to maximize their own God-given potential. In a business context where people can be valued more as balance sheets than balanced beings, empowerment requires a wholesale change of employee treatment. In a ministry context, this concept flies in the face of traditional clergy-laity distinctions, and requires new breed leaders to overcome the great resistance that stands against this model. Whereas the old model limits both the development of the body of Christ and the growth of the church, the new model equips the people of God for the work of God. Jesus "...gave some to be apostles...pastors and teachers, for the equipping of the saints for the work of ministry, for the edifying of the body of Christ" (Ephesians 4:11-12). Thank God for the new breed of leader who seeks to empower rather than drain people!

Empowering Leaders—Loyal Followers

There are two primary benefits the new breed of leader reaps from an empowering leadership style. First, it endears their followers to them. What we mean is that there is no other leadership behavior which resonates so deeply and results so positively in loyal followers as does empowering. People love it!

The Creator implanted each human with a desire to be fruitful and to use their gifts and talents for the common good. In my 30 years of experience as a pastor, the people which I empowered the most were the most grateful and the most loyal to me as their leader. For a group of people in a church, business, or any setting to become a healthy and functional organism, a high percentage of them need to be doing the work. Every opportunity should be taken to create new opportunities for participants with varying gifts, temperaments, and passions to become involved in meaningful service. This is a key leadership task that the new breed of leader embraces wholeheartedly.

Second, empowerment builds things that endure. Anybody can build a business or ministry to last for ten or twenty years, but only leaders who have learned the art of empowerment build enduring organizations that pass the test of time. Apparently, building lasting work was important to Christ, as seen in the parable of the two houses and two builders (Luke 6:46-49). Shame was cast on the man whose work fell during the storm!

If leaders never give the people ownership of the vision, it remains only a "mom and pop" operation. When empowered people gain ownership—meaning they have freedom to help shape and drive the future of the organization in a profound way—the organization is transformed into a living organism that lives beyond its pioneering leader.

Building on the Ashes of Failure

I learned this best from my early church planting efforts. The case of my Austin, Texas church plant stands out. After laboring tirelessly for five years, the church exploded into a multifaceted ministry serving 1300 people each weekend. Having resigned the church to move into missionary initiatives, the successor took the reins and moved immediately to put his stamp on the church. Within six months attendance and giving plummeted. Within a year the church filed for bankruptcy.

Why should I, the former pastor, feel the burden of this failure? Because it was a statement about my leadership. The embarrassment of the failure drove me to the Lord for answers. After months of reflection and prayer, I realized that my style of leadership—a reliance on my personal charisma and gifts—had become a deterrent to empowerment. The church had been built on me, and it fell!

Years later, my pastorate in Virginia Beach, Virginia went differently. I applied a new empowerment paradigm. It worked, and the church grew into a healthy, reproducing ministry center. I drew wisdom from several peer mentors and coaches to ensure that former mistakes were not repeated.

Coaching served as a protective guardrail for traveling down the leadership road again. The final proof of success came when I transitioned from pastoral ministry to an apostolic ministry four years ago. To my delight the church endured the transition and remains healthy today. Empowerment produces lasting results. The new breed of leader wants lasting results, and so he practices empowerment!

Coaching: A Mark and Method of the New Breed of Leaders

As I have demonstrated, the new breed of leader exhibits many important qualities—all of which are supported by coaching relationships. In his grace and foreknowledge, God knew that we could not become the new breed in our own strength. So, in addition to supplying his Spirit, he has given us one another. To the degree we rely on one another in relationships we enjoy leadership transformation. The coach-client relationship is one no serious-minded leader should live without.

If conducted properly, the coaching relationship is like a B-12 shot in the arm of the client. By bringing the new breed of leader into close relationship with a like-minded coach, the energy of iron sharpening iron infuses the will of the client. Over time, at each bend in the road where moving to the next leadership level seems impossible, the coach is able to supplement the leader's will and cheer him on so he can make the leap.

We must emphasize that the coach is a complement to the leader. The new breed of leader recognizes that no hired gun or lifelong buddy can do the work for him. A coach is a partner, not a crutch or magic rocket. He also knows there is no secret formula for transformation, but a coaching relationship provides the leader with a guiding hand of support, encouragement, and accountability for the pilgrimage.

A coaching relationship is the perfect complement for any leader whose aspiration includes development and growth. The days of plateaued potential can be replaced with a pilgrim's progress up the hill to the horizon of God's destiny. You too can be a member of this new breed! It's not an exclusive breeding—it is available to any leader with a heart for grasping God's best and the willingness to change.

Reflection and Discussion Questions
Chapter Six: A New Breed of Leaders—
How Coaching is Transforming the Way
Leaders Lead

1. Which two leadership qualities of a new breed of leader do you or your leadership team need to prioritize over the next six months?

2. How would a transformational coach help make this leadership a sustainable change for you?

3. Outside and layered accountability may not be processes that you have experienced in your personal or organizational life. Can you identify two individuals in each of these categories that you presently have or plan on having to fulfill this key aspect of successful leadership?

4. How would you rate your "authenticity levels" with your key leaders in your organization? How could you improve that rating over the next nine months?

5. TLC Korea also serves their nation with the Natural Church Development (NCD) assessment. According them, of their eight quality characteristics of a healthy church or organization the "empowering leaders" is a key factor for which many organizations fall below the standard measure for ongoing growth. Our Korean partners have discovered that the number one way to empower leaders is through transformational coaching.

How might coaching assist you and your organization in its need to empower and release quality leaders?

CHAPTER SEVEN

Convergence Coaching— How God is Using Coaching Values and Methodology to Bridge Strategic Leaders into Purpose and Destiny

By Doug Fike

Recently I co-hosted a five-day retreat for some forty-odd artists—musicians and songwriters, painters and filmmakers, writers and poets. The participants were all followers of Jesus, drawn together by a hunger to make sense of their journey. They came together to wrestle disparate life experiences into some sort of coherence, grow personally as artists, and connect with others on a similar journey.

To varying degrees, they all shared both the exhilaration and frustration of the creative process. They flirt with a sense of destiny while sparring with a sense of futility. They hunger for authentic relationships, but identify a pervasive and persistent sense of isolation, particularly regarding the secret places of the heart, and most chronically "in church." Sometimes they dream dreams—rarely shared with others—but battle the fear that their dreams will be still-born, never living to see the light of day.

One of the enduring images from this rather intense

gathering was the look on the faces of many of the participants following a session led by a resource person previously
unknown to them. That look is hard to describe—stunned
delight, head-shaking amazement, relief, and disbelief in
equal proportions. I mingled and chatted during the break,
tracking a growing awareness that, for several, this was
suddenly holy ground. They were sucking the rarified air of a
life-changing moment deep into their lungs, like a half-
drowned man tossed by a wave onto dry land.

The presenter—we'll call him Pat, because he would
likely be uncomfortable with what I will say about him
next—had just shared a bit of his journey, his heart, his
passion and agony and questions and musings, and some
hard-fought learnings. His sharing was powerful enough, but
the real impact, the blow to their gut, was simply who he IS.
Husband, father, friend. Churchman, prophet, artist. Pastor,
gadfly, teacher. He walks with a limp, not a swagger, but still
walks with the assurance of one who knows he is going
somewhere—if not always totally clear where "there" is. But,
by God's grace—and he really means that—he will go there,
and he seems to believe God is indeed able to lead the way.

The weekend progressed, and the artists (mostly Gen-X
or younger), interacted with Pat: tentatively, or hungrily, or
intensely, but never indifferently. Some just stood back,
watched, and mused. Why the commotion? What were they
seeing? This guy was doing something they were not sure
could really be done. No, not "doing something"—**living**
something. **Being** something they had seen too little of.

For the quarter of a century that I have known him, Pat
has been on a journey into convergence. Over the years, he
has wrestled to understand, discipline, embrace, celebrate
and, ultimately, steward the call of God on his life. Some
pieces along the way seemed awkward or just didn't seem to
fit, but they were part of his being nonetheless. At critical
junctures I watched as he staked his life on the God who

first wove together those inward parts in his mother's womb, and would yet weave a thing of beauty out of the scattered threads of his life.

The arts-retreat participants experienced that sudden-intake-of-breath thing that happens the first time you really stop and look at a high-quality diamond. It dawns on you that there is more going on in that rock than you first suspected—much more. Light bounces off a nearly-invisible facet with startling brilliance ("Where did *that* come from?"). The gemstone plays with the light, first devoid of distracting color, then overwhelming the senses with a multi-hued barrage. The rough stone has become a crafted thing, a multi-faceted gem reflecting a harmony of light and color. But you have to slow down and tune in to see it.

The startled, relieved looks on the faces of those artists came in response to Pat, but they weren't really about him. At the end of the day the question was not, and is not, "Who is Pat?" but "Who am I?" What they saw, and struggled to articulate, was living, breathing evidence that "it" can work. Their conversation and their countenance betrayed a surge of hope that some of life's incoherence can be deciphered, that perhaps this creeping sense of futility can give way to a deeper, and more stubborn, sense of purpose.

They had just heard from a guy who through the years has defied categorization, resisted amputation, rejected emasculation, and actually seemed to have found some sort of integration. In his own agonized prophetic-artist-churchman sort of way, he seemed to be truly enjoying himself. Moreover, he had driven ten hours to make himself available to them, fueled by the obvious conviction that God Himself places inestimable value on His workmanship in each of our lives. Now he was hanging around, asking good questions publicly and privately, sharing vulnerably and providing thought-provoking material to ponder. Between sessions he remained interested and available, drawing on his own journey but focused on empowering them for theirs.

Through the course of the weekend they began to really see that their own highly individual, intimately personal journey into convergence is inextricably intertwined with God's larger purposes throughout time and space. The unfolding of their personal mystery and the mystery of the ages are forged together: it is precisely through His people, the Church, that the "complicated, many-sided wisdom of God in all its infinite variety and innumerable aspects" will be made known (Ephesians 3:9-10, Amplified Bible). They were not as alone as they often felt, marginal to "church" and the purposes of God. In fact, precisely at the vulnerable heart of this journey, they discovered a place of resonance, of connectedness, of belonging.

Later on, the assembled artists were invited to write letters to "the Church." "So many of us," wrote one of them, "live **so alone**. Friends, yes. Small groups, maybe. Churches, yes. But we need more. We need to be with people who we can be torn open in front of and they will help us see how God is putting us back together. This time has shown me what these relationships can be like. We've tasted it now—and once you've tasted truly excellent wine, why would you go back to packet Kool-Aid?" Another wrote, "I meet a person every now and then with authority. They look you in the eyes and you start crying. They tell the truth."

They nailed it. This journey into convergence is not designed to be traveled alone. We all need safe, nurturing, iron-sharpens-iron relationships that encourage our hearts—people we seek out, invest in, and draw on along the way. Leaders need support, encouragement, and accountability (generally more than we already have) to help us grow and maintain a Kingdom perspective through the seasons. These relational patterns, these joint-and-ligament connections which are to help us "grow up in all aspects into Christ" and come to maturity, are in fact intended to be normal, and normative, in the Body of Christ (Ephesians 4:15-16, NASB). The unfortunate reality is that this standard has been eroded by such an impoverished relational paradigm in most of our church cultures that our "chance" encounters with Pat and his "tribe" startle us, making us scratch our head and try to figure out what just hit us.

I was at the retreat because I too am on that journey, and enjoy gut-level interaction with people who are serious about "going there." I have been in a coaching or more informal mentoring relationship with several of the participants, so I have been encouraging both the hunger and the hope for this "something more." But I too was caught a bit off guard, not by Pat's sharing per se, but by the intensity and depth of the group's response. It rolled through me like an aftershock of a trembler in the next county—and an echo of more distant rumblings throughout the Body of Christ, well beyond artists and pastors. That little gathering in the Virginia mountains was simply a microcosm of a growing hunger throughout the Body of Christ worldwide for clarity and convergence, for fresh discovery of meaning and life purpose, and for the kind of empowering relationships we all need to help us go there.

Cultivating Empowering Relationships

God exposes us to leaders like Pat to get our attention, and draw us into a more intentional journey into the full expression of His purpose for our lives. He touches our heart and stirs hope and vision for our own future. He moves us beyond the generic "I want to be a good Christian" posture into the proactive "...lay hold of that for which Christ Jesus has also laid hold of me." stance (Philippians 3:12). Pat's own journey into convergence modeled, for the gathered artists, life-patterns and choices that God uses to help us finish well. And his catalytic interaction during the retreat modeled the kinds of ongoing relationships we all need to help us along the way.

If we will go there, God will leverage this kind of inspiration to help us build into our lives the patterns and relationships necessary for long-term transformation. Like Mary in Luke 1:26-56, we all need Elizabeths who will say to us, "You are blessed! Blessed is that which you carry in your womb, and blessed are you who believe that the things the Lord has spoken will be fulfilled!" We need a "band of brothers"24—not many, but enough, who stay with us in the battle, cover our backs, and help us discern the Lord's strategy through the din of warfare. Perhaps just as importantly, they help us sharpen and maintain our strategic focus in the midst of life's daily routines and the mind-numbing periods of waiting in the trenches.

These key relationships can take a number of forms. The Lord can and will provide a variety of covenant relationships throughout the seasons of our lives, which may include spouses, key friends, family members, partners, mentors, and coaches. The more clear we become about our need for a core of mission-critical companions, the more specific we become in our requests to God, more alert as He provides them, more aggressive about doing our part to find them, and more intentional about cultivating and valuing those He provides.

J. Robert Clinton, Associate Professor of Leadership at Fuller Theological Seminary, has researched and written extensively on how God forms leaders throughout their lifetimes. His work on "finishing well" is particularly helpful in identifying key elements which enhance good finishes. His research indicates that, from ancient biblical history to the present time, fewer than one in three Kingdom leaders "finish well" (using his thought-provoking definition for the term25)—a startling and sobering conclusion. He distills five items that appear repeatedly in the lives of leaders who do finish well:

- effective leaders view present ministry in terms of a lifetime *perspective*
- leaders who are effective over a lifetime have repeated *renewal* experiences
- effective leaders cultivate spiritual *discipline*s
- leaders who finish well maintain a life-long *learning posture*
- leaders who finish well welcome and cultivate mentoring relationships.26

The writer of the Proverbs reminds us, "Where there is no guidance the people fall, but in the abundance of counselors there is safety" (Proverbs 11:14, NASB). Simply put, effective leaders who finish well have taken this ancient wisdom to heart. They ask God for, seek out, recognize, invest in, and take seriously the relational resources they need for the journey. These resources may not be immediately obvious, and the journey will surely include some relational disappointments, to put it mildly. But, if this becomes a do-or-die value, it's worth the price.

Clinton's identification of mentoring as indispensable relational empowerment underscores a key leadership principle:

Healthy, effective leaders proactively cultivate empowering relationships in every season of life.

"Mentoring," Clinton writes, "is available if one looks for specific functions and people who can do them (rather than an ideal mentor who can do all)."27 Both in the marketplace and in church leadership circles, coaching is emerging as one important resource for leaders intent on doing this.28

More specifically, life-coaching (as distinct from coaching focused on a particular task or role) can make a tip-the-scales difference, particularly during critical times of transition or redefinition in a leader's life. TLC's *Life Focus* core (part of TLC's coach-certification process) was created precisely in response to this kind of need, first in our own lives, then in exponentially expanding circles of leaders in the 20+ years since then.

The response to the *Life Focus* process confirms that leaders—across cultures and continents, women and men, from the silent generation to the millennial generation—are hungry to wrestle with core purpose questions in the context of a lifetime perspective. They sense the need to develop life-patterns rooted in a growing understanding of God's design and purpose, and need tools to help pull together the errant pieces of their lives into some sort of coherent framework. Perhaps most fundamentally, they—*we!*—hunger for someone to walk with on that too-often lonely journey of the heart.

Convergence Thinking, Convergence Coaching

Jeremy was in his mid-twenties when his life seemed to go awry. A born leader, his creative energy had been the catalyst for a series of out-of-the-box ventures marked by innovation and the blessing of God. His most recent project, however, started with a bang but ended up in a tangle of frustration and bruised relationships. Longstanding friendships were thrown into question, and Jeremy began to question himself, his sense of call, and his understanding of God and His guidance.

To both Jeremy and his wife Karen, it appeared that this Christian life and leadership thing may not actually work as advertised. They felt they had stepped out in obedience to God's call, and sincerely endeavored to follow His direction each step of the way. Others who had joined them in the venture were similarly motivated. They felt they had received clear confirmation that they were on course, and anticipated God's blessing as they had experienced it in the past.

Instead, the project became embroiled in relational conflict. The backlash against Jeremy's leadership was particularly severe, unexpected, and disheartening. The only available category in Jeremy and Karen's thinking for this experience involved failure and, by implication, disqualification from future ministry.

I had met Jeremy a few years earlier. At that time his flag was flying high, his ship sailing full steam ahead. This time around Jeremy was asking a whole new set of questions, triggered by this experience where nothing seemed to fit. We took a long walk in the woods as he shared his painful story. What went wrong? Where was God in all this?

Near the end of the trail I shared an experience I had back in college, which God used to teach me the "Doing Business with God First" principle. Simply stated, leaders grow in character and effectiveness when they learn to "do business with God" first and foremost, in every situation, and only then with the other players or circumstances. Jeremy's categories of "success" and "failure" were ripe for redefinition, and he eagerly embraced the challenge to do some reading and reflecting that would open up new perspectives on his formation as a leader. The ministry meltdown became the doorway to a whole new way of thinking about God's unfolding purpose in his life. We agreed to continue to meet from time to time to explore this journey together.

Shortly thereafter, Jeremy and Karen enrolled in an internship program designed to provide an integrative framework for leaders during critical times of redefinition. They learned to build mentoring patterns and principles into their lifestyle and, assisted by personal coaches, worked through TLC's *Life Focus* track. What had previously seemed to be disconnected experiences and irrelevant fragments began to yield patterns of convergence and meaning. Discouragement began to give way to the hope that God may indeed have a life-giving and life-shaping purpose that they could discern and lay hold of. To their delight, they discovered that they not been disqualified, but were actually being offered an upside-down-Kingdom opportunity for growth, increased effectiveness, and eventual promotion.

For these young leaders the intervening years have seen a remarkable transformation, defined not by unblemished track records and shimmering "success" stories, but by a growing confidence in God and His mysterious but trustworthy ways. They have developed the skills of reflection and mentoring, and learned to engage in "convergence thinking" that mines insights from past and present experience, and begins to make connections between dimensions of life and being that previously seemed to have nothing to do with their life purpose. "The understanding that you meet God in **every** situation and experience, including the negative ones," notes Jeremy, "was the foundation or prerequisite for convergence thinking in my life."

Convergence thinking comes more naturally for some persons—and personality types—than others, but it is a skill which can be learned, cultivated, and practiced. "The convergence concept," says Jeremy, "took a natural inclination of mine and gave it a context and framework that I had been lacking, one that made the gathering of meaning even more useful and, ultimately, more significant. I started to see purposefulness in the events of my life, including those that I had previously dismissed as irrelevant or completely negative."

The coaching relationship served as an ongoing catalyst to help Jeremy assemble the pieces and see them as part of a meaningful whole. He uses the metaphor of a scrap collector who previously believed he was simply collecting bits of junk, but then discovered a diagram illustrating what the pieces will ultimately fit into, and thus begins to see their current value. One tangible outcome: "You become much more excited about what God is building!"

A convergence-oriented life coach walks with the client through a rhythm of experience and reflection, where the client eventually sees disparate insights begin to come together in a more coherent tapestry of meaning and purpose. Thus,

> *Convergence coaching helps the client weave previously scattered, random, or divergent threads into an integrated framework. The client gains new perspective on past and present life experience, and is better prepared to glean convergence insights and themes from future experience.*

The resulting long-term perspective can invest life with a greater sense of purpose, while simultaneously tempering the mixed-motive tendency to try to squeeze undue significance out of the experience.. In effect, it both ennobles our daily lives and checks our (usually premature) desire for lasting significance. Jeremy recalls: "The relief of seeing my life in perspective, realizing that my primary contribution was years in the future, took a lot of pressure off of my daily life." But, rather than taking the wind out of his sails, "this has made me willing to take smaller, strategic steps toward my life purpose without expecting every experience to **be** my life purpose, which means that now I feel freer to **take** steps, and am actually doing so."

As our long-term perspective increases, so does our staying power. Developing an integrative framework for life's barrage of experiences is empowering enough. But discovering tools and paradigms that enable us to proactively partner with God, in anticipation of finishing well, can anchor and energize us through whatever our flesh, the nay-sayers, and the enemy of our souls may throw our way.

The discovery-turned-conviction that our lives are indeed going somewhere in the providence of God, and that our choices and actions will affect the outcome, can provide that something extra we often need to run the race with excellence. One result will be greater patience and resilience as God labors as a craftsman in our lives to bring us to a place of maximum effectiveness and fruitfulness—bearing fruit that lasts.29

Thus, convergence coaching empowers the client to make more sense out of past experiences, discovering unrecognized value in what previously may have seemed routine or even disruptive. But the greatest impact is usually on the client's sense of purpose. Discovery, rebirth, or renewal of a sense of life purpose will transform our perspective on the future, with resounding implications for emerging life-patterns and critical choices.

The Power of Purpose

When faced with bewildering or painful circumstances, we Christians often encourage one another with a "bumper sticker" slogan that is so easy to repeat. We've probably all heard it, maybe even said it. "You know," we say, knowingly, "God works all things together for good!" Does He? How? Why? What does that really mean, and how, exactly, might we find comfort and encouragement in that thought?

Scripture, of course, provides critical context that can move us from quip-for-the-day exchanges to life-changing revelation. God's working of all things together for good in the lives of those who love Him is grounded in the revelation of His **purpose.** It is not simply a disconnected, have-a-happy-day reality, but an expression of His very nature, beginning with His unwavering intent to conform us to the image of His Son. (Romans 8:28-29)

This is the Father's purpose, and it is *about* purpose, not simply about survival or making it through or "holding on till Jesus comes." It is His purpose—to transform us, conform us into the image of Jesus, and ultimately to reveal Himself to creation through us in a unique and remarkable way—that invests our lives, and every experience, with meaning. Along the way, lots of things that don't make sense at the moment are transformed. Some may not yield a full explanation until we no longer "know in part" (and therefore also "guess in part"?), but everything takes on a different light when we begin to understand ourselves as expressions of His careful and purposeful craftsmanship (Ephesians 2:8-10). We can live with some unanswered questions if we are confident of His intimate and persistent involvement in our lives, and don't lose sight of His purpose.

It was Jesus' understanding of His **purpose** that helped Him choose the Father's will over a counterfeit—but less costly—course (John 12:23-28). It was clear perspective on who He was, where He came from, and where He was going that enabled Him to choose servanthood over self-preservation, and wash his disciples' feet in the midst of profound betrayal (John 13: 1-4). A similar revelation—both of God's general purpose and His specific, personal purpose and calling—emboldened the apostle Paul to "suffer for the gospel according to the power of God," and to exhort Timothy also to "guard the treasure" entrusted to him (II Timothy 1:8-14, NASB).

"Look carefully then how you walk!" Paul writes to the Ephesians. "Live purposefully and worthily and accurately … making the very most of the time—buying up each opportunity" (Ephesians 5:15-16, Amplified Bible). Unfortunately, despite such powerful biblical exhortation and modeling, we contemporary followers of Jesus often find ourselves tentative and uncertain about whether such life-patterns are indeed within reach. Rather than being fueled by clarity and conviction about our life purpose, we find ourselves being "vague and thoughtless and foolish" rather than "understanding and firmly grasping" God's will for our life (vs. 17). The need to refocus and regain life-purpose perspective becomes particularly critical during times of transition or major season-changes in our lives.

Focusing In

After 15 years as a high school teacher, Deborah was burnt out. The wife of a globe-trotting ministry leader and mother of four high-energy kids, she unexpectedly found herself in an emotional and spiritual wilderness with little left to give. Her youngest was nearing graduation from high school; her older children were already out exploring their own new worlds. She struggled to make sense of this alien place: old familiar road signs seemed pointless, old assumptions about her life and calling seemed suffocating, old roles no longer seemed to fit. She sensed the need to refocus and redefine herself, but wasn't sure how to do so or whether she even had the energy. Worse, she was unsure whether doing so was even kosher. She heard about a *Life Focus* seminar and decided to give it a try.

The seminar provided the tools, the support, and the opportunity for her to do some much-needed reflection about her life—past, present, and future. Perhaps most importantly, it provided some new ways of thinking about questions of purpose and destiny. One premise was particularly revolutionary: that God has already been speaking, throughout our lifetimes; revealing clues to His design and purpose that we have not adequately recognized or valued. We already have more information than we think, about God's purpose and calling! Learning to discern and assemble the clues, and tapping others' perspectives, leads to greater clarity and empowerment to fulfill God's call.

"Learning the process of identifying God's voice in your destiny was very helpful," Deborah recalls, "and coming to understand the *cumulative effect* of seeing God at work in all circumstances was critical." Convergence thinking played a key role in redeeming her "secular" past, helping her recognize God's care and design in situations that she had previously dismissed as negative or at best irrelevant. "I was released from exclusively 'spiritual' forms of hearing God," she says, which opened up huge areas of her life to an exciting, Spirit-led process of discovery.

While compiling a list of fruitful vs. "barren" or unfulfilling life experiences, she identified a consistent pattern of life-giving, fruitful experiences in areas that she had long considered "non-spiritual." "Convergence thinking," says Deborah, "gave me permission to accept this reality, and really wrestle with the implications." This led to a fresh examination of her "spiritual vs. non-spiritual" categories, and to some life-changing insights about God's design and purpose for her life.

Deborah integrated these fresh insights into the goal-setting phase which culminates the *Life Focus* process, and launched into a new season of personal growth and discovery. Eventually, she completed all the TLC coach-training tracks and focused some of her new-found energy into coaching. The impact of convergence thinking in her own life naturally cast a new light on her interaction with others. "Understanding my own design in light of experiences that were all leading toward convergence led me to see other's lives the same way," Deborah recalls. She became convinced that an understanding of one's design and purpose was "accessible and discernable through this process," and decided to explore the option of a coaching career.

Deborah found, to her surprise, that no matter the circumstances, character, personality, or history of the person she coached, "it always worked!" She found a consistency and commonality to the questions many people are asking, or wanting to ask. "I felt particularly called to coaching at this specific juncture in the life of the Church.

The coaching model, specifically in the context of convergence thinking, provides tools and paradigms the Church needs at this time in history. It provides answers to questions and needs that real people have."

TLC's *Life Focus* process begins with coached reflection exercises where the client conducts a life-purpose inventory. He or she collects "gleanings" by reviewing past life experiences within a particular data-gathering framework, looking for potential life-purpose clues in eight designated spheres. Most of these are not new insights in and of themselves, but have often been overlooked or have remained unexamined in the light of a life-purpose discovery process. The client is encouraged to follow the exercises even if many of their findings initially seem mundane or under-whelming.

The clues are then assembled using a "convergence diagram" that begins to gather and visually relate the life-purpose data while it continues to be gathered, sifted, and sorted. The coach then introduces the critical concept of "mini-convergences": energizing experiences where a number of life-purpose spheres overlap, providing a foretaste of—and critical insights into—the client's life purpose. The client learns how to identify and "unpack" mini-convergences, mining them for the valuable nuggets of life-purpose information they invariably contain. Fresh insights regarding God's design, life-purpose patterns and themes, life-messages, and ultimately about the client's emerging core life purpose are distilled and inventoried.

Concurrent with the life-purpose thread, the client engages a similar guided reflection process focusing on personal dreams. The dreaming process itself is explored, and dream-busters are identified and addressed that overtly or covertly undermine the client's ability to dream. Dreams are inventoried and prioritized, and fresh insights about God's design, or about the client's life-purpose themes, are distilled.

The client then pursues a values-discovery process, identifying personal core values in ten distinct life categories, ranging from personal development and spiritual life to work, family, and finances. He or she crafts values statements, and then defines ongoing life-patterns that express or flesh out these values. The values and pattern statements serve as personal plumb lines as the client then embarks on a goal-setting process—establishing both long-range and short-term goals, and creating an annual action plan with a 90-day planning cycle. The life purpose and dream inventories, in tandem with the client's values and desired life-patterns, provide content, motivation, and grounding as the client works at developing a convergence lifestyle, living purposefully and continuing to glean key insights, in anticipation of ultimately finishing well.

CD input sessions provides biblical grounding, adding a vision-raising and paradigm-shifting backdrop for these processes. Themes such as God's purposes in history and in our personal lives, God's unique design in every person, the art and discipline of dreaming, identifying and overcoming dream-busters, and our signature freedom as members of God's family to fulfill His purposes are explored. CD sessions also provide practical handles to aid in the values discovery and goal-setting processes. A one-day *Life Focus* seminar provides group coaching and interaction as the client enters the final (goal-setting) phase.

Throughout the process, a trained coach interacts with the client on a regular basis. The client is also paired with a peer mentor, another *Life Focus* participant on a similar journey. Peer mentoring adds yet another dimension to the support, encouragement, and accountability provided by the coach, and generally creates a fertile environment for the emerging crop of life focus insights. The coach serves as a sounding board and stimulus, introducing and following up on each exercise, probing and listening and asking questions as the client navigates what are sometimes unfamiliar waters.

Keys to Empowerment

TLC's certified coaches have themselves embraced an ongoing journey of personal transformation. They continue to reflect and grow, cultivate mentoring and coaching relationships in their own lives, identify and learn from mini-convergence experiences, and live purposefully toward the fulfillment of God's purposes in their own lives. Along the way, they are trained to come alongside others to help them also develop convergence thinking and convergence lifestyle patterns, toward the ultimate objective of finishing well. Specifically,

> *TLC's certified coaches offer ongoing empowerment to those they serve, providing timely PERMISSION, a defined PROCESS, clear PARAMETERS, and critical PERSPECTIVE on the journey toward convergence.*

Permission

Sometimes each of us simply needs encouragement to "go there"—to listen to our hearts, take inventory of our dreams, dare to believe that God has been active in our lives and is preparing us for a future that will be a delight both to Him and to us. We need the courage to name what is inside us, to articulate that inner yearning or elusive sense of call, to own up to who we really are, regardless of how we think it will sound to others. Sometimes we simply need a push to give it a try, explore an idea, and think out of the box. We may not technically "need" permission from anyone, but a timely nudge from someone who has come to know and believe in us can be just ticket to get us in gear.

Interaction with a coach and peers can provide a safe

place for this, and powerful dynamics often set in motion when this happens. Years ago I walked a group of young church leaders through the goal-setting phase of *Life Focus*, encouraging them to begin taking steps to explore the dreams they had begun to name during the prior phase. One young couple shared a dream they had discussed and prayed about but never knew what to do with. They had been drawn to join an international missions organization specializing in Bible translation among unreached people groups, but had not pursued the idea due to a number of looming obstacles. The reflection exercises and personal inventories had again brought it to the forefront.

We celebrated the dream with them, and encouraged them to take some exploratory steps simply to test the idea and see what God might do. They set some modest goals for the next couple of months and went away excited at the prospect of finally doing something about these persistent stirrings. They contacted us, breathlessly, a few weeks later, to share their good news. Things had fallen together in ways well beyond their ability to orchestrate them. Within a matter of months things were moving forward, and they eventually moved into a fruitful term of service with that missions organization.

During the same sessions, another young couple shared their dream of receiving the "Master Farmer" designation for their farming operation—recognition for leadership in agricultural development and production, innovation in techniques and process, and community involvement. The language of Scott and Sharon's dream was new to many of their church friends, but we encouraged them in their pursuit of something that was obviously "hard-wired" into their God-given design. They got much-needed "permission" to pull out the stops and go after this thing that had been quietly percolating in them for some time.

"We set a 10-year goal to become Master Farmers,"

Scott remembers. "We began arranging more local and national speaking engagements, expanding our 'field days' for the local community, and networking with local universities and USDA organizations." Their expanded efforts were the trigger for a series of remarkable developments. Within the next couple of years, their farming operation was featured on a television documentary, and Scott was featured as a speaker for several overseas agricultural conventions. The goal that seemed so audacious when shared in that church fellowship hall became a reality in only seven years. But it all began with permission and encouragement to really go after what was in their heart.

Process

Life Focus coaches walk clients through a defined and tested discovery process. The methodology is effective, but not magical. Like many personal development tools, some portions are unique to this process and truly original, while others incorporate principles and processes in widespread use.

The critical thing is that handles are provided to grab hold of and wrestle with, making it possible for persons to "go there" without having to re-invent the wheel. Questions and growth areas that might otherwise languish on the shelf are brought into clear focus. The structure and support systems can also provide needed reinforcement to help a client press through challenging issues that may come to light, which might otherwise be put off amidst the clamor of everyday life.

Katie was in her late thirties, a home-schooling mom with three highly extroverted children and an equally extroverted husband, Matt. Despite her own natural bent toward introversion, Katie did a remarkable job of anticipating the needs and demands of the family, effectively juggling roles as wife, mother, teacher, and household manager. She and

Matt were both extremely gifted, trained musicians. Together they nurtured a desire to develop their own music-related business, as an avenue to pursue their call in music and the creative arts.

After fruitful terms with several churches and parachurch ministries, Matt resigned his church staff role and began to freelance. Matt and Katie went into a period of transition, during which they both engaged the *Life Focus* process. With everything in flux, how do you step back, get perspective, work at redefinition and sort out priorities for a new season? It can be challenging to work on such issues when everything seems up in the air and energy is already in short supply. But this may also be the time when doing so is of the essence.

"Without *Life Focus'* structured process," Katie observes, "I would probably have settled for maintaining some semblance of normalcy in our home, and just hung on. I wouldn't have 'gone for it'—or kept going when the going was tough. My *Life Focus* coach helped me wrestle with questions I really needed to look at, but didn't know how. It also provided the tools and support we needed to work through some things as a couple that in the long run will make this new season much healthier, and more enjoyable, for all of us."

In particular, the life-purpose gleanings process and dream inventories gave Katie handles to work on some much-needed personal re-definition for this new phase. She had become adept at being the person others needed or expected her to be—in church, at home, in her marriage. Her *Life Focus* coach now became a friend and mentor in the ongoing process of figuring out who she really was; finding healthy and life-giving ways to integrate her past formation, present responsibilities, and future sense of call.

Ideally, what begins as a structured process will evolve into a set of inherent life-skills, and into new ways of seeing, thinking, and responding to life experience. The *Life Focus* reflection exercises help develop new mental and spiritual "muscles" that will serve the client well for the long haul. And the coaching interaction can open up new personal paradigms that become integral to who we are. But it begins with a coached process that minimizes the up-front guess-work, and frees the client to probe, wrestle, and explore.

Parameters

The reflection and discovery process at the heart of *Life Focus* can be a wild and wonderful thing. Clients often experience an awakening of the heart across the board, mustering thoughts and dreams and reflections that may have languished for years without a voice or champion. What begins as meager droplets from a seemingly rusted faucet can unexpectedly turn into a gusher. Conversely, the client may find it a struggle to come up with responses to a given exercise.

Coaches cultivate a "let it flow" posture, encouraging clients to jot down the array of thoughts stirred by the reflection exercises. Ever so gently, they attempt to help clients move beyond grooved thinking patterns to tap into areas of the heart that may not have been visited for a while. It can be difficult to avoid slipping into rutted responses or mindsets. We sometimes need support and accountability to help us go to the place of honesty, or vulnerability, or freshness that our heart longs for.

Whether by design or neglect, sometimes it seems we've forgotten how to have an honest conversation with our own heart. We may have de-valued entire portions of our being to the point of convincing ourselves they are not even there. The support of a *Life Focus* coach is designed, in part, to help us re-discover our own hearts, providing tools and parameters to help us along the way.

Terry and Corrie sought out *Life Focus* coaching during

a major transition. Married just three years, they met in Bible school and had served in an array of formal and informal ministry roles. Their passion to serve the Lord was contagious, and they entered the process with a bucket of ready responses to the questions about future ministry that often came their way. They were hungry, and eager to lay hold of that for which Jesus had laid hold of them.

Early in the *Life Focus* process, their responses were heavy with spiritual language and ministerial references. While this may be admirable at one level, they each found it difficult, initially, to move out of the realm of church ministry—both in reflecting about their past lives and dreaming about the future. Independently, their *Life Focus* coaches began to encourage both of them to think outside the ministry "box." This included their "BC" years—before making a lordship committal to Christ. How was God at work, even then? What could they discern about God's design in their lives, even in that raw, unredeemed state, that might have a bearing on how and why He created them?

This, in *Life Focus* lingo, is an essential part of "reclaiming the land": coming to see God's active involvement throughout all preceding seasons and experiences. We are called to serve God with our whole being, proclaiming His excellencies in every dimension of our lives, in every arena of society and human endeavor. Clients may struggle, at the outset, to see purpose in certain seasons of their lives, or see value in some aspects of who they are. They may be slow to push out into the full terrain available to them. The coach's gentle but persistent encouragement to take another look— do some journaling, ask for the Holy Spirit's help in bringing missing pieces to mind, try it from another direction, chew on some new questions—can be critical.

Slowly at first, Terry and Corrie each warmed to the task, then began to trip over new discoveries and insights. Terry began to see a consistent pattern stretching back to his childhood, with his leadership gifts and prophetic motivation much in evidence. His passion for "real" music, for authentic experience, for honest relationships, extended far beyond the "ministry" sphere. Corrie began to see her past experiences and perceived "failures" (in her "former" life) as a valuable asset, and began naming aspects of her heart and personality that had grown dormant. Both independently and together, their dreaming took on a fresh, out-of-the-box flavor. They began to envision a future that more fully maximizes their God-given design and, frankly, will be a lot more fun! But, paradoxically, the catalyst for this newfound freedom was the discipline of the *Life Focus* process.

Staying within the parameters of the process, at least during the initial discovery round, develops a discipline that will serve the client well long after the coach has faded from the picture. The process itself includes built-in plumb lines, which the client develops and learns to apply to his or her own emerging goals. The core values statements alone have the potential to enable the client to stay on course and avoid pitfalls that have shipwrecked many. En route to success as a Master Farmer, Scott recalls, "Clearly defining our values helped me to intentionally maintain our value of family as priority, and of finding ways to include the family in my goals." Today, Scott and Sharon's thriving family gives evidence of the parameters that they developed and internalized with the assistance of their *Life Focus* coaches, now long gone.

Perspective

Perhaps the most empowering assistance a *Life Focus* coach provides comes in the form of timely perspective. We are often simply too close, too immersed in our own experience, too aware of our own failures and shortcomings to adequately recognize the value-laden raw material of our lives for what it is. We commit the "sin of familiarity" first and foremost against ourselves! The assault is numbing: against our God-designed uniqueness, our God-delighting passion, our God-blessed identity, our God-inspired dreams, and our God-promised future. Against this relentless tide, a coach's outside perspective can be a critical God-given gift.

Shannon signed up for TLC's *Life Focus* track in response to her husband's persistent prodding. She had been through the prior track in the TLC coach-training sequence and, while she found it enjoyable, "it didn't connect at a deep level." Shaking her head, she says, "I didn't really 'get it'!" Coaching was something her husband was into. She had her hands full with a thriving nutritional consulting business, and did not anticipate continuing with the TLC training process past this second track.

A few weeks into it, she participated in a three-way call with her peer mentor and her *Life Focus* coach. During the call she interacted with her peer, effectively helping her sort through some blockages she had encountered. Afterwards her coach called her: "Do you realize you just coached her through that? Coaching is in you; you already do this instinctively, just in different areas."

"I didn't see it until then," Shannon remembers. "But after she said that, I began to think about it. I began to see intersections with what God had already been doing in my life. I was doing nutritional coaching in my business, but had never connected the two. That is my business; it's what I do. This is coaching. I hadn't seen the pattern, or really valued how God had designed me in this way. I certainly hadn't envisioned myself as a coach, at that time or in the future. I went on to complete the TLC training, and I continue coaching today. If she hadn't planted that seed, and given me that perspective, I would have just stopped after the second track and chalked it all up to experience!"

A coach can help us see when we are simply too close to

make sense out of our own experience. Sometimes it is as simple as connecting the dots: discovering linkages between experiences, discerning larger patterns, recognizing and naming ongoing themes. Often it triggers a redefinition of our categories of "success" and "failure," embracing language and paradigms more attuned to God's ways, less governed by those of surrounding culture. Usually it involves a fresh discovery of God's sovereign goodness—His relentless love and untiring commitment to conform us to the image of His Son. But the essence of the transaction is the same: the redemptive gift of perspective, providing just what is needed, at the moment, to carry on.

The Convergence Imperative

Discerning and embracing our life purpose, and developing lifelong convergence patterns are, at the core, a profoundly personal process. It involves the essential stewardship of our lives, our ultimate answer to the ultimate question: "What did you do with what I gave you?" It even goes beyond the issue of leaving our legacy, as important as that is. It has to do with how we live life here and now—abundantly, creatively, purposefully, playfully, abandoned to God in all His loving ways. We have been given the unique privilege of representing our Family in all we do. The growing convergence of our lives reflects the presence of Him in Whom all things cohere and hold together (Colossians 1:17), the One in whom history itself finds its consummation (Ephesians 1:10).

But the challenge of personal convergence has implications beyond our own lives, even beyond our immediate sphere of influence. Our willingness—or not!—to live deeply, to integrate the diverse dimensions of our own being, to "press toward the goal for the prize of the upward call of God in Christ Jesus" (Philippians 3:14), and to seek out the empowering relationships we need to do so, sends a clear message to next-gen leaders who are even now determining the nature of their own journey. The jury is still out on whether the church can or will be the place where they pursue their own callings, wrestle with what it means to be followers of Jesus, and engage their own convergence journey.

Pat's impact on the group of young artists at the Virginia retreat highlighted, for me, the power of hope in inviting each successive generation to dare to believe God for his highest and best, for themselves and for their generation. But such encounters need not be so rare as to take one's breath away. Convergence coaching is one means God is using to empower increasing numbers of His people on the road to convergence. And every life in obvious convergence will have a disproportionate effect on those they touch. Such encounters become doorways for the God of hope to "fill [us] with all joy and peace in believing, that [we] may abound in hope by the power of the Holy Spirit" (Romans 15:13).

Reflection and Discussion Questions
Chapter Seven: Convergence Coaching—
How God is using Coaching Values and Methodology to
Bridge Strategic Leaders into Purpose and Destiny.

1. Of the five principles for "finishing well" from Clinton's classic work that is mentioned by the author in this chapter, which stands out to you as the most lacking in your life right now? Which of these might you most need a coach to help you bring up to speed?

2. In what areas of your life do you most need to follow the proposed principle, "Doing business with God first?" How might that have changed an outcome that you wish was different? If a coach had been in your life to put that principle before you how might you have reacted then and now?

3. I have defined "perspective power" as the ability to see what God is up to in the midst of difficult circumstances. Can you recall a conversation that enabled you to see things with a renewed perspective? Have you evidenced an ability to bring a perspective power to others? In what ways might this be an evidence of a "calling" to coaching for you?

4. Who do you know that is in need of "convergence" in their lives? After reading this chapter how might a *Life Focus* coach help them in this process? If it is someone you really care about, what if you were to go through this process with them as a peer with a coach?

5. Which part of the discussion of the *Life Focus* coaching most intrigued you? TLC coaches will be glad to give you a complimentary coaching session in this compelling area to bring you more understanding and appreciation for the power of this process.

CHAPTER EIGHT

Bridges of Transformation— How the TLC Approach Develops Transformational Coaches

By Tony Stoltzfus

+≍+

The Pursuit of Transformation

"Even though I went out and got a degree in violence prevention, through the TLC process I've seen that the real violence that needed to be eradicated was in me..."

What kind of training produces coaches who consistently see their clients' lives transformed? If one of my coaching clients was searching for an answer to that question, I might respond with a question of my own: "Where in the past have you been effective in transforming others? What did you learn that made that possible; and how did you learn it?"

That question takes me back to my own pilgrimage as a coach. I spent my formative years in a radical church that started on a college campus. It was an amazing place to be in those days: passionate services, exciting worship, and a deep sense of community. I remember traveling around the country in a van with ten other people to do worship renewal services— leaving at 5:00 pm on Friday, driving all night, doing three programs over the weekend, and then coming back for work on Monday. I lived in community in a men's discipleship house that a friend and I bought inexpensively in a rough part of town and remodeled together. We taught guys younger than us to pray, pay their bills, take responsibility for punching a hole in the wall when they were angry, even to cook (some of the meals they made were terrible!).

All of us had a deep sense of destiny in those days. We were part of something important; something that was going to change the world, and we were ready to give our lives for it. We had wonderfully transparent relationships with one another and were growing by leaps and bounds in our abilities and capacity. The fact that most of us were single and had very little responsibility certainly offered a lot of time and energy to pursue those goals!

Unfortunately, the world didn't change that much, but our lives did: we got married, got real jobs, had children, and bought houses. All of a sudden we had responsibilities. About the same time a major conflict caused about half the church's members to leave, and afterward things weren't the same. Most of the components that had made that environment so transformational—the transparent relationships, the sense of destiny, the learning community, and the high expectations—had disappeared.

That was a blow. After what I'd experienced, it was hard to settle down and live an average Christian life and endure mediocre "How are you?" "I'm fine!" relationships. During that time I set out on a 10-year quest to discover how to create that kind of transformational environment for others. I learned about gifting and personality types, experimented with developing learning communities, got heavily involved in mentoring and leadership development, and worked with life purpose and destiny issues with others. That search culminated in my opportunity to participate in the development of the TLC system. Along the way I hit upon several key insights that have shaped the way we've designed coach-training experiences.

Part I: Foundations of the Transformational Process

Key Principles: Authentic Relationships Produce Transformation

> *"The most significant learning experience has been developing authentic relationships with another person. Being accountable to someone else has showed me how important this is for assisting someone in reaching their goals and purpose in life. This whole experience made me feel lighter because I no longer felt I had to hide things. I guess the word is liberation."*

The first insight was the importance of transparent relationships in transforming people. Authentic relationships allow us to be who we really are, and in them we see ourselves much more clearly for who we really are. The fact that we are not in hiding or on the defensive or trying to control the impressions others have of us allows honest dialogue to take place about where we are at in life, what we do well and where we need to be transformed. Real conversations with real people are a far more likely place to meet God than in a spin-controlled image we are holding up for public consumption. Authentic relationships give God access to our lives in a way few other experiences do.

Half-way through each TLC training course we have an appointment where the trainer checks in on the peer relationships to see if everything is going well. One of our trainers had a trainee who seemed reluctant to talk about her peer. She talked about the good things that were happening, but the non-verbal signals were communicating something was wrong. It finally came out that this woman's peer wasn't really doing the work—she would come with it half completed and then try to cover it up. She wasn't really opening up or engaging the relationship, and was basically going through the motions of completing the program. Our standard procedure in this kind of situation is to ask the trainees to take responsibility for the situation. So the trainer asked, "What can you do about this situation?"

There was an awkward pause. The trainer didn't know it, but she had just touched a raw nerve. This woman had never confronted anyone directly in her life, and she was petrified. At that kind of moment, a decision is made: we can cover up and go on to something else, work at things at a surface level, or really be vulnerable and maybe experience a life-changing transformation. The difference is relationship. In this situation, the relationship between the trainer and the trainee enabled them to keep going—the trainee opened up about what was going on inside her, and the trainer was able to walk with her through the painful process of learning to confront.

It's a tough thing to really look at yourself honestly when you don't look good. Authentic relationships provide the safety, acceptance, and perspective we need to go there. Here the trainee was able to ask for help for the first time, beginning a process that finally resulted in bold new changes in her other relationships; a breakthrough personal transformation. That one coaching conversation ended up launching this woman into the fulfillment of her destiny.

In an authentic relationship, the other person sees me for who I am and loves me anyway. Acceptance and love are such deep needs for human beings that we are willing to twist ourselves into all manner of unreal and unnatural shapes to get them. An individual who has authentic relationships is much less dominated by the need to be loved, and is more apt to be motivated by destiny and service than by the kind of endemic drivenness that causes us to spend our lives on things that ultimately don't satisfy. I am filled, not empty; therefore my focus can shift elsewhere.

When the need for acceptance is met, all the energy that was being expended keeping up an image or hunger for acceptance can be transferred to living a more purposeful life. Therefore, if all a coach does is provide an authentic relationship and unconditional acceptance to a client, that client will be able to reach higher and go farther than they ever could without a coach.

One of the questions on our TLC training evaluation form is, 'What was the most significant or transforming thing in the coaching process so far?" One of the most common answers is something like, "My relationship with my coach!" or "Just being listened to." As trainers we first prioritize that trainees are people, and that simply having great relationships in their lives will increase their performance. An authentic relationship between a coach and client in and of itself is transformational.

Coaching as a discipline is very relational to begin with, and relational and conversational skills are a normal part of coach training. TLC takes that a step further in saying that the ability of a coach to quickly catalyze relationships with an unusually deep level of transparency is a key element in making a coaching relationship unusually transformational. Therefore, an important component of our program is training and first-hand experience in authenticity.

Key Principles: Transformation is an Experiential Process

> *"[The impact of TLC training] has been universal—I ask many more probing questions: "What's*

God doing in this, what's God want to show you?"...I guess I occasionally used to do that before as a last resort, but now it's kind of common."

The second insight was about the training process itself. I saw in myself and others a tendency to learn something through an extended life process, but then attempt to transmit it to others by presenting those experiential truths only as information sound bites in a summary form. For instance, I remember once giving a series of messages on meeting God in your day. I had just taken a three-month sabbatical at a silent retreat center, and becoming more aware of God throughout the day had been a powerful experience for me. So I took the tool that I had used on retreat and taught a series on how to use it. A few people latched on to it, but most people never really took it to heart. A month later they were still chugging along in their lives as if I'd never said a word.

Then a light came on: if I learned something one way, why was I trying to transmit it in another? I had grasped this by going away on retreat, surrounded by others who were working at the same thing, being constantly reminded by a spiritual director to work at a slower pace and enjoy the moment. If that's what it took for me to get it, why did I expect that I could condense an entire summer into three sermons and get the same impact on others?

In other words, the problem wasn't the trainees, it was the way I was training. I began to pay close attention not just to *what* needed to be learned but the whole process of *how people learn.* To consistently produce transformation, training needs to replicate the life processes involved in changing who people are.

This insight evolved into making a critical distinction between teaching and training. In the TLC model, teaching provides the basic *content* or information for developing coaches: the values, principles, and techniques that form the discipline of coaching. Training is the *entire process*, including teaching, of transmitting that content so that it produces transformation of the *being* (values, habits, core beliefs, worldview) of the trainee. When who you are changes, changes in your actions inevitably and naturally follow. Therefore, coach training had to be much more of a life process to produce the transformation I was looking for.

For example, a fundamental change for every prospective coach is to get out of advice-giving mode and start to really listen and ask questions. We start the process of working at that in TLC training by demonstrating the difference between asking and telling in a role-play session. The trainer gets a volunteer to come up front and be coached on a real issue, then proceeds to demonstrate in front of others how not to respond as a coach. The trainer jumps to conclusions, asks closed questions, uses the times the client is talking to formulate his or her own responses instead of listening, and finishes the session with a burst of advice-giving. Usually after only four or five minutes of this, the "client" is visibly frustrated.

Then we debrief, using the question, "What did you hate about what the coach just did?" This question brings up the times we've gotten unsolicited advice from others and hated it. Most groups in our training criticize what the coach did with obvious relish! Once we've identified what we all find repulsive about advice-giving, we redo the role-play, with the coach listening intently and asking probing questions. The difference is huge. Usually the conversation goes to a totally different place than it did the first time, and the "client" will often have a real breakthrough.

The power of this role-playing approach is that it provides a learning process instead of just an informational summary. Trainees see what it looks like to be coached by "Mr. Fix-it"; they identify with the disappointment of getting another pat answer, and see the difference in effectiveness between advice-giving and the coaching approach. Seeing, discussing, feeling, experiencing, and doing are components of a process that yields real transformation in the form of value and habit changes. We learn much more from this kind of teachable moment than we ever do from just hearing a trainer say, "Don't give advice!"

TLC training is based on the idea that if your heart or core values start changing, your actions will soon follow, and change in a natural and unstrained way. If you live the lifestyle of a coach—an accountable, authentic, reflective, curious, purposeful life—then your natural life patterns will flow over into the way you coach others. When you do what comes natural to you, you *will* be coaching. We express this value as *"Ministry flows out of being."*

By contrast, if coaching is utilized as a set of techniques or skills by someone who doesn't lead the lifestyle of a coach, it will be difficult to maintain even the skill-set over time. The gravitational pull of the person's real values and habits erode what was learned in coach training, and sooner or later who we really are comes out. In the parable of the talents, the servant who was asked to invest but didn't have the values or character of an investor eventually lost his place as a servant and his opportunity was given to someone else. *"...To everyone who has will be given; and from him who does not have, even what he has will be taken away from him" (Luke 19:26).*

Key Principles: Train for Character and Competence

> *"This had been life changing...the whole experience has been like a real-time case study. [TLC training] doesn't just add a couple of tools, it spreads out into all the other tools I already had and adds another dimension to them."*   *(Corporate VP)*

In the TLC training approach, the foundation of great coaching is living the lifestyle of a coach (we also talk about this as "having the heart of a coach"). Since transformational coaching flows most freely out of a transformed life, we have chosen to target how to train coaches in character. Skills are essential as well: they are the walls and roof of the house and one without the other is ineffective. Skills and techniques built on a foundation of character will last for the long haul and have a great impact on those we coach. Therefore, training in competencies and training in character need to go hand in hand.

The problem with training in skills alone is that technique without character results in manipulation. I may have great listening skills, the ability to make my client feel totally heard, and an exceptional knack for asking the question that unlocks a new perspective. But if, for instance, my real motive is to look successful as a coach, the coaching relationship becomes about my needs and not the client's. I'm not giving freely to the client; I'm giving because I get something in return. Instead of offering unconditional love and belief, I'm offering a bargain: I'll love you and believe in you *if* you perform up to my expectations and make me look good. Paul talks about the outcome of this bargain in First Corinthians 13: If I have tremendous skills and ability but don't have love, I'm nothing and I accomplish nothing. Much of the power of the coaching relationship is based on the coach's having the depth of character to offer something unconditional.

On the other hand, character without skill is just clumsiness. It's like having all the money you need to buy a new car, but having it locked up in a long term investment so you can't get at it when the vehicle you have breaks down. If I really believe in my clients but have poor listening skills, the way I relate to them may actually be communicating that I *don't* believe in them. My excellent motives are thwarted by my lack of practical ability.

At one of our training workshops I was observing a role play where the trainee was having a terrible time listening well. She interrupted, finished the client's sentences, and just couldn't restrain herself from giving advice. It was so painful that during the debriefing I had to point out to her the different places she'd missed the mark. She wondered out loud whether she was ever going to get this. That afternoon I came back to watch her do another role play, and the difference was like night and day. She listened intently, her questions flowed out of what the client was saying, she didn't interrupt—it was a very powerful and empowering session. I was intrigued and enthusiastically blurted out "You did such a great job this time! What made this so different than the role play you did this morning?"

"Well," she replied after thinking for a bit, "I guess I was so interested in what this client was talking about." It was a perfect teachable moment for her: when her heart was in the right place, when she was genuinely interested in what the client was saying, she coached well without even trying. When she tried to focus on doing things right and looking good as a coach, the wheels came off and she had crashed. For her, learning the character of a coach and the skills of a coach happened together.

When you train for character and competence at the same time, each reinforces the other in a way that the sum is greater than the parts. Skills (if practiced repeatedly over time as disciplines) become habits, and habits are part of character. "Doing" experienced enough becomes "being." Working in the other direction, when an individual is transformed through the coach training process, coaching becomes deeply embedded in their value system, providing a strong motivation and life-long rationale for practicing the coaching skills. Changes in '"being" produce long-term changes in "doing."

Summary: Key Training Principles

In summary, here are the three key principles that shape the TLC training approach:

- Training will happen in the *context* of a learning community of authentic relationships.
- We will train for character and competence (the *content* of the program) together.
- Training will be an experiential, transformational *process* that engages all of life.

Part II: Designing a Transformational Training Program

What does a training program based on these principles look like in real life? Let's first take a quick overview of the program, and then walk through how the three key principles above play out in the way the program is structured. Finally, we'll dig into the nuts and bolts of one particular skill, how we train for it, and what kind of impact TLC training has had on those who've been through it.

The TLC coach training program certifies transformational coaches through a 40-week process offering approximately 180 hours of training. The program is divided into three 13-week courses:

- *Formation*, which covers foundational coaching skills and developing the lifestyle of a coach.
- *Life Focus*, which offers a set of tools for life purpose coaching while the trainee is being coached on their own life focus.
- *Implementation*, which provides advanced coaching skills and ample opportunities for skills practice with feedback.

The program is delivered primarily through one-on-one appointments, workshops, and independent study exercises using an extensive training manual in an exercise format. Each trainee goes through the program with a peer and a personal coach trainer. About 30% of total program time is from workshop sessions and teaching input, while 70% is integration, application, and practice.

The *context* or venue of the training is relationships; the *content* of the program is the character and competencies to be developed (summed up in our values and training outcomes); and the *process* is made experiential and transformational through real-life application.

Context: The Relationships

> *"I was extremely skeptical [about working with an unfamiliar peer]...but I believe I grew more as a person by working with someone who didn't know me... It began to imbue me with the confidence to more aggressively pursue strong, spiritual, intimate relationship with other men, which doesn't happen in my culture."*

The first clue for most of our trainees that this program is going to be a little different than the norm is the emphasis on relationships. Each trainee meets bi-weekly with a personal coach/trainer and bi-weekly with a peer mentor (a fellow student or "client") throughout the 40-weeks of training. In other words, every week the trainee has a one-on-one appointment with his or her coach or peer. *These relationships are the primary venue for the training.* The program includes six classroom sessions and three workshop days in 40 weeks, but it has 44 peer or coaching appointments.

One of the first objectives in the training is to establish these relationships and foster a high level of transparency in them. The interaction with the trainer is the crucial ingredient in this process. Most individuals believe that deep relationships can form only after a long period of knowing each other and building trust. In the coaching appointments the trainer models something totally different—that authenticity is a lifestyle where one simply chooses unilaterally to be open with others. The openness of the trainer quickly catalyzes an unusual degree of openness in the trainees. For instance, an apostolic or denominational leader going through TLC training with a group of pastors under his oversight reported, "Because the relational process [with the peer mentor] is so intentional...within a short time we touched more areas in depth than I have with any of the other pastors I oversee." (He made this comment only seven weeks into the process!) Trainees often report that by the end of three months their peer relationship has become one of the most open and significant relationships in their life.

This accomplishes two important objectives. First, authenticity opens the door for the trainees' own lives to be transformed. Second, the trainees begin to live more authentic lives themselves. As they become more comfortable with transparency they develop the ability to catalyze transparency in others. This powerful skill will greatly enhance their effectiveness in coaching others through transformation.

One of our trainees related his experience of starting through the TLC training process with someone he didn't know from another part of the country. "I was extremely skeptical about working with an unfamiliar peer...but I believe I grew more as a person by working with someone who didn't know me... It began to imbue me with the confidence to more aggressively pursue strong, spiritual, intimate relationship with other men, which doesn't happen in my culture." The ability to confidently develop those kinds of relationships became an important part of this individual's ability to see others transformed through coaching.

Content: Values and Outcomes

> *"When I started this coach training program, I thought of it as routine, just another thing to do for my job. But now that I've seen the power of it...if I had a coach like you when I was 20 or 30, my life would be so different! So I want to be a coach and do this for other people."*

The content of TLC training is embodied in a set of training outcomes and coaching values that the program was designed around. While there is a lot of overlap between the two, in broad terms the values represent the "character" part of the training, while the outcomes represent the "competencies" (or skills). The aim is to produce people with a certain kind of DNA, people who embody this set of values and who have the practical competence to walk them out.

Values

Listed below are five of the thirteen coaching values from the TLC training program:

- **Transformation Happens Experientially**
  The things that really shape us happen experientially, not by accumulating information.
- **Ministry Flows out of Being**
  Who I am is what I have to give.
- **Own-life Stewardship**
  God has entrusted each person with the stewardship of his or her own life.
- **Learning Community**
  Growth and change are maximized within an accountable learning community of authentic relationships.

- **Leaders Take Responsibility for Their Own Growth**
  Instead of waiting for others to care for them, leaders take responsibility for their own growth.

These values shape everything about the training program, right down to the logistics. For instance, trainees make all the phone calls to their trainer and not vice versa, because *Leaders take responsibility for their own growth.* Having trainees make the call is a way of helping them experience the value in action. In the same way, if there is a relational breakdown between peers, instead of immediately intervening, the trainer challenges the peers to take responsibility and solve the problem. Every exercise trainees do is explicitly tied to at least one of the values, and they are talked about in each appointment. As the students experience the training process the values that guide it are brought out, so understanding of the values is tied to powerful experiences that they are having. Trainees come to "value the values" because their own lives have been transformed by them. Since our values reflect what is most important to us, something important, something transformational has to happen for us to take on new values.

Outcomes
Below are five of the ten training outcomes from the Formation course:

1) Understand and be able to articulate the thirteen TLC core coaching values.
2) Understand and experience accountability and value it as crucial to reaching one's potential and finishing well.
3) Learn practical ways to foster change by providing S.E.A. (Support, Encouragement and Accountability) in an accountability relationship.

4) Understand and experience authenticity, and know how to create transparent, growth-centered relationships.
5) Learn to ask powerful coaching questions.

Outcomes represent the major skills to be learned in the course. Instead of focusing on one skill each week and then moving on to the next, courses are made up of "threads" (a series of learning experiences on one topic) that extend through many weeks or even an entire course. By working on the same skill a little bit each week, it begins to become an ingrained pattern instead of something we just talk about.

Here's an example. To work on listening skills, trainees:

• Watch several listening role plays where the skill is modeled.
• Experience being listened to week after week by their coach.
• Take in an input session on listening.
• Role play listening skills with their peer with feedback from the coach.
• Do several exercises where they practice listening to friends or co-workers.
• Do two more sets of role plays with groups of other trainees.

If the goal was merely cognition (head-knowledge), simply listening to the input session would be enough. But listening is a habit; therefore time, practice with feedback, and real-world application are needed to change the way we actually listen.

One of the challenges in listening skills training is that most people don't feel like they have much of a need to improve. So we developed a surprise session called the "Ambush Role-Play" to give trainees a true picture of how they listen. A coaching appointment usually starts with five minutes of just "clearing the air": "How are you?," "What have you been up to since we last met?" and such. During those five minutes of clearing the trainer works in a little story about what he's been up to that week. Then the actual coaching appointment starts, the trainees give their progress reports and five or ten minutes later the trainer springs the ambush: "Remember that little story I told at the beginning of the appointment about the couple I was working with? I'd like you to tell that back to me with as many of the details as you can remember."

After a moment of stunned silence, the trainees attempt to reconstruct the story. Sometimes they do pretty well; other times they leave out whole sections, get the names wrong, or jumble the different parts together. Then we start to unearth their listening obstacles by looking at what they were thinking about while the trainer was talking, whether they had fully disengaged from their last activity, or what in their environment was distracting them from really listening. Often the trainees come out of the exercise with a step or two that they are highly motivated to take to improve their listening.

The Process: Application and Teachable Moments

What we've done with the ambush role play is to create a **teachable moment**; a multi-sensory experience where trainees were able to *see* for themselves what their listening skills were like instead of just being told. Teachable moments allow people to draw their own lessons from an experience. Learning this way is more memorable, so it stays with us longer, and it is more motivating, so we are much more likely to act on it.

One of our overseas trainees shared a teachable moment from his training with us:

> *"I did this [listening] exercise with my*

wife...Through 23 years of marriage, finally she really started for the first time to tell me her mind...She was very honest and it was my first time to meet with her spiritually. It felt like two jars of water being poured into each other. It was such a good experience...I realized that through 23 years of marriage I had never listened to her and that we did not have a deep relationship. This is a present from God."

In essence, the TLC training process is also a container designed to incubate teachable moments. Each exercise, training event, and coaching appointment builds the trainee's skills and abilities, but every so often a moment comes along that takes things to a whole new level. Suddenly, something profound happens and the trainee really understands the value of relationships, or sees for the first time why others react to him, or realizes what the way she lives says about what her priorities really are.

We create certain types of experiences and foster authentic relationships as a greenhouse to nurture these transforming moments, but we can't produce the transformation itself. It's not something predictable that you can schedule or manufacture—transformation happens at the confluence of relationship, experience, and the work of God in a person's life. In fact, some of the most powerful experiences people have had in TLC training have happened when something has gone wrong.

As trainers we talk about "trusting the process" to get the work of transformation done. What we mean by that is that if you put your seed in the ground of authentic relationships, you water it with meaningful training experiences and fertilize it with powerful questions, sooner or later the trainee will meet God and be transformed. We don't know when or where that will happen, but the fact that it consistently does is something we depend on. We tend the plant, but God gives the growth.

The power of these transforming experiences is that they happen at such a deep level that their impact is felt in many different areas of life. One significant moment like this can produce as much change in a trainee's life as a whole semester of input, application and practice. In TLC we want both: the skills, the practice, the habits formed by working systematically through an intensive training curriculum, but also the lightning strike of transformation that changes everything in a moment. One of the key roles of the trainer in the TLC process is to help the trainee identify and get the most out of the teachable moments life creates. Too often we have these breakthrough moments in our lives, but without the support or follow-up of a coaching relationship the moment is lost. As coaches, our goal is to give the individual the best chance they've ever had to meet God in an area of their life and respond well.

Results

> *"I've had these values [accountability, authenticity, relationship] for most of my life, but there is a relief to having actually lived them out; to have walked my talk and to feel the integrity of doing it."*

In the last five years TLC has trained close to six hundred coaches in the US and abroad. In program evaluations, trainees consistently rank it very high (4 or 5 on a scale of one to five) on various ways the TLC program has impacted them personally. The program has consistently had a transforming effect on the lives of trainees. While the skill and experience of the trainer certainly make a different, the process works even with relatively inexperienced trainers. It has also worked across cultures and national boundaries.

However, I think the best way to capture the impact is in the words of the trainees.

> *"The hour I spend with this guy I'm coaching is the best hour of my week—this is the best investment I'm making."*

> *"I had lots of good friends, but none who were helping me in the areas I needed to grow...I could fool a lot of people because I'm authentic up to a point. In this course I found that I wasn't as transparent as I thought... and that God wants me to have those kinds of relationships in my life."*

> *"The greatest thing I'm learning from this is how to work at change while keeping others responsible...After 22 years of pastoral experience giving people advice and providing answers, this is a whole different way of working with people...[and] I've gotten a taste now of what it can do."*

> *"I can't say this much, so I take it seriously when I do: Thank you for changing my life. My family (wife and kids), school work, perspective and even my goals are the better for having gone through this process. Thank you."*

Reflection and Discussion Questions
Chapter Eight: Bridges of Transformation—
How the TLC Approach Develops
Transformational Coaches

1. Think back to relationships that have been genuinely authentic in your life. What was it that made this possible? Who took responsibility to initiate the relationship to that level? Can you imagine a skilled coach who could take you there in a short time? What would happen in your existing relationships if you developed that coaching heart and skill?

2. "Ministry flows out of being" is a TLC value that, if lived out in our lives, would make huge differences in the way we learn and train others. What part of your life already reflects a coaching heart towards others? Where might you seek to be transformed within to have more than a learned skill but an enlarged heart towards others?

3. Where has any of your past training taken place in the context of a learning community of authentic relationships? What would your church or organization look like if there was a small community of "coaches-in-training" as part of the future development of people and leaders?

What would it look like if you were a key person to bring coaching into your organization?

4. Which of the five TLC core values listed in this chapter is most missing in your life or organization? How might coaching address this for you in a way that other ways of development has fallen short of the mark?

5. As you reflect on the process that TLC uses in coach training for listening skills, what comes to mind about how this kind of process of training compares with other methods you have experienced? What would it be like for you to experience the coach training process as a way to train you for the process of training in other areas besides coaching?

Section Three:
A Prophetic, Biblical, and
Personal Call to the Marketplace

Introduction

I cringed as I anticipated yet again the familiar story of the preacher as he got really worked up in the pulpit. I could feel my resistors kicking in as I anticipated almost word for word what he was about to say to the educators, media personnel, artists, government workers, and business executives who sat there wanting so badly to hear how they could fulfill their destiny as they felt God's pleasure over them in their careers. That day, like many before, they would be disappointed as the high tech audio system penetrated our lives with his words:

> *"I used to be a successful businessman until God called me to serve Him with all my heart. I would never go back to those fishing nets like the first disciples. I gave up all that for the highest calling to serve God full-time in the church ministry!"*

There is a problem with the line of thinking that asserts that the only way to serve God full-time with all of our hearts is by being a pastor or missionary or some other professional ministry career available to serious church members today. Anything less than that is second class, back of the bus, leftovers, used parts...you get the picture. Not only does this stem from a narrow theology of the people of God as a kingdom of priests in all spheres of the Kingdom of God, it also comes from a church culture that lives a dualistic, even Gnostic, lifestyle from Monday through Saturday.

Recently I noted over 85 books that are readdressing this error that ministry happens in the arena of the stained glass instead of the arena of plain glass.30 More people are embracing their call to serve God outside the church and more churches are serving their members in that call. Pastors are showing up on site at board rooms to get insight of how their executive level church members have to live out their faith daily. More leaders are being "commissioned" into their workplaces, as they did in Antioch in Acts 15, as pastors are declaring that "it seemed good to the Holy Spirit and to us" (Acts 15:28).

The challenge in this Kingdom of God emphasis is that many do not have a solid foundation on which to stand as they go after their vocations in the spirit of Caleb when he proclaimed, "Give me that mountain" (Joshua 14:12)! It is not about being the best so we can have the best and then somehow gain the credibility of our faith to share. It is much more about being agents of transformation so that we can make a difference where we are planted. It worked in ancient civilizations and it works today.

Many of us have studied the characters in the Bible in only a one-dimensional manner. We have looked for the secrets of their spiritual lives only missing the obvious evidence of the emotional and relational skills that did not nullify what was in their spirit, but instead magnified their spiritual influence on the lives of those around them. What they had is what transformational coaches are trained to experience and replicate in others.

Emotional intelligence is an exciting new field of inquiry.31 I am in dialogue with several scholars who are doing original research in this area. Many excellent coaches model the principles of this emerging discipline and help their clients embrace them in their personal and work lives.

Transformational coaching is seeking to step it up a notch by incorporating the biblical realities of wisdom and favor into this practice. The result of this is the promise of an uncommon advantage for those in the marketplace and an uncommon result for those who are coached transformationally.

I have a David and Jonathan partnership with one of the most powerful presenters of this transformational advantage. Lance Wallnau and I have seen the truth of the next chapters as we have worked in an international arena to bridge God's favor across cultural barriers to marketplace leaders. There is no one I have met who combines the latest research in emotional intelligence with the biblical, supernatural, and sustainable impact of wisdom and favor in the work and ministry arenas.32

As you work through the next section, take time to reflect on what you are reading. Take personal notes as to what will be conceived in you—a creative insight, a breakthrough innovation, a loosening of a log jam, a tying together of loose ends. Marketplace ministry that will take mountains begins at the biblical base camp of the lives of those who have gone before us. Transformational coaching operating in the principles of these chapters is a force that cannot be stopped, a fire that cannot be quenched. You are about to enter into a no-whining, no- complaining, no-turning-back zone.

Let us know if we under-promised and over-delivered.

CHAPTER NINE

Marketplace Invasion—
A Prophetic Call to Transforming
the Workplace

By Lance Wallnau

Shatter The Fish Tank

It was like any other summer day as I walked into that house in Levittown, Pennsylvania. I was designing programs that netted millions of dollars for retail oil companies that were in the process of reinventing themselves as "energy conservation" companies. While interviewing a homeowner for my project, I glanced at his fish tank and saw a most unusual, almost exotic looking fish. "What kind of fish is that?" I asked. "That is a Japanese Oranda fish," the owner replied with evident pride. The fish seemed a bit larger than any tropical fish I had seen, so I asked, "How big will it grow?" "That depends," the owner answered thoughtfully. "Depends on what?" I mumbled absentmindedly as I observed the different colors of the scales. "Depends on the size tank you put it in. Stick him in a 50-gallon tank he is six inches, but put him in 100-gallon tank and he grows to nine. Without a tank he can be a foot long."

I jerked my head and stared at him for a minute, weighing the impact of what I heard. I knew there was something profound in his statement, but could not tell what exactly it was. On the way home I asked the Lord to help me understand what lesson He put into nature and revealed through this fish. Like a flash-*bam*! I caught it. "You are that fish— and you will grow to the size revelation you are swimming in!" The fish swims till it reaches its clear glass boundary. Somehow nature sends a signal to the fish brain that says, "don't grow past four inches" and the fish obeys. Likewise a believer grows to the size revelation he or she embraces. If you are only taught about a Jesus who saves, you will grow to the size of a saved believer, but not much more. If you are taught that Jesus wants to transform world kingdoms through you—it will stretch you to your full potential.

I asked myself, "What size revelation am I swimming in?" Or more specifically, what are the boundaries I need to shatter? What are the personal constraints I must break through to become what is God's dream for me of becoming? Immediately, I saw that most of my vision for ministry was limited to my life in church. Apart from attending Sunday morning, my main business in life was to live a good life, occasionally witness to a lost soul, and give my money to worthy church projects and ministries. As I thought about my vision for ministry it just seemed so...boring. Is this what God expects? A quick examination of the life of Christ however yields a much different picture of things.

A friend once sent me a quote saying: *"Jesus made 132 public appearances in the New Testament and 122 of them were in the marketplace. Of the 52 parables Jesus told, 45 had a workplace context. Jesus spent his adult life until age 30 in the profession of a carpenter. From there he began a preaching ministry, not in the synagogue but in the workplace. The workplace is where a majority of a church congregation spends a majority of their time, interacting with a majority of the unchurched world. This is the front lines of the advancing army of Christ."*

Billy Graham says, *"I believe one of the next great moves of God is going to be through the believers in the workplace."*33 God is about to shatter the fish tank.

27 Minutes Dead—Then Brought Back to Life!

State Senator Mike Crotts of Georgia knows what it means to have his fish tank shattered. The speaker was South African born prophet, Kim Clement. There was excitement and anticipation in the atmosphere as Kim pointed in the direction Phyllis Crotts, the senator's wife, and declared that the Lord had called her and Mike to have a son named Caleb who they would raise together, and that this son would walk in the same political steps of his father. The Crotts and Kim had never met prior to this meeting, but the word of the Lord confirmed Mike's personal vision to run for state senator.

Life however did not go on as usual for the Crotts. While campaigning a month later, he had a heart attack. Rushed to the emergency room, the medical team of specialists sought in vain to revive him. His vital signs were fading, and then...stopped. The monitor recording his vital signs flattened out for thirty-six minutes. Phyllis had to literally fight guards and claw her way to her husband's side. Pushing the exasperated medical team to one side she took hold of her husband's leg and proclaimed the prophetic word from Kim. With all the faith she could summon she began to proclaim "You can not die because the word of the Lord says we will have a son named Caleb and we will raise him *together*..." She continued proclaiming the word God gave over and over with authority while the doctors tried to ignore the desperate but futile attempt to alter the inevitable fact of death.

But the senator was not entirely gone; he was in another realm, seeing an entirely different scene. The scene he viewed was one that would change his life.

Standing before him he beheld a great endless ocean when suddenly islands appeared, and these islands became mountains. He could sense the presence of Jesus next to him, and stood transfixed on the sight before his eyes. There were seven islands in all and they rose out of the ocean, growing to become great mountains. Suddenly an eighth island mountain emerged in the midst of the seven and began to grow and grow until it dominated and over-shadowed the others. A voice rang out audibly in his ear, "These islands are world kingdoms. This great mountain in the midst of them is the Kingdom of God and it is greater than every other mountain. And that mountain," Jesus pointed to one in the midst of the seven mountains.... "is the political mountain and *you are called to go into it...but* there must be *agreement!*"

As Jesus said the word "agreement" the senator's wife stopped proclaiming the prophetic word of the Lord over her husband's lifeless body and in one last desperate shout of faith proclaimed, "Mike! I command your spirit to come back into this body." The next sound that filled the stunned emergency room was the bleep-bleep of the monitor finally locating a human heartbeat. The senator opened his eyes, but the physicians told the wife that any man without a heartbeat for 27 minutes was sure to be oxygen-starved and brain-dead. At first she feared she had made a great mistake by commanding her husband's spirit to return, but Mike settled the issue by speaking to everyone's astonishment... "Where is my son Caleb?"

He went home a new man. Mike Crotts was given back more than his life on that day; he was given an assignment to invade a mountain—a political mountain. Mike went on to become a state senator and adopted a little boy named Caleb, who will no doubt walk in the political steps of his father.

What are the Seven Mountains?

As I contemplated the senator's vision I kept asking the Lord, "If one of the mountains is a political mountain, what are the other six?" My quest for the identity of the mountains concluded a few months later in the form of a divine appointment with Loren Cunningham, the esteemed founder of Youth With A Mission. He told me how he came to know the seven mountains and their names. He and Bill Bright, founder of Campus Crusade for Christ, were scheduled to meet one day for lunch, but before they met the Lord had visited each of them and spoken to them about the seven mountains, or world kingdoms of this current era of time.

God spoke to each of them: "If the world is to be won, these are the mountains that mold the culture and the minds of men. Whoever controls these mountains controls the direction of the world, and the harvest fields therein." Each man wrote his impression of what the seven mountains were; though their language was different their conclusions were the same. These seven mountains are kingdoms that shape the minds of men—they are the "mind molders" that form the culture and the spiritual climate of each nation. They are:

1. *Church*
2. *Family*
3. *Education*
4. *Government and law*
5. *Media (includes all communication: TV, radio, newspaper, internet)*
6. *Arts, entertainment, sports*
7. *Commerce, science and technology*

Suddenly it seemed clear. The harvest and the culture are connected. Satan penetrates the minds of men through the mind molders, setting up strongholds in the institutions that shape society. From these heights he can command vast regions of influence, manipulating the false reasoning that shapes the minds of a nation's inhabitants. It was these very "imaginations" Paul targeted as the first priority of apostolic warfare in Corinth. Paul had a two-stage strategy. In the first stage he cast down deceptions that hindered the conversion of people. The apostle began his work in a territory by doing the work of an evangelist claiming, "I determined to know nothing among you except Jesus Christ and Him crucified." (1 Corinthians 2:2)

Once a beachhead was established, however, Paul commenced to the second level of combat against strongholds as he discipled the believers into a new way of thinking. "But we speak the wisdom of God in a mystery, the hidden wisdom which God ordained before the ages for our glory, which none of the rulers of this age knew..." (1 Corinthians 2:7-8). Paul saw this mind-renewing process as indispensable to the establishment of disciples who could impact the culture of Corinth. Stage two is the strategic stage necessary to accomplish the occupation Jesus desires for every nation, tribe, or ethnic community. The battle to occupy the mind molders is the real reason why American political contests have been so incendiary since the year 2000. This ideological conflict is in fact a cultural war whose battle lines are shaped primarily in the mind molders.

Probe each mountain and you can locate the infrastructure of heaven and hell engaged in desperate struggle somewhere in the high ground. For instance, examine the education mountains in the United States. In universities and colleges like the renowned Duke University, the bias in hiring liberal deans and department heads is as high as 17 liberals to 1 conservative. Look at the arts mountain and witness the startling resistance felt by Mel Gibson when he sought financial backing from Hollywood for his movie, *The Passion of the Christ*. A powerful elite core group of tinsel town bankers and producers locked arms on the top of this mountain and almost succeeded in keeping the movie from ever being released. Today they are kicking themselves up and down Hollywood Boulevard as they watch the Gibson film become a historic, record-breaking, all time best grossing R-rated movie—at $625,000,000 and rising!

So why is there so much resistance? The Hollywood of Cecil B. DeMille shifted ownership somewhere during the last 40 years. The change is clear when you consider that movies mocking Christ, such as *The Last Temptation*, received Golden Globe status and movies based on Christ's actual life such as *The Passion* struggle for distribution. There was once a time in history when the Church dominated the arts and popular culture. Plays, poetry, paintings and popular music were flavored with moral messages to the multitudes. Sculpture depicted biblical characters and stories. Sadly, like the parable of the tares and wheat reveals to us, while the church slept Satan planted his people in the high ground of each of these powerful spheres of influence. Those poetic, artistic, and dramatic prophets who once brought the world into warm contact with the unseen world that they saw have lost their voice. The world has never lost its desire for awe, wonder, and adventure. When productions incorporate the values of the Kingdom they invariably make money. Popular author Steven King said, you "can't even do a good horror movie unless you first know what good is."

How did American universities and Hollywood studios ever become so hostile to God? Wasn't Harvard originally established as a college dedicated to the shaping of ministers? Consider that pastors started 183 of the first 186 U.S. colleges for the education of Christians in society! But the Church has given up its place, preferring to let the world view us as the disgruntled critics of a decaying culture. As a result we have surrendered, uncontested, the current day mind molders to the powers of darkness only to have to recover in conflict, tooth and nail, what we occupied at the turn of the 20th century. The world needs our salt. Jesus said "salt" is "good." The Lord has rights to all lands, cultures, and systems. Arts and entertainment is perhaps the most significant because all other mind molders are necessary, but arts are the only field in which people spend their money for love of the experience. Since the arts exist for recreation, it's a wonder that those who know their Creator do not dominate the field of re-creation. Why do we back up from the culture?

To the religious mind, these mind molders are viewed as territory that is "off limits." Some even go further to call everything in this world outside of the local church or revival meetings the work of the devil. These viewpoints are built upon a subtle but serious error, namely, attributing to the devil or fallen man the ability to create anything—government, communication, technology, agriculture, arts, literature and science—on his own, without God. Neither man nor the devil can do anything really original. Man cannot even sin without using something God has provided and pervert its use. What is lust but the abuse of the gift of sexuality? What is gluttony but overeating? What is greed but the abuse of the power of acquisition? What is manipulation but the abuse of the gift of persuasion? Even murder is rooted in anger, which is meant to alert us to a rule that is in violation or to supply us with resolve to deal with a problem. Behind every sin there is a God-given gift being distorted.

What to do with the World?

For years the Church made the mistake of conveying a sort of second-class citizenship upon those who felt called to the world of business or arts rather than ministry. We have in various ways fed the idea that there is a separation between the secular and the sacred in terms of career tracks. Where does this come from? Perhaps confusion in understanding what Scripture teaches about the "world."

On the one hand the Bible says, "Friendship with the world is enmity with God" (James 4:4), yet another verse tells us "God so loved the world that He gave His only begotten son…" (John 3:16). So when the Bible tells us, "do not love the world" (I John 2:15), what is it saying? Which world should we love and which one should we not love? This is important if I am called to be in the world but not of the world. The word used in Greek for *world* is *kosmos*. Thayer's Greek Lexicon breaks out the various uses of the word *kosmos* as:

> *"1. An apt and harmonious arrangement or constitution, order, ornament, decoration, adornment: 1 Peter 3:3*
> *2. The world, i.e. the universe: Acts 17:24; Romans 4:13*
> *3. The inhabitants of the world: 1 Corinthians 4:9*
> *4. The ungodly multitude; the whole mass of men alienated from God, and therefore hostile to the cause of Christ John 7:7*
> *5. Worldly affairs; the aggregate of things earthly; the whole circle of earthly goods, endowments, riches, advantages, pleasures, etc., which, although hollow and frail and fleeting, stir desire, seduce from God and are obstacles to the cause of Christ: Galatians 6:14"*

From this we can see that the *world* God loves refers to the mass of lost humanity. Based on another definition we see that there is an orderly arrangement to the *kosmos* that is not evil on its own, but has fallen under the influence of the dominion of darkness. Satan has invaded this *kosmos* or orderly system of the earth. It is not the mind molders that are evil; the evil is in the spirit that is at work in fallen man that animates these systems that can be called the spirit of this world. To the extent that you are in friendship with that spirit you are at enmity with God in any system, including a religious one.

Or to put it into plain language, Doug Fortune states, "the kosmos speaks of the 'worldly system,' that which originates from carnality."34 Jesus said, I came into this world (kosmos) for judgment, as a Separator..." (John 9:39 Amplified Bible). Jesus came as a Separator to bring judgment, to bring a separation to the *kosmos* of the "worldly system," to bring a separation to all that originates from carnality. His intention is that "The kingdoms of this world (*kosmos* in Greek) are become the Kingdoms of our Lord, and of his Christ; and he shall reign for ever and ever" (Revelation 11:15). Yes, He came to the *kosmos* to bring separation, in order that the kosmos (all that originates from carnality) be consumed in the Kingdom."

Paul states: *"and you He made alive, who were dead in trespasses and sins, in which you once walked according to the course of this world, according to the prince of the power of the air, the spirit who now works in the sons of disobedience"* (Ephesians 2:1-2).

Why Christians are Obligated to Transform Their Culture

The Ephesians 2 verse, quoted above, says that when you were a sinner, you walked according to an organized course in this world, the satanic cosmos. Unsaved people, whether they are religious, agnostic, or atheistic, think they are doing their *own* thing. Nothing could be further from the truth. They live lives manipulated and led by the god of this world, Satan. Much like the movie *Matrix,* these people are unaware that they are plugged into a system that controls them. They are far from doing their own thing; they are walking according to the prince of the air. This power is a fallen angel that rules over the spirits that traffic in the heavenly realm.

> *"Among whom also we all once conducted our-*
> *selves in the lusts of our flesh, fulfilling the desires of*
> *the flesh and of the mind, and were by nature children*
> *of wrath, just as the others. But God, who is rich in*
> *mercy, because of His great love with which He loved*
> *us, even when we were dead in trespasses, made us*
> *alive together with Christ"* (Ephesians 2:3-5).

This verse says that before you were born again, the flesh and the mind controlled you. More importantly, notice that the *spirit* of man is *not* referred to. Fallen man is under the control of the nature of the flesh and the unrenewed mind. All this changes when we are "made alive together" with Christ. His death and resurrection makes *a new spirit* possible for fallen man. It is this new spirit creature alone that is able to serve the needs of mankind as a royal priesthood. This person with a born again human spirit has dual citizenship, one in their nation of origin and another in the kingdom of Heaven. They alone have power to stand in the gap between their nation and God and defy the corrupting influence of the Prince of the air.

With this understanding, we can see how the Bible tells us to be "*in* the world," but not *of* the world. We are born again. We do not live for the same ends as those who do not know God. We see eternity, but they do not. We feel and resist the pull of satanic schemes and adamic corruption, they cannot. We who are new creatures know that we are called to a higher standard of life than the mere gratification of our senses, or the acquisition of things, or measuring our success by how it appears in the eyes of others. We live by the standard of God's Word and know that our lives will be reviewed at the judgment seat of Christ. We live out of another dimension of life; our happiness is not tied to the *kosmos* of this world.

So who should rule the earth? The only people who can safely be trusted with the influence of mind molders are those who live for the well being of the whole and not for the gratification of themselves. That call is best answered by a transformed leader. The Christian who withdraws from their role of influence is in fact denying that they love mankind, because to do so would be to intentionally leave a vacuum for the devil to occupy with a counterfeit priesthood. One might ask the question, how much is Satan able to do simply because the Church does not rise to its role in the culture? Ask Germany what filled the vacuum years after God blessed their nation with the Reformation and the Guttenberg Press for the printing of Bibles? What filled the void in the culture once the Church ceased to be relevant? Into the void came a demon-possessed Austrian with a counterfeit gospel of National Socialism. The spiritual vacuum produced a Hitler and plunged the world into a war that ushered 56 million souls into eternity.

The Real Battleground

One of the greatest revivals of the 20th century took place in Wales at the turn of the last century. Entire towns and villages were forced to close down pubs and jails because of the sweeping impact of this move of God. So prominent were the events of the revival that newspapers covered the story on the front page for over a year. In 2004 the revival enthusiasts celebrated the 100th anniversary of this awesome move of God. How many people in Wales attend church today? On any given Sunday, less than 2% of the nation can be found in church. What happened? Christians fully occupied the church mountain, but failed to transform the workplace.

Compare this to the impact of the Reformation, which

we still feel today. It was the Reformation, particularly in the city of Geneva, where the gospel went beyond a private experience to one that would impact the culture. What is the difference between what happened in Wales and what happened in Geneva?

Calvin and Luther took time to work out the implications of the lessons learned during the reformation and considered how these would effect the entire society. As a result the education systems we now have, as well as our current banking systems, owe their existence to the labors of reformers who worked out a bridge between the insights gleaned in the Word of God during their time of restoration and their application to the culture. Certainly we need revivalists, because they help believers recover their passion for God. Reformation, however, must follow revival, because reformers focus on the lasting application of recovered truth to the culture.

In these last days, reformation-minded Christians are desperately needed to take their place in the current systems of business, banking, industry, communication, science, education, politics, and so on with the confident conviction that they are in the perfect will of God; and that their work is spiritual and sacred, even though it is secular. In fact, the workplace is the front line of the expanding Kingdom of Christ. It is the next great missionary front line. This integration of faith and work brings an infusion of purpose and power into places that are lifeless until Christians show up, use their gifts, and let their light shine. We need to open our eyes and see that believers have been routed from the commanding heights of culture and that God is intent on taking back territory. The workplace is about to be transformed!

Who Really Controls These Mountains?

Make no mistake, the mind molders are the strategic

battleground in our day. Satan boasts of the authority to dominate these mountains as it pleases him. This was made clear in the exchange that took place between Satan and Jesus in the wilderness

> *"Then the devil, taking Him up on a high mountain, showed Him all the kingdoms of the world in a moment of time. And the devil said to Him, 'All this authority I will give You, and their glory; for this has been delivered to me, and I give it to whomever I wish'."* (Luke 4:5-6)

When Adam fell, Satan was given authority to rule over these kingdoms. Once in position, hell began to systematically occupy and defile these fountains of civilization. Satan populated the mind molders with those humans who he could control. Not being omnipresent, he placed fallen angels over nations in order to assure their servitude. All the miserable history of man's wars, oppression, and suffering are due largely to the unbridled lusts and egos of demonized leaders. But what was working behind these leaders? We only need to look at the facts of history 70 years ago to see Hitler, Stalin, and Mao as the unwitting instruments of malicious wicked spirits. Read the atrocities in history further back and you see more than the misdeeds of fallen man; you see the suffering that reflects the kind of kingdom that fallen angels will shape over nations to suit their pleasure if unchallenged by the authority of the believer.

Satan Offers Jesus the Kingdoms

> *The Gospel of Matthew's account states: "Again the devil took Him up on an exceeding high mountain and showed Him all the kingdoms of the world and their glory"* (Matthew 4:8).

Why did the devil not show Jesus all the souls of the world and their suffering? Why the "kingdoms of the world and their glory"? Would not lost humanity be better bait for temptation? The only answer is that he who rules the kingdoms has the souls.

As Jesus stood on the mount of temptation his eye could survey the vast expanse of the great kingdoms: past, present and those yet to come. He could see them rising in succession. He saw the might of Rome, the great dynasties of China and India, and the succession of empires that would rise through the ages—all under the dominion of darkness, and all longing to be liberated by Him, their creator. As the King, he quite naturally would feel the intense longing to reign over all He created.

As He saw the kingdoms you must remember that this was a real temptation, but not as most suppose. Many think that the kingdoms of this world were presented to Jesus like contraband offered as a bribe, as though Jesus had to choose between the world's kingdoms or the kingdom to come. But these kingdoms were not the devil's creation; they were created by Jesus for Jesus. All of this was made by Him and for Him (see Hebrews. 2:10). The triumphant cry in the last book of Scripture declares, "The kingdoms of *this world* (not the world to come) have become the Kingdoms of our Lord and of His Christ" (Revelation. 11:15). The temptation was to entice Jesus to take to himself what indeed belonged to Him, but at the wrong time and in a way that would dishonor his submission to the Father. In the end, Jesus died to inherit both our souls and the nations—because the nations belong to Him.

The Father gave the Son permission to take over the earth in Psalm 2:8: "Ask of me and I will give you the nations for your inheritance, and the ends of the earth for your possession." We need only look at how things operate in the book of Revelation to see how God desires things to work. In the new heaven and new earth there will be *nations* on earth, for eternity, that will bring their glory into the city of God. (Revelation. 22) Earth, its nations, and kingdoms are—for reasons only known to God—the central focus of the celestial drama that encompasses history until the consummation of the ages. And Jesus was destined to be the Lord of this world.

A Power Contest

These Kingdoms belong to Jesus and therefore by virtue of His obedience they now belong to us. Notice that Satan boasted that "I give them to whom I will," (Luke 4:6) but Jesus told His followers "the kingdom of heaven suffers violence, and the violent take it by force" (Mark 11:12). Note that Satan "gives it," but believers "take it" by force. Clearly, this shows us that God reserves the right to overrule Satan's will and "He puts down one and exalts another" (Psalm 75:7). This is the power struggle that is going to intensify until the end of this era, culminating in convulsions in nature, conflicts of nations, and conversion of multitudes.

When Jesus said, "All authority has been given to Me in heaven and in earth, go therefore and make disciples of all nations…" (Matthew 28:18, 19), He was inviting believers to participate in the overthrow of satanic strongholds over entire people groups through prayer, the preaching of the Gospel, and the transformational discipling of nations. In truth, as first century believers went forth with their trade into foreign cities, they conquered them. The Roman Road was their pathway into the nations, and today's globalized economy is our highway into the entire world to take our trade into nations, and to subdue kingdoms.

A New Breed of Leaders

I am meeting a new kind of leader in the Church, particularly among third world nations. These are leaders who have shattered the fish tank of limited vision. They are not aiming to just build bigger churches or even to transform of their cities. Their goal is even more ambitious. They seek to serve as an apostolic voice to the president, king or chief mullah and his cabinet. They will not stop until they have a transformed nation. Like John Knox who cried, "Give me Scotland or I die," these men are a species of apostolic reformer leaders that make hell nervous.

How do we go about reclaiming the mind molders of nations, and what does this have to do with you and your calling in the marketplace? Everything! You are about to be drafted into an elite unit of marketplace commandos. These are men and women who are answering the call to penetrate and transform vast fields of secular influence. You are about to be thrust into transformational training so that you can handle the temptations and opportunities that accompany a position of massive preeminence in your field.

Here is how you start. Look at your occupational field and see it as a mountain. What companies and people are at the top of that mountain? Why are they at the top? What skills, knowledge and personal characteristics are needed to occupy that position? What would need to exist for you to occupy the top of that mountain? Look at where you presently are and look at where you plan to go. How will you build a bridge into the future? Begin now to ask the Holy Spirit for help. God will begin to confirm His calling and start to link you to new resources. The question you must ask first is this: are you willing to pay the price to be preeminent in your field?

Reflection and Discussion Questions
Chapter Nine: Marketplace Invasion—
A Prophetic Call to
Transforming the Workplace

1. What are the implications of the statistic that Jesus Christ intentionally appeared 122 times in the marketplace in all of His 132 appearances recorded in the New Testament? How does that reality merge with the "come and grow with us" methodology of many church enterprises? What do you sense is happening in the next years as the Church approaches the places where their members work as a mandate to "go into all the world... beginning first in Judea..."

2. What theology or attitude have you most been exposed to regarding the world? How has this affected the way you view your career? What would happen to you and others if we changed our perspective about our career calling to the view that this chapter is expressing? How might a transformational coach help us to make this shift?

3. How has the description of the seven mountains and those who most influence them caused you to see the role of your church or marketplace career in a different perspective? How has this prophetic insight from the

author helped you to see yourself in the marketplace with a call to ministry in the same manner that pastors and missionaries see their call to the mountain of the church?

4. Who do you know that needs to be validated on their calling to one of these seven mountains? How might a transformational coach help them to embrace and celebrate that call rather than merely tolerate it?

5. In what ways might transformational coaching become a bridge between the church mountain and the other six mountains? How might the language, values, and methodology of coaching itself enhance the sense of the prophetic priorities of God to transform believers in order that they may reform and transform their mountains for the glory of God?

CHAPTER TEN

The Uncommon Advantage— Biblical Characteristics of Transformational Marketplace Leaders

By Lance Wallnau

From our research we believe that there are certain characteristics possessed by those God uses to transform the marketplace. Each of these is engaged by a transformational coach who can alert the leader to its critical value to success. All of these are found in biblical accounts and form a foundation of what God is up to in our careers. In combination these form an unusual and uncommon advantage for those who are coached into stewarding them. These are called the "excellent spirit," the force of divine "favor," and divine "assignments." Let's look briefly at how these operate.

The Excellent Spirit

Daniel was promoted because he had "an excellent spirit" (Daniel 6:3). The Hebrew word *excellent* here is *yateer* and refers to "that which juts out further, like a coastline or mountain top."35 Biblical excellence is a unique merger of skill, knowledge, and character in such a way that it causes the person to rise up above all others. It is a prerequisite for someone who intends to make it to the top of the mountain. A curious contrast to the picture of excellence as a mountaintop can be found in the word *mediocre* which in Latin means "halfway up the mountain." Only those with the spirit of excellence are able to "jut out" in such a way that they make others mediocre by contrast. The excellent spirit can actually pierce the darkness that seeks to dominate the environment. It is a quality that causes its possessor to rise to the top of the mountain he or she is assigned to take. In Daniel's, David's, and Esther's cases, it was a political mountain. Yours might be sales, church growth, education, a small business, or simply rising to be a center of influence in your own hometown, school, or music group.

There is an anointing on those whom God graces with an excellent spirit. Those who acquire this have an extraordinary degree of personal competence in the area of their gifting and expression. The reason why many who are gifted are not called to greater things is because talent and gifting will get you into areas where your character can't keep you. Remember the part of the Lord's Prayer that says, "And do not lead us into temptation, but deliver us from the evil one" (Matthew 6:13). You may not feel that God is advancing you as fast as you like, but God has an obligation to keep you from temptation. The higher you go into the systems of this world, the more legal access the enemy has to test you. Only those of developed gifting and proven character can advance to the point of displacing ruling spirits. Many are called and few are chosen because few are willing to choose the high call at a high price.

Assignment

The very word "sanctify" means to set apart. Those whom God uses greatly are usually set apart for specific purposes. This is an important concept because we often read the lives of Bible heroes and make the mistake of thinking that we are reading of the exploits of individuals who did amazing things for God. In reality, what we find is an amazing God who delights to invite consecrated people to join Him in that which He is about to do! Consider the matter and you can see that Moses' dramatic call at the burning bush has less to do with Moses' personal destiny than it does with the activity of heaven at that time, for God tells him, "I have surely seen the oppression of My people…and have heard their cry…So I have come down to deliver them…" (Exodus 3:7-8). Moses tried to deliver the Jews earlier in his life and the mission failed miserably. Now God was summoning him and the resulting deliverance would shape history.

Why could Moses not do the thing earlier? In a word it was timing. At the right time Moses was summoned to fulfill a previous prophetic promise made to Abraham in Genesis 15: 13, "Then He said to Abram: 'Know certainly that your descendants will be strangers in a land that is not theirs, and will serve them, and they will afflict them four hundred years.'" After four hundred years of captivity God moved and invited Moses to join Him. Had Moses not heeded the call, God would have brought deliverance through another.

What of the generation following Moses? What can we learn about divine assignments in the life of his young associate Joshua? The title of the book may be "Joshua," but the book is really the record of the activity of God who commanded the young man saying, "go over this Jordan, you and all this people, to the land which I am giving to them—the children of Israel" (Joshua 1:2). Had Joshua not been obedient to answer the summons to God's activity in that specific time in history, it would have been the book of Caleb we would be reading. Again, the timing is set like clockwork. The great crossing over of Israel was set to take place exactly 40 years after the initial failed calling to cross

Jordan and to possess the enemy's cities. Joshua 5:6 says, "For the children of Israel walked forty years in the wilderness, till all the people that were men of war, who came out of Egypt, were consumed, because they did not obey the voice of the Lord."

God shaped both Moses and Joshua for a specific destiny, yet they would not be able to fulfill that destiny until God invited them into participation. In both cases, God had a specific timing. If we focus too much on the individual, we miss the realization that God is the one who initiates the great advances of His cause in the earth. In the first stages of the high call of God it is not our job to create a great destiny, but rather to discover the invitation of God to join Him in what He is about to do.

In Bible times, the most significant historic events occurred in set times and cycles of history. God works according to heaven's timetable of times and seasons. Moses was called exactly 400 years after captivity. Joshua crossed into Canaan 40 years after the last generation failed. Saul reigned exactly 40 years. David likewise reigned exactly 40 years. Solomon reigned 40 years. God has a strategic plan and leads us at the right time.

What about Nehemiah, the great cupbearer turned governor of Israel? What accounts for his emergence in Bible history? He was raised up at exactly the time Daniel had prophesied the wall of Jerusalem would be rebuilt. Had it not been God's desire to build a wall, there would have been no Nehemiah to talk about. Had Daniel not prophesied the matter in detail, we would not have known that Nehemiah emerged in precisely the time in history that God determined to rebuild a wall and restore Jerusalem.

What about Joseph? His memorable journey from a pit to the throne was really the story of a remarkable assignment God had in mind to save his people and the people of Egypt. The book of Genesis tells us that Joseph's brothers sold him to slavery, but the Psalmist gives heaven's perspective saying that God "sent a man before them—Joseph—who was sold as a slave" (Psalm 105:17), and used to preserve his brothers' lives. It may sound like a cute play on words, but God shapes your personal *history* to fulfill *His Story* as it is lived through your assignment. Joseph, the rejected brother, becomes the ruler who forgives and saves his brothers. Sounds like Jesus' story, doesn't it?

Likewise, Esther is not the story of an exceptional Hebrew woman; it is the story of God's providence. As God went ahead in the history of the Jews to provide a Joseph, even so, He placed a Hebrew in a position with the power of influence to move a king on behalf of her persecuted people. Her uncle Mordecai saw clearly the finger of providence saying "who knows whether you have come to the kingdom for such a time as this?" (Esther 4:14). Indeed, Esther, like Joseph, was promoted to a role of power for precisely that moment in history in order to save a nation. Likewise, places of secular power and influence are being offered to God's people today as the battle for the advancement of His Kingdom.

A great destiny is attached to a great assignment. We have seen that God moves in specific times and seasons throughout history. Most of the time, it is not the man who makes the season, but the season in history that makes the man. This is certainly true in the case of each of those listed earlier in this chapter. What about our current time and season? We are living in a period where there will be more key assignments given with greater acceleration in spiritual and natural developments than any other period of time. In our day, as the Church crosses the threshold of two thousand years of history and enters its three thousandth year, or third day of its own history, the time is ripe for heroes of faith to receive fresh instruction and new assignments.

Would you like to qualify as a vessel of noble use? Since

90% of the body of Christ is not called to the role of full-time pastoral or teaching ministry, it is logical to expect that at least 90% of these assignments will be issued in the workplace. Certainly Abraham, Isaac, Jacob, Joseph, Daniel, David, and Nehemiah would testify that their main ministry was lived out through their employment in a secular arena. These were cattle farmers, landowners, and political rulers. This did not hinder them from being leaders in the Kingdom.

God is no respecter of persons. He desires to use you. He is distributing assignments today. Do you want to be one that is ready for an invitation? Paul told Timothy, "Therefore if anyone cleanses himself from the latter, he will be a vessel for honor, sanctified and useful for the Master, prepared for every good work" (2 Timothy 2:21). The word here for *purge* is taken from the word we use for *catheterize*. A catheter is used in the hospital for the removal of toxins. Paul is saying to Timothy that it is his responsibility to eliminate the toxins of lust, selfishness, and greed from his system so that he can be a vessel fit for noble assignments. As you purify your heart and bring divine order into your life, a change starts to happen. You draw near to God and He draws near to you. God is issuing assignments to penetrate every mind molder in every nation. Assignments are issued to those whose hearts have been prepared and whose gifts have been developed. They come to those who are ready to pay the price to "jut out further" and take territory by the spirit of excellence engaged in a divine assignment.

Some feel a strong pull of destiny but lack clarity in the exact nature of the assignment. The good news is that you are in the destiny process just as surely whether you know your ultimate calling or not. Remember, your calling will always involve a problem that needs to be solved. David, for instance, could always comfort himself in the midst of his persecutions by knowing the problem he was being shaped to solve. He was to replace a failed king and protect and expand the boundaries of Israel.

But what if you don't know your assignment, or put more clearly, what if you don't know the problem you are called to solve? Joseph had this dilemma. His journey started with a dream, but he had no knowledge of the problem he was called to solve. In fact, he almost succeeded in aborting the plan of God while in prison. He negotiated with a high-ranking official to get him out of prison so he could return home to his father and brothers. Talk about a dysfunctional family reunion! Had he succeeded, he would have returned to Jacob's tent, divided his family, and died along with them in a famine seven or so years later. However, Joseph did not need to know fully what was going on; he only needed to know that God was with him. Once Joseph was in Pharaoh's court and heard the king's dream, he began to answer the problem he was being prepared for 15 years to solve.

Blessed are those who know the problem they are being shaped to solve. More blessed yet are those who do not know the problem they are called to solve, yet nonetheless fully embrace the process of being shaped into the vessel that can solve it! Be patient and be faithful to that which is your present assignment, knowing "He who is faithful in what is least is faithful also in much" (Luke 16:10). We have talked about the excellent spirit and the power of a divine assignment, but something else is needed. When the time is right, you will find yourself catapulted into new realms of promotion through the force of favor.

What Exactly is Favor?

The third quality we found common to those whom God calls to noble use is wrapped up in the word *favor*. Not everyone who demonstrates skill or competence makes a permanent and lasting impression. Something else is needed to penetrate, occupy, and tip a mind molder. The display of excellence gets you access, it gains a platform, but favor adds an intangible "likeability" factor that makes people want to connect with you. Even then, it's one thing to make a likeable impression—anyone with charisma can do that—and it is another to make an impression that "sticks" in such a way that others are enlisted in your cause. Favor is the key to the "stickiness factor." Why? It is because favor is the charisma of Christ that wraps itself around a person when they are engaged in a heavenly transaction.

> *Or put another way, favor is*
> *the attraction of God to you*
> *that releases an influence through you, so*
> *that other people are inclined to like, trust,*
> *and cooperate with you in the assignment*
> *God gave you.*

The New Testament word *grace* carries within its many folds aspects of this unmerited favor of God toward us. Through the grace of the Lord Jesus Christ, your standing with God is equal to the standing of Christ. In Christ, you have as much favor with the Father as He has. This is a mind numbing concept, and hard to grasp. Most believers have an understanding that Christ died for them, but comparatively few truly understand the other dual implications of the substitutionary work of Christ, namely: Christ lives *in you* and Christ died *as you!* Therefore, the favor of God is already upon you once you are born again because God sees you as an entity "hidden with Christ in God" (Colossians 3:3).

The reason most believers do not see massive displays of manifested favor is because this level of favor becomes most evident in your external circumstance when you start to walk in maturity as a son or daughter. Sonship is the key. Many of us behave as orphans. An orphan mentality does not rest in the full awareness of unconditional acceptance. In Christ, the moment you are saved you are as accepted in God's eyes as Jesus is accepted. The moment you are born again the issue is no longer one of acceptance with God, the issue is *maturity*. The mature are given assignments, and the assignments connect you to the force of favor at a whole new level. For this reason, there may be an extended season of growth in character and competence before favor becomes evident. God releases the inheritance of Christ to His mature sons and daughters. An inheritance is not something you work for, like wages; it is something you receive. Orphans work for things like high achievers, but sons walk in the grace of high receivers. They walk in favor at a higher level and they need it because of the nature of the challenges and dangers in the assignments they have embraced.

Excellence and favor are a formidable combination. Joseph combined excellence with favor and was raised overnight to become the second most powerful man in Egypt. This is the combination the devil fears most. This level of favor, once released, acts like a magnet to the blessing and promotion of God.

I remember an image that came to my mind most forcibly one day as I struggled to make this concept understandable to a group of people. I seemed to see all at once a person standing in a sort of wind tunnel with papers flying all around and bouncing off them. Suddenly this person was under a deluge of honey and the papers, as they continued to fly, would stick to this person on contact. The Lord impressed upon me that favor comes when He dips you into the honey of His presence so that all the blessings that seemed to elude you earlier now stick to you. This seemed to explain the idea much better than my other attempts. This is when I saw favor as a "stickiness factor."

Favor at this level, however, is always attached to a purpose and comes with a price. The word for favor, *charis* is first mentioned in the New Testament when Mary is greeted by the archangel Gabriel proclaiming, "Rejoice highly favored one, the Lord is with you..." (Luke 1:28) and again, "Do not be afraid, Mary, for you have found favor with God. And behold you will conceive..." (Luke 1:30, 31). The Greek word for favor is by definition a two-fold operation. One part describes a divine influence that comes upon you, and the other describes the reflection of that *charis* or favor flowing through you.

In Mary's life, we see exactly how this happens. As you draw near to God, He draws near to you. As you seek Him, He comes to visit you. When He comes to visit you, He leaves you different than before He came. In Mary's case, she was left pregnant! As my friend Randy Clark says, God thus reveals that in addition to His many names of the Old Testament, Jehovah Rophi and Jehovah Nisi, He is also Jehovah "sneaky"! When He visits you, He impregnates you with a vision, an assignment, and a mission. You may not understand it all at first, but once the favor of God comes, the assignment begins to form within you. You start to care about something.

Are you still uncertain of your assignment? When you spend prolonged time in God's presence, it is natural that at some point you conceive His desire. When you walk in favor, God gives you the desire of His heart. And as you walk out His will, He honors the desires of your heart; frequently incorporating your heart's desire into the work He is doing through you. Once believers understand this principle, they can have greater boldness in asking whatever they desire with certainty that it will be done for them. That is why I said that the first step in the High Calling of God is to discern His invitation to join Him in what He is doing.

---

*Once you are engaged in your
calling and gifting
the Lord gives remarkable latitude and
scope to entertaining your desires and
vision in accomplishing the assignment.*

Contradicted Assignments and the "Favor Backlash"

Returning to Mary as an example, once she spoke "Let it be to me according to your word," (Luke 1:38) the transaction was complete. Mary became pregnant with heaven's assignment in a very tangible way. The road ahead, however, was not entirely convenient. Mary and Joseph will have to make many adjustments to accommodate this work of God. It is a peculiar feature of both divine assignments and the force of favor that they arrive and progress in the midst of contradictions.

Circumstances are often inhospitable to God's assignments for a clear reason. The world system is a *"kosmos"* under Lucifer's control, an entire system animated by self interest, infiltrated and dominated by people under the influence of a fallen nature and the demons that are assigned to keep them captive. Do not expect planet earth to roll out a welcome carpet to the assignment you carry. The writer of Hebrews 12:3 encourages us to "consider him who endured such hostility from sinners against himself, lest you become weary and discouraged in your souls" (Hebrews 12:3). This contradiction occurred throughout His ministry. "You are those who have continued with me in my trials" (Luke 22: 28). Though Jesus was draped in favor, his entire journey was fraught with opposition.

When Paul wrote to the Romans, he prayed for a "prosperous journey" to Rome (Romans 1:10). How is this prayer answered? Through the ignorance and arrogance of men in authority on the ship to Rome, the warnings of Paul were not heeded and they were shipwrecked! Though he had insufficient favor or influence with the ship's owner, captain and Roman centurion, the situation would change. In the midst of the contradiction, you can see the pervasive power of favor beginning to do its work. The centurion spared Paul's life when the soldiers wanted to kill the prisoners once the ship started sinking, and they listened to him when he told him to cut off the smaller escape ships.

When they swam their way to shore, the contradiction continued as a viper leapt out of the heat from a fire Paul built and fastened on his hand. The whole island saw this as an omen that Paul was a man under the special judgment of God. Ten minutes later they see him unharmed and concluded that he must be a man under the peculiar blessing of God! In that moment, God began a massive reversing of the contradiction. In the next moment, Paul will carry a healing gift to the island chief. Many others were healed and saved.

As with all such contradictions in scripture, once you have endured the backlash, there is a divine balancing of accounts and the force of favor is unleashed to an extravagant degree. In Paul's case, the fugitive fire starter became an island celebrity and no doubt treated with peculiar honor and wonder by all on board the ship for the remainder of his return ride to Rome. Talk about a captive audience for evangelism! Paul's prayer for a prosperous journey to Rome was answered, but hardly in the manner expected. The force of favor is God's equalizer in a hostile world.

Again with Mary, you remember the Christmas story of Jesus' birth. There was no room for them in the inn. As Mary and Joseph bore the contradiction of the manger and wrestled with the burden of what appeared to be an untimely birth, every conceivable resource needed for the assignment was already on its way in a caravan of kings! If they had eyes to see, they would have noted that there were rulers from the east laden with treasure coming straight toward them. The Magi were en route on their journey before Mary even left. The problem was that their journey would require months. And the same is true for those with heaven's assignments in our day, even as you deal with your challenge, inconvenience, inadequate resource, or people problem; everything you need is being drawn toward you. Though it tarries, it shall come. The force of favor on the assignment is drawing it to you. Just stay put and prepare your manger for a visitation. Everything you need is coming to you as you obey.

What did these kings bear? The kings brought gifts, dreams, and direction. They came laden with provision and revelation of the next step. Joseph will soon need to take his family and flee to Egypt. However, thanks to these kings, God has given them everything they need for an all expense paid vacation! Here is the lesson: Once you endure the contradiction, the force of favor will enable you to receive protection for the assignment, provision for the journey, and direction going out and coming into God's perfect timing. So if you have obeyed God and feel stuck, be still and stand fast because everything you need is coming to you, drawn by the irresistible favor that accompanies your divine assignment.

Favor Transferred in a Failed Assignment!

1 Samuel 16:17-24 tells us that David was not the first choice of his family, the mighty prophet Samuel, or even the Lord for that matter. The original call of kingship was given to Saul. It is a sobering thought to note that David would have never been called had Saul not failed in his assignment. Saul's assignment is clear as the prophet Samuel is told specifically, "Tomorrow about this time I will send you a man from the land of Benjamin, and you shall anoint him commander over My people Israel, that he may save My people from the hand of the Philistines; for I have looked upon My people, because their cry has come to me" (1 Samuel 9:16).

Saul however became focused on his office rather than his assignment, and the assignment was taken from him and given to a neighbor more worthy. This is the real reason Saul could not face the giant Goliath. Without the anointing, he was intimidated. The anointing that qualified him to handle the national crisis was no longer on him. It had been transferred to David. We make much of little David's exploits on that day he faced the giant, but in reality it was the anointing that Saul rejected which empowered David to become famous.

Had Saul stayed true to his assignment, the gift of faith would have been in operation in him and he would have faced Goliath without intimidation and no doubt killed him. It was this internal realization that fueled his jealousy toward David. The crowds would have sung of Saul's fame, as they soon did David's, and Jonathan, his son who was every bit as qualified as David, would have made an excellent next generation ruler at the end of Saul's 40-year reign. The tearing of Samuel's garment in Saul's hands is symbolic of more than a tearing of the kingdom from him to another. God had to dismember the entire DNA of all Saul's descendants from the royal house they were called to be part of, and re-member the garment around the house of David. These consequences of either a failed assignment or a fulfilled assignment will effect generations to come.

This introduces another mysterious aspect to the force of favor. If David, in 1 Samuel 9:16, is given Saul's assignment because of Saul's failed stewardship, then you and I, dare I say, are expendable as well. What is not expendable is the assignment! This is no doubt the sober meaning behind the words "hold fast what you have, that no one may take your crown" (Revelation 3:11). What is this crown? Your crown is the reward and recognition status that awaits you in eternity because of the successful completion of the assignment God gave you to accomplish on earth. To lose your crown is to have someone else take your assignment because you were disqualified from the mission.

Favor first comes to you, and David did this as he captured God's heart in worship on the hillside. Once David received his prophetic commission from Samuel, he was anointed to set the nation free, but how is he to do so from a hillside working with a few sheep in a family business? God must move him into alignment with his assignment, and the force of favor combined with a divine appointment is about to go to work. The moment of truth comes in 1 Samuel 16 when Saul sees David. Instantly the favor of God hits the situation, and Saul is seized by a celestial affection for David. He wants him as his own armor bearer and son-in-law.

A closer look at this reveals one of the mysteries of the force of favor. A person who is advancing in the force of favor experiences divine appointments that enable them to enter new spheres of opportunity. They also experience a corresponding advance of spiritual authority to match the assignment. In fact, authority and favor are woven together and tailored meticulously to fit the exact measure of the assignment you are presently walking in. As the assignment grows, so does the measure of authority and favor.

Samuel the prophet received a new coat each year as he grew. He was a type of Christ as the scripture states, "and Jesus *increased* in wisdom and stature, and in *favor* with God and man" (Luke 2:52). Jesus increased! That pictures an ongoing process in itself. Favor and wisdom did not just come down in one massive installment in the manger, with good reason—it was not needed. Premature release would have attracted premature attention. No, He "increased" in favor and wisdom and stature till the "fullness of time" came for release to His assignment. If Jesus experienced progressive increase in wisdom, stature, and favor, you will no doubt experience progressive release as well.

Disobedience to destiny comes with a price. When Saul

forfeited his assignment, he became a man tormented by demons. However, as Saul's demons came into the radius of David's authority, they were bound and silenced. The anointing on David bound the forces of Satan in Saul. The tormenting chatter that tortured the king was silenced in David's presence. As David ministered to Saul on a harp, the power of hell was broken.

While it is true that David's music released an anointing that broke the king's oppression, it was not the instrument alone that was at work. It was his authority. Spiritual authority and favor flow out from the area of your gifting that accompanies your assignment. God touches the hearts of people and joins them to your vision. As the time came for David to lead an army, there were men who were supernaturally added to him. When those who are connected to your destiny come into your presence, you have an anointing and authority to impact them. You will experience the same thing that David experienced. There will be people who will come into your circle of influence who will feel better just being with you, just as it happened to Saul in the presence of David. You will see Satan bound and favor create an opportunity for you to do business for God. This is why hell attacks those they perceive have favor from on high.

God prospers you through the gifts and talents He has given you. This was true of David whether he fought or played his music. Authority and favor begin to take over your environment as you operate in the gifting that God has given for the work you are set apart to do, whether that is speaking, singing, selling, operating equipment or writing music. While you are demonstrating your gifts, the favor of God will come upon you to make the right connection with the right people. In David's case, one moment it was a sling shot that God anointed, in another it was a musical instrument. The point is that the force of favor worked with David's gifting, and David had evidently developed a diversity of gifts to the point of excellence in exhibition. In the end however, it was neither the slingshot nor the musical instrument that was the key, but the anointing that came upon a shepherd boy who attracted the attention of God through his worship. Never forget—it is the heart that God is drawn toward.

The Key to Acceleration

We have talked about patience, but up till now we have not mentioned the accelerator, the one factor that can ensure that you are keeping pace with destiny. Jesus wept openly over Jerusalem because they missed their opportune time of visitation. What about you? How can you be sure you are growing at the maximum rate? Are you presently operating in the level of gifting and calling or fruitfulness you are called to produce? What is the key to development?

Joshua had Moses, Elisa had Elijah, and the disciples had the Master. So the key to staying on track and moving at top speed is now as it always has been: a quality relationship with someone who will support you and hold you to the standard of excellence needed to fulfill your assignment. This is the fuel that sustains the flame of the uncommon advantage that God has given to righteous men and women in the marketplace. A transformational coach that enables us to stop, look, listen, and activate the favor, excellent spirit, anointing, and assignment given to us to fulfill God's destiny in and through us.

We can accelerate our journey with a transformational coach. This coach will call forth in us what God has made available to us. We have everything we need to take our mountains and a transformational coach will fight for you to access the potential you carry. As your journey progresses, you will have more than one coach, but there is no doubt that they will be there as you wake up to the key role they will play in your life calling. Every great athlete and peak performer can trace their success, or lack thereof, to the role of a personal coach, a trainer, mentor, or father who held them to a high standard and helped them reach it. Who is the next person to do this in your life?

All that has been described in this chapter, the excellent spirit, qualification and discerning of divine assignments, and alignment with the force of wisdom and favor are learnable skills. If they are learnable, you need to ask yourself where you are going to go to acquire them. The wise thing to accelerate that learning is to find a transformational coach who will work with you on a tailor made growth plan to get you there. Solomon tells us that wisdom is the principle thing. There is an often-overlooked aspect to this wisdom that must be possessed or the calling of God will never be fully attained. In fact, the next chapter will outline the five components that make up the quality of uncommon wisdom that made David, Joseph, and Daniel unstoppable in the face of fierce opposition.

Reflection and Discussion Questions
Chapter Ten: The Uncommon Advantage—
Biblical Characteristics
of Transformational Marketplace Leaders

1. Who stands out in your circle of relationships or extended network that you would describe as having an "excellent spirit"? What influences in their lives brought this about? Why not find out and ask them? How might transformational coaching do so for you?

2. Much about life coaching tends to dwell on our individual dream and destiny. In this biblical description of God's "assignment" we see that it is not our job to come up with a destiny, but to discover the invitation of God to join Him in what He is about to do. This is the distinction of transformational coaching. How might a transformational coach assist you in identifying and embracing God's assignment for you? What if you had the joy and significance in helping others do the same?

3. Where are you seeing the favor of the Lord in your workplace career? If you are not seeing it, how might a coach enable you to see and steward this key commodity of the Kingdom of God in the marketplace?

4. Where have you seen favor backlash in your life and in your career? How could a transformational coach have helped you in the interpretation of what was happening? Where could you be part of someone's destiny by helping them see what they have been experiencing from this perspective?

5. Interview executives, entrepreneurs, or marketplace leaders who have had the benefit of a coaching relationship. What difference did it make in their advancement and promotion to influence their mountain? How might a transformational coach be the accelerator in your life to restore years of circling a mountain and take you to the top?

CHAPTER ELEVEN

Transformational Coaching for the Uncommon Advantage— Foundations of the Favor-Wisdom Connection

By Lance Wallnau

Wisdom—The Intelligence Factor

The book of Acts tells us "[God] gave [Joseph] favor and wisdom in the presence of Pharaoh, king of Egypt" (Acts 7:10). The favor that God extends is intended to operate in two directions, vertically toward God *and* horizontally toward man. Jesus covers both dimensions. Therefore all the favor that Jesus has with the Father is given to us as we walk "in Him." As we think with the mind of Christ and are led by the Spirit of Christ, we will experience the phenomenal force of favor. Why do we not hear more about force of favor and its related exploits today? A lack of wisdom is the sole explanation why many who are anointed with favor toward God and man, seem to blow it… with man.

What was this uncommon wisdom that Joseph demonstrated in front of Pharaoh? I suggest it was a three-fold capacity: *supernatural intelligence*, *natural intelligence,* and *emotional intelligence*. This wisdom was put on display as a result of a divine appointment that brought to a perfect culmination a long process of preparation in the young man who never failed to complete a divine assignment. God had given Pharaoh a supernatural dream containing an economic forecast of the future, but he had no power to interpret it. Joseph alone had wisdom from above for the task. Through the gift of divine interpretation, he was able to understand and explain the dream. This could be categorized as supernatural wisdom in its most conspicuous form, like a word of knowledge or gift of prophecy that reaches into a realm beyond man, accessing the realm of God.

He follows this up however with a display of wisdom of a different sort as he lays out a shrewd course of action that would not only save the people from famine, but also radically prosper and expand the ruler's power base in the Middle East. This sort of wisdom could be classified as innovative thinking, or the ability to develop a strategic plan based on available information. It is but one of many aspects of supernaturally enhanced natural wisdom.

However there was yet another species of wisdom that preceded this impressive display. Note these words: "Then Pharaoh sent and called Joseph, and they brought him hastily out of the dungeon; *and he shaved himself, and changed his raiment*, and came in unto Pharaoh" (Genesis 41:14).

Joseph took the time to prepare his personal appearance so that he presented himself to Pharaoh in the context and language that Pharaoh understood. This is all the more remarkable when seen in light of his specific request two years earlier to have his unjust imprisonment brought before the ruler for his release. Though he had waited two years for an opportunity to plead his case, he was willing to wait fifteen minutes more. Why? It takes only two minutes of interaction for a person to form an initial first impression.

To a Hebrew, facial hair is a sign of maturity. To an

Egyptian, it is an offense. Joseph presented himself to Pharaoh's court in the manner his audience would find easiest to relate. Joseph entered an Egyptian place with an Egyptian face. This is understood today as the art of "rapport"—that is, the ability to establish a connection with another so that they are comfortable and therefore more receptive to your ideas. If a first impression is formed in two minutes, how many exposures does it take to undo a bad first impression? *Twenty*! That's right; twenty *good* impressions I might add. There is a certain way to establish initial rapport, gesture, talk, react, listen, ask questions, and affirm that can exponentially increase your impact on others. Research repeatedly confirms that people interpret 55% of your message by your facial expression and body language and 38 % based on your voice: tone, pitch, volume, and variation. Only 7 % of your persuasion power is determined by the literal words. Put all this together in a way that makes people feel rapport and you have what Roger Ailes, the communication expert who coached Ronald Reagan for his debates, refers to as "the magic bullet." What is it? It is the "likeability" factor.

Likeability however is not enough. Without competence, likeability can get you blessed with a job or promotion you can't keep. Competence without likeability is the combination that leads to bitterness as you see others with less competence often promoted before you. But, likeability combined with personal competence is a dynamic combination that is guaranteed to thrust you beyond others! Under the anointing it becomes an uncommon advantage.

It's also guaranteed to evoke a backlash. Joseph had so much favor in Potiphar's house that his boss's wife tried to seduce him. Once spurned, she set him up for imprisonment with false accusation. Great favor, like great wealth, is a double-edged sword. One side produces blessing; the other side has the power to lead you into temptation. God however teaches us through Joseph that our career journey may have many turns in the road that do not make sense at the time. There are promotions that look like reversals and reversals that lead to promotions later. With such vicissitudes, the only safe way to manage a supernatural career is to have a transformational perspective—to be thankful in all things.

That's right, simple as it sounds, once you give your life to Christ you can be thankful in every situation because everything the devil throws at you is coded to contribute to your personal formation and your formation is connected to your ultimate assignment. Therefore the devil was the instrument that God manipulated to shape Joseph into the man who crushed the serpent's skull. It is easy to have this transformational perspective when we study his life from this side of his story. What is important to us is that we gain that perspective while we are in the middle of our story—the very role that a transformational coach seeks to fulfill in our lives.

From Joseph we learn that your capacity to honestly and openly handle the temptations of your current level of assignment determine whether or not you receive an invitation to go up another level to the next assignment. The capacity to sustain motivation and keep serving in the midst of cruel reversals was what eventually made Joseph impossible to defeat. Like cream, people with the right combination of attitude and skill always rise to the top. Joseph may have looked like he was going backward, but a discernable theme was woven through all his experiences. He was gifted with the ability to make those he served outrageously successful. This is clear as you track his advance from serving his father, to Potiphar, the prison warden, and ultimately Pharaoh. He was given an excellent spirit of wisdom in order to complete the potential of others. With this gift his circle of stewardship expanded until he handled everything in the domain of those he served until his sphere of service encompassed nations. Joseph's setbacks run hand in hand with his triumphs. These themes of service, favor, rejection, betrayal, and promotion are the strands that weave together to make up his "life message." Blessed is he who does not stumble at the process of his own promotion.

In Joseph's handling of setbacks we see a wisdom that was multifaceted. He knew how to stay open to learning even in the midst of turmoil. Consider his adjustment to a foreign country and language, rising from an agricultural slave to manager of the fields. From the fields of management he went to prison. Soon enough he learned something about prison administration and became the manager of that domain. It all culminated in a moment where he drew on his entire experience and combined his learning in agriculture and government administration to become the vice president of Egypt. At each level he learned something that was indispensable to the next level of promotion.

Scripture tells us that "the fear of the Lord is the beginning of wisdom" (Proverbs 9:10). Had Joseph not feared God, he never would have made it past the agricultural stage of destiny. How so? He had the wisdom to remove himself from the presence of sexual temptation. This sort of wisdom is directly connected in Scripture with the fear of the Lord. In a sense he became a prisoner of destiny because he feared God. But this awareness of God also produced a comforting awareness of God's presence. Thus, in every setback or twist of plot he had the ability to manage his response and adapt to new challenges in positive ways.

Joseph's story is meant to teach you the pathway of promotion to the top of your mountain. Seen from the vantage point of the end of his journey we learn to access greatness through serving others and to embrace life's reversals and contradictions by holding fast to the fear of the Lord and the comfort of the Holy Spirit.

Understanding this and walking in a relationship with a personal coach who can keep you in remembrance of these principles is a major part of what 21st century transformational leadership coaching is all about. As one lonely man told me who was struggling to make it without a coach, "sometimes you just need Jesus with skin on." We all need the support, encouragement and accountability of a friend who supports us in the difficult times.

Favor – Emotional Intelligence Connection

Let's explore the wisdom and favor connection from yet another angle.

Research by Dr. Daniel Goldman36 and others on the subject point out with statistical evidence that a majority of CEO's and entrepreneurs have people with higher IQ's working for them. It is not that the CEO's are less intelligent, but rather that have an intelligence of a different type. The entrepreneurs and CEO's surveyed by Goldman were bright but had comparatively average IQ's. Their strength was emotional intelligence (EQ) rather than an intellectual intelligence.

This is the type of intelligence displayed consistently by those who exercised extraordinary influence with God and man in their period of history. David for example displayed wisdom as a faculty of behavior rather than scholarship. Scripture says: "And David behaved wisely in all his ways, and the LORD was with him. Therefore, when Saul saw that he behaved very wisely, he was afraid of him" (1 Samuel 18:14, 15).

It is insightful to read that Saul feared David when he saw that he *behaved* himself wisely. Notice that the wisdom here spoken of is *behavioral wisdom* and **not intellect**. It's as though *Saul was not afraid of David's anointing, not even his favor, but when he saw that the anointing and favor were married to wise behavior he was terrified!* This should give us a glimpse into the realm of spiritual warfare and tell us what frightens the devil. What is "behavioral" wisdom? David's wisdom was revealed in his ability to know how to act in order to get a desired outcome. Later in his career, historians recorded that David's chief counselor, Ahithophel, was the real intellectual firepower behind David's dynasty. Again, it is more often the case that behavioral EQ is a greater factor in promotion, than academic IQ. David's dynasty confirms Dr. Goldman's research.

How are favor and emotional intelligence linked? When favor occurs it's as if God dips you into the honey of His presence so that a "stickiness" factor begins to come into your life. With favor, key people connect with you and are inclined to like or trust you. What you attract however, you must have wisdom to maintain. D.L. Moody said, "Love works the most, faith gets the most, but humility keeps the most."37 It might be added that wisdom knows how to handle the most. In particular, emotional intelligence is measured by your ability to manage two things: awareness and relationships. EQ research tells us that you need to be both self aware and socially aware at the same time. Then you must take this awareness and do something at almost intuitive speed—manage yourself and your relationships based on your awareness.

Put another way, emotional intelligence is all about personal and interpersonal skills. On a personal level, this skill is expressed thru three characteristics: personal EQ: self-awareness, personal responsibility and sustained motivation.

- At a relational level a different set of skills are needed.
- Interpersonal EQ: empathy and rapport.

Let's see how these operate in real life situations. King

David revealed the qualities of self-awareness and personal responsibility early in his career when he made his first disastrous strategic error while running from Saul straight to the wrong king for refuge.

> *"And the servants of Achish said unto him, Is not this David the king of the land? did they not sing one to another of him in dances, saying, Saul hath slain his thousands, and David his ten thousands? And David laid up these words in his heart, and was sore afraid of Achish the king of Gath. And he changed his behaviour before them, and feigned himself mad in their hands, and scrabbled on the doors of the gate, and let his spittle fall down upon his beard. Then said Achish unto his servants, Lo, ye see the man is mad: wherefore then have ye brought him to me? Have I need of mad men, that ye have brought this fellow to play the mad man in my presence? shall this fellow come into my house? David therefore departed thence, and escaped to the cave Adullam."* (1 Samuel 21:11-22:1)

Driven from Saul, David made a desperate dash toward Saul's enemy in hope of finding a sympathetic refuge. In a heartbeat however, David discerned the thoughts of the men in the king's court and perceived that he had run directly into a death trap. He scanned the environment, read the social situation quickly, and saw his strategy was not wise—they were going to kill him and make him an offering to Saul for peace.

What happens next is *self-awareness* and *social awareness* in action. Remember, EQ knows how to act in order to create the desired outcome. In an instant, David adjusted his behavior to get out of the situation. How? By simply acting insane, right on down to the spit drooling out of his mouth as he clawed the walls. This is a brilliant, if not hilarious demonstration of *personal responsibility*. He adjusted his behavior to get the desired outcome…repulsion and rejection. One cannot help but wonder what the men of this foreign court thought as years later they again encountered David in the midst of his conquests as he vanquished the surrounding territories and solidified Israel in peace and prosperity. You could hear them ask "How could that slobbering mad man be so successful?" *Personal responsibility is the ability to own your own behavior, every thought, word, action and feeling. It is the willingness to accept that you and you alone are responsible for your circumstances and have the ability to respond; hence, responsibility. It is the 100% utilization of all your personal power.*

Personal responsibility is the key to knowledge because reproofs and corrections come to us all, but only the truly wise learn from mistakes so they don't repeat them in the future. This is the essence of nearly half the Proverbs of Solomon. You never learn from an experience that you deny responsibility over. In fact, the moment you catch yourself explaining, justifying, and defending yourself, it's a sure indication that you are denying personal responsibility and thereby surrendering your personal power. What happens when you complain and blame your setbacks on circumstances or "warfare" with the devil? If you own only 50% of your problem you leave a 50% opening for the devil to have influence over your life. Own all your personal power and make your confession that the enemy has no power over your life. This makes every setback a learning experience.

The third personal aspect of EQ involves *sustained motivation*. Anyone can start an enterprise, but it takes a certain quality of emotional fitness to sustain a high level of motivation in the face of setbacks and reversals. David demonstrated this quality of wisdom as an aspect of emotional intelligence when he dealt with the set back at Ziklag. As you recall, the men returned from battle only to find all their possessions including their wives and children taken captive by a much stronger enemy. David was himself overwhelmed with grief, but he became socially aware very quickly as his own men began talking about killing him.

> *"And David was greatly distressed; for the people spake of stoning him, because the soul of all the people was grieved, every man for his sons and for his daughters: but David encouraged himself in the LORD his God."* (1 Samuel 30:6)

As with the earlier incident with King Achish, David's problem was solved the moment he took personal responsibility for his situation and redirected his emotions to a more productive activity, like focusing on a solution. As he turned his attention to God he received fresh strength and instruction. He summoned the priest and consulted the *urim* and *thumim* where God gave him assurance that if he rose up and acted he would recover his losses. To this day there is a bit of mystery surrounding the *urim* and *thumim*. Most likely they were two stones kept within the breast pocket of the priestly ephod. The names in Hebrew mean "lights and perfections." This clearly speaks of the Holy Spirit who resides in the heart of every believer priest and promises to give us counsel from heaven. David took counsel from the Spirit, rising up he proactively pursued his enemies, tore into their flanks and recovered not only all of his losses, but a share of the enemy's spoils as well.

Throughout his long career David continued his pursuit of God in the midst of hardships. He left the treasured legacy of his emotional journey for us in the Psalms. In those sacred pages we see a man very much in touch with his emotional life. We also see a man who would not allow his emotions to determine his behavior. In fact we often discover statements such as, "When I am afraid, I will trust in you" (Psalm 56:3), or "why art thou cast down, O my soul? ...hope thou in God" (Psalm 42:11). What was the secret behind David's emotional self-mastery? He demonstrated that the secret springs of *sustained motivation* were supplied from the depth of his private devotional life. His venting of feeling was directed toward God in a life of worship and prayer fused in the poetic expression of the Psalms. David also revealed that his wisdom came from his meditation on the Word of God: "You, through Your commandments, make me wiser than my enemies" (Psalm 119:98). David's admirable capacity for *personal responsibility* came from the humility with which he embraced both his strengths and his weaknesses before God in prayer, drawing comfort from his knowledge that God is both infinitely just and infinitely kind. His frequent crying out to God is evidence of a man who took responsibility for his actions while always seeking supernatural assistance to work out his overwhelming problems.

In each case we see how David possessed these EQ attributes as a leader, but more importantly, we see how he supernaturally enhanced them through his dependence on God. Anyone seeking to attain significant victories in life will need to master these three aspects of wisdom: self-awareness, personal responsibility, and sustained motivation. David solidified this in his early transformational relationship with Jonathan. We can do this today with a transformational coaching relationship.

Reflection and Discussion Questions
Chapter Eleven: Transformational Coaching for the
Uncommon Advantage—Foundations of the
Favor-Wisdom Connection

1. The unique description of wisdom as the combination of
   the dimensions of supernatural, natural, and emotional
   intelligence is a convergence of what seems like opposite
   rather than parallel streams of thought. How has the
   description of this in Joseph's life helped you to see this
   combination in an illuminating way? In what other biblical or historical characters can you see this combination?
   In what ways are you having your eyes opened to see
   what was there all the time?

2. A biblical key to wisdom from God is the fear of the
   Lord. How does the relational accountability of a godly,
   supportive, transformational coach contribute to that
   healthy fear of God in our lives? Why is it a mistake to
   have so personalized the fear of God that we have
   isolated ourselves from this kind of transparent relationship that is the foundation of transformation? Could this
   have been the source of David's downfall when he lost
   his peer coach in Jonathan's death?

3. Empathy and rapport have been discussed as keys to
   emotional intelligence. In what ways have you assessed
   these areas in your life, recognizing that these do not

reveal themselves by self-analysis? A transformational coach models these skills and enables you to see yourself in relation to the interpersonal exchanges with your coach. How might coaching in this area enable you to see more of the uncommon advantage in your career calling?

4. All of us can get motivated by an event or experience. What do you do in your life and work to enhance a sustained motivation over time? Since it is critical to those who want to move to the top of their mountains, how would a transformational coach help you in areas where you lost your focus or motivation at critical junctures in the past?

5. Where have you not taken personal responsibility for change, but rather have pinned the responsibility on someone or something else? In what ways might this have limited your personal power? How has this chapter encouraged you to take another look at those areas in your life?

CHAPTER TWELVE

Transformational Coaching for Sustained Motivation— Unlocking the Advantage for Success

By Lance Wallnau

W e need to know what kind of an environment has the greatest power to motivate us. Great exertion, long hours, and much conflict tend to accompany the journey of anyone who seeks to ascend to the top of a mind molder, especially where the spoils involve a dispossessing of strongholds. The better you know yourself (self-awareness) the easier it is to know your ideal work environment. According to data validated by 40 million people who have participated in surveys on behavioral styles, there are only four basic types of motivational settings. Pick the one that you would feel energized working in. That is the easiest place for you to experience sustained motivation!

Some prefer an environment that addresses their need for: (pick one)

1. Significance through the accomplishment of goals with a minimum of supervision, a wide scope of operations, fresh challenges, and the rewards of increased authority,

power, and prestige. Sometimes called a high dominant or "D" personality.

- This person is energized in a role that empowers them to shape an environment, overcome challenges, and accomplish results.

2. Significance through public recognition of ability, freedom from control, and a variety of stimuli. Opportunities to use their considerable verbal and creative skills to make a difference. Sometimes called a high influencing or "I" personality.

- This person is energized when shaping an environment through their personal influence and persuasion.

3. Certainty and opportunity to demonstrate personal expertise. High need to control all factors affecting performance, reserved and business-like environment. A role allowing for careful planning and exact standards of evaluation. Sometimes called a "Conscientious" or High "C" personality.

- This person is energized by a role that allows them to ensure quality, accuracy, and excellence according to their standards.

4. Connection in an environment of minimal conflict, team orientation, predictable patterns, genuine relationships, sincere appreciation, and opportunity to develop and demonstrate personal expertise. Sometimes called a "steady" or High "S" personality.

- This person is energized when cooperating with others in the execution of tasks.

At some point in your career you will need to enter a convergence of *role* and *field of expertise* in order to be your best. Your role will perfectly match one of these motivational environments or you will experience greater challenges to sustained motivation.

We have discussed the **personal** attributes of wisdom when seen as aspects of emotional intelligence. What about the **interpersonal** aspects of wisdom: *empathy* and *rapport*? On an interpersonal level people need wisdom in order to accurately read people. One skill that enables this is called empathy. In fact, the acquisition of this single quality is so important that it explains the mystery behind some of the suffering that comes into our lives. Paul said to the Corinthians,

> *"Blessed be the God and Father of our Lord Jesus Christ, the Father of mercies and God of all comfort, who comforts us in all our tribulation, that we may be able to comfort those who are in any trouble, with the comfort with which we ourselves are comforted by God."* (2 Corinthians 1:3-5)

Paul starts off his career as a bull-headed, one-man church wrecking machine. A religious terrorist with little regard for the sufferings and losses he inflicted on others....till he met Jesus. In fact Jesus made a point of linking suffering to Paul's mission when He commanded Ananias to befriend him, saying go, "for I will show him how many things he must suffer for my name's sake" (Acts 9:16). Paul soon learned the quality of empathy by converting his personal struggles into an opportunity to understand the pain of others.

Empathetic people have a wide range of emotional awareness, and can read other people's states fairly quickly. Empathy is the power to understand what others are feeling. Sympathy, on the other hand, is the power to feel what others feel. Some people who gush with sympathy are nonetheless people-illiterate because they are dominated by their feelings. To operate with EQ you don't need sympathy, but empathy. It was this well-developed capacity in David that led Nathan to set him up for a moment of divine correction. Nathan needed to confront David's commission of adultery and murder. He told the king about a man who had a very dear sheep that was raised from a lamb, but was taken by a stronger man and killed. David was incensed and ordered the offending man to be killed. At this point the prophet cried out "thou art the man" (II Samuel 12:7), and exposed his affair with Bathsheba and the murder of her husband Uriah. David's capacity for empathy was the key to finally seeing the horrific nature of his sin, thus leading him to repentance.

The other critical interpersonal skill is the ability to build bridges of influence through **trust**. It is one thing to know how to read people's feelings, and another to know how to create an environment so that people feel safe and trust you. How important is trust? Without trust, all the people-reading skills in the earth will avail nothing. You cannot influence others without the ability to build trust. From the beginning of his career David demonstrated a capacity to form relational covenants with others, even former adversaries. David's capacity for trust building was such that upon Saul's death, his chief military commander, Abner, defected to David and entered into a covenant friendship. When one of David's generals, Joab betrayed that covenant of protection under David and killed Abner, David felt such a violation of trust was committed that Joab paid for this breach with his life.

There are two rules to remember when dealing with interpersonal EQ. The first rule involves the relationship formula:

Rule #1: Respect + Trust = Commitment

Without respect people won't care about what you have to say. Without trust they won't listen, even if they believe you know what you are talking about. Without both respect and trust, you will never gain significant commitment from anyone.

Your gifts and talents can command respect, but only your interpersonal skills build trust. Trust building is wisdom's master key to influencing others into alignment with your assignment.

This is especially critical for believers to understand, because not all those who know how to gain trust are trustworthy. In the last days many empty talkers and deceivers will influence people. This poses an interesting question: is it automatically true that people who are trustworthy know how to build trust with others? Isn't it often the case that people who are untrustworthy have the uncanny ability to influence others? From con artists to pimps and unscrupulous salesman or politicians, trust building is a skill that can be learned—even by the untrustworthy. In the last days those who have the ability to build trust will persuade many for good or evil. To succeed in your field you will need to be not only trustworthy, you must have the master skill of winning the trust of others.

At times you may get frustrated working with other people and desire to strike out and "go it alone," but that is when you must remember rule #2.

Rule #2 Relationship Builds Capacity

This rule is described in the scriptures as the principle of

agreement, and is so woven into God's design that it is difficult to see how often we miss the application. As wonderful
as your gifting is, there are complementary gifts in others
that can release you to a whole new level of productivity
when you join them to yours. Nature makes this obvious.
Combine nitro and glycerin and you create enough energy
to explode mountains. Combine a man and a woman
together in relationship and you trigger the capacity for
reproducing a child. What is the capacity of that child?
Again, this depends on the relationships it is exposed to.
Provide nurture and love to that child and it will contribute
back to the world; abuse that child and you foster a capacity
for hate and destruction.

You see the connection between relationship and
capacity in every field. In the arts field, music teams like
Leonard Bernstein and Stephen Sondheim combine music
with lyrics to create classics for stage; in military history
we see Robert E Lee and Stonewall Jackson forming an
invincible alliance in America's Civil War. In Scripture
you can explore the early model of Jesus sending the
mighty apostles in teams of two, such as Peter alongside
John or Barnabas with Paul. Time and again we see that
relationship does not double our capacity; it multiplies and
often reconfigures entirely the product we are able to
deliver. The relationship you have with your bank or with
the right business coach or consultant will be the difference between mediocrity or preeminence in your field.
How well you attract and keep these relationships is a
function of your EQ.

Putting it all together we learn that emotional intelligence matters. It is critical. It is an aspect of wisdom that
describes how you handle yourself on a personal and interpersonal level. It calls upon your capacity to manage awareness of yourself and your social environment. It calls upon
you to manage your behavior and relationships. It becomes

the one factor that determines how high you go and how long you stay.

Let's review. If you are a person who intends to walk in favor and fulfill divine assignments you will need to cultivate the wisdom of emotional intelligence. It all starts with self-awareness. Learn to step outside yourself and consider what you look and sound like from another person's perspective. Remember you make a first impression in two minutes. The moment you see that what you are doing is not working, adjust it! That's the essence of personal responsibility—the ability to take full ownership of everything you think, see, feel and do, thus giving you the ability to respond differently if what you are doing is not working. He who has the greatest range of behavioral flexibility always wins. Its simple mathematics!

The person with the greatest diversity of response gets to try more options. Eventually one of those options will work. Be flexible so that you can make the adjustment needed to get the outcomes you want. With high self-awareness you don't have to wait until later, you can do so in the moment.

Finally, sustain the effort. Excellence in short bursts does not work. A sustained effort has power. The power of consistent effort is the emotional intelligence power of sustained motivation. For long-term motivation, become clear on the type of environment you work best in and either find it somewhere or create it yourself. Align your gifting with the right role in the right environment and you are on the fast track to career convergence.

Remember, the force of favor works with God and man according to the measure of wisdom being applied. Watch how you interact with others. It matters little how talented or gifted you are if you cannot read people accurately you will not know how to establish rapport. You will come off as if you are speaking a foreign language at the emotional level.

How can you adjust your interaction if you do not know how to put yourself in the other person's shoes and relate to what they are feeling? Empathy is the power to understand what they feel. Empathy and trust-building form the complete link of interpersonal EQ. What is at the core of this skill? It's simply the ability to behave in such a way that others feel safe with you. It is the science of rapport. R.A.P.P.O.R.T. is also an acronym for: Really All People Prefer Others Reflecting Themselves. Those who know how to connect with others by setting them at ease in their presence demonstrate mastery in building rapport and gaining trust. This is a skill that can be learned.

I have used both David and Joseph as examples because their experience illustrates principles that are relevant to believers in the workplace today. These young men invaded the dominant political and economic mountains of their day and dispossessed the enemy from his high places. They show us how to walk in favor with both God and man. They illustrate the power of true spiritual leadership, which is the willingness to set aside your own agenda in order to take up an agenda of service empowered by the Spirit of God. They model the relationship between anointed expertise and its intended end—service to others. David was made king "for Israel's sake" and Joseph was sent by God to Egypt to "preserve his people" from future calamity. In the course of their service to others they plundered hell and occupied the mind molders of their generation.

Much has been made of late regarding the "transfer of wealth" that is expected to accompany the last-day's harvest. The Bible promises that treasures hidden in darkness will be given to those who walk in God's calling. The Josephs, Davids, Nehemiahs, Daniels, and Esthers of yesterday serve as the biblical role models for the last-days church. They show us how to pick every one of Satan's locks, penetrate the gates of hell, and plunder the treasures of darkness. These are treasures of influence, access, and assets to get the job done. These believers will stand at the tipping point of their arena and penetrate world kingdoms. They are the royal priests exerting authority in the realm of the spirit and gaining access to places Satan would prefer to appoint others to occupy. As royal priests they have the privilege to use their authority in prayer to shut the gates of hell and open the gates of heaven. In the wake of their influence they will birth sheep nations.

A New Language of Achievement

Every new science requires a new language. In a sense we are learning a new language today as Transformational Leadership coaches talk about: tipping points, mind molders, high places, royal priesthoods, "*yateer*" or the excellent spirit, assignments, desire, favor, contradictions, backlash, divine appointments, gift-mix, career convergence, and wisdom expressed through emotional self management,. We can see how these components properly understood come together and combine like a professional boxer to unleash explosive potential. Learn to apply these concepts and you are certain to experience the most exhilarating career journey any believer could desire. The outcome of all this will become career preeminence.

Again, let's observe some of these elements and watch how they converge in the lives of Joseph and David. First we note their commitment to *serving* demonstrated by their willingness to work to make others successful. Note, they served in the area of their *gifting* with resultant *excellence*. The supernatural blessing of God came upon their labors and caused them to "jut out further" than all others. As one stage of *assignment* ended, another stage opened up through *divine appointments* frequently veiled in the guise of crisis. It started for David as he progressed from the sheepfold to the king's palace through various *displays of gifting* (slingshot and harp), till driven off to a cave (*favor backlash*) where he shepherded misfits (*character formation*) till they turned into warriors working as a unit. These relationships however *trusted* him and were the key to *building his capacity* to govern the nation and expand the territory. During this period of prophetic *contradiction* running from Saul, God was shaping the man and enlarging his *measure of rule* from captain to king. Having survived the *contradictions* and *backlash* that came with his calling, he emerged with a kingdom finally put into his hand and stood atop the great political, economic and religious mountain called Israel.

Joseph likewise *served* his father Jacob; then *served* Potiphar with an *excellent spirit*; then *served* the prison warden and finally Pharaoh through a *divine appointment* and *display of gifting,* where he emerged in such a display of supernatural *competence* and *favor* that he was immediately declared the second greatest ruler in the land. He entered *career convergence* in a moment. Joseph's setbacks and crises were in fact all *assignments* that developed him in his gifting and character even as he ascended further into his ultimate high calling as a *royal priest* at the top of the great *mind molder* of his day—Egypt.

Both Joseph and David advanced with *favor* and ruled with *wisdom* that produced national peace and prosperity. Yet they could only do so because they endured the contradictions of envy and accusation that put one in prison and the other on the run as a fugitive. The favor *backlash* involving Potiphar's wife and the backlash of Saul's jealousy were the *contradictions* each endured as the hand of providence set up circumstances for the future of each. These contradictions were necessary and strategic. Joseph's imprisonment set him up to meet the king's butler, and the king's butler was the key to Joseph's promotion! The *wisdom* and forgiveness with which Joseph behaved in the midst of personal hurt set him up for greatness. Both Joseph and

David became *tipping points* for the survival and prosperity of Israel and the advancement of God's plan. All Joseph's setbacks worked together to position him to fulfill his original *assignment*: "And God sent me before you to preserve a posterity for you in the earth, and to save your lives by a great deliverance" (Genesis 45:7).

What about David? Having endured the exile from Saul's house he matured to live out a successful 40-year career as king over all Israel. Thus he fulfilled the *assignment taken* from Saul, "to save [God's] people from the hand of the Philistines" (I Samuel 9:16). Each man lived to see the *desire* of his heart made manifest. Joseph was reunited with his father and his brother Benjamin, and David was given seven glorious years with open access to the ark of God. In the end he also received the blueprint and the resources to build the house of his dreams for God. Even then God went beyond his dreams to grant him a place in the royal line through which the messiah would be born and rule perpetually from the house of David.

As you see all these principles combine, it becomes clear that there is a system, a science if you will, to personal advancement in taking the Kingdom. As the late Ed Cole was fond of saying, "everything God does is according to a pattern and based on a principle of His Kingdom. Find God's pattern, base your faith on his principles, and success is guaranteed."38

The pattern and principles are clear. To penetrate the realm of the high calling of God you must be willing to go deep with God. All conception is a byproduct of intimacy. Desire is conceived according to the atmosphere you commune with. Becoming a true worshiper of God is the first step toward creating the kind of environment in which sacred desires are conceived and divine desires are developed. As you develop your God-given gifts and invest them in making others successful, a spirit of excellence will come upon you. As you are faithful in small assignments, God will bring you greater assignments and each one will bring further definition and development to your strengths and direction to your calling. These assignments also come with increased deposits of divine favor as God opens doors and networks you with whatever you need to finish the work He gave you to do. In order to survive the contradictions, sustain motivation and maximize opportunities for advancement in the assignments of Heaven we will need to operate in a high degree of personal and interpersonal wisdom. We call that particular type of wisdom *emotional intelligence.*

Remember, a divine assignment is nothing less than the invitation of God to join Him in that that which He is about to do. It's not about you— it is about his activity and his invitation. In a sense, God is in the business of shaping history through the assignments given to His people. At the same time He is in the process of shaping individuals lives in secret so that He can prepare them for greater invitations to assignments. Destiny is fulfilled as private preparation intersects public opportunity. In the end destiny is fulfilled to the degree we fulfill assignments for which we were created.

The Twelve Strategies to Unlock the Believer's Advantage

Thus far we have described the language of advancing toward career convergence and taking mind molders, but we have not yet discussed the specific strategies available to believers who take their weapons of spiritual warfare into a secular application. To date we have uncovered twelve powerful strategies available solely to the believer that can shift the territorial balance in favor of the saints in the workplace. We call them "Marketplace Force Multipliers" because they explode your potential to do business supernaturally. We explore them only in part here.

1. *What about the power of prayer in the workplace?* Can we not bind and lose in our career as we would in an evangelism event? Are there no devils in the workplace? Is it not likely that the strongholds over media, arts, and education are every bit as ferocious and determined as the strongman assigned to major cities or the principalities of nations? Is it possible to map out the infrastructure of a stronghold in business and address it in prayer? Can God use your spouse as a powerful vehicle to discern and amplify the voice of God when it's time to prayerfully pick an associate or make an investment?

2. *Can believers move in supernatural gifts as they engage in commerce?* Can they be given specific words of knowledge to guide them in bids or prices or markets to access or people to contact?

3. *Can the Holy Spirit quicken specific promises from Scripture that can be held forth over career situations* much like Moses stretched forth the rod of God over the Red Sea or Joshua holding forth the rod of his authority over a battlefield called Ai? As Jeremiah was called to prophesy to the earth, what happens when we learn to speak by the Spirit to the very earth we are called to occupy?

4. *Is it possible to walk through an office or meet with people and be able to discern accurately what spirit they are operating with or in what way they are being attacked or harassed?* Can God not give you insight through this discerning so that you know how to pray for others and minister to them?

5. *Can God speak through you in a very natural manner a word of wisdom or prophetic utterance in the midst of*

your work with people? Can He so anoint your communication that people are made receptive to your ideas?

6. *Will angels open doors for divine appointments in
your life* as they did for Abraham's servant when he
was led to the exact location where the future bride of
Isaac would meet him?

7. *Can favor so encompass you during a sales presentation that the very atmosphere of the room shifts or the
state of a person you are speaking to is altered?*

8. *Is it possible that you, like Joseph or Daniel of old,
can access the mind of Christ to solve a virtually
unsolvable problem your boss or client is facing?* Can
God show you new inventions in dreams, help a musi-
cian hear music coming from the worshiping realms of
heaven, or do artwork that is enhanced by a gift for
visions?

9. *Can an anointing come upon you to pioneer new territory in your community* so that a major problem like
poverty, violence, drugs, pregnancy, abortion, hunger,
or illiteracy is decisively dealt with through new
entrepreneurial initiatives? Can believers in a business
come together and so map out the operation that they
begin to dismantle the works of Hell and open the gates
of Heaven?

10. *How about Christians in the workplace coming
together to coach, support, challenge, and pray for
one another till a corporate excellence comes upon a
whole company?* Can the body of Christ build itself up
by helping one another take Kingdom territory in the
marketplace through excellence and peer coaching?

11. ***Will a day come when God calls forth Kingdom leaders of the church and workplace into a citywide coalition of compassion to pray for and change the very spiritual climate of the city by targeting the mind molders?*** What would happen if these leaders of church and commerce were to meet together with an understanding of divine assignments? What if leaders committed to pray for God to show them what He was doing in their city and where He was inviting His people to join Him? What if they were to focus on the tipping point God reveals in the city? If nations can be born in a day, is it too much to believe that entire cities can reach collective tipping points in a day? In the Welsh revival the leaders would travel and pray seeking the "thin places." These were places in the nation which had less resistance and hence more potential for breakthrough. God knows where the "thin places" are in the enemy's camp and can align his workplace and church generals to attack. It may be an attack against poverty, racism, teenage crime, or childless youth. God knows which gate makes Hell most vulnerable.

12. ***As we talk about the transfer of wealth, what will happen when Gods people begin to build their faith to access the blessing that is already upon them because of tithes and offerings?*** What happens as wealth is transferred in its fullest form: wealth of influence, access, ability, and assets? As believers sow finances, money goes into their future to prepare a way for them. Your giving works like a bulldozer to plow up satanic obstacles. It clears your path and prepares an access for you into heaven's resources. Many times this access comes through windows of heaven being opened with God-sized ideas and divine appointments that if acted on will produce massive increase. Three times in the Old

Testament, numerous times God promises that the reward of giving will be a supernatural blessing on "the work of your hands." Notice it is *your work* that is supernaturally blessed, not your finances or your prayers that are blessed. God blesses the work of your hands.

Do these twelve strategies work? Based on the increasing number of testimonies from believers around the world we give a resounding—*yes*!

In fact, the breakthroughs accelerate as more believers become conversant about these principles and walk out their practical application. Something more than a revival can take place—this movement has the potential to produce a tipping point in the national culture. The impact will result in a reformation, and a reformation in the last days is what precedes the establishment of sheep nations.

Entire nations will tip one way or the other before Jesus returns because there will be sheep nations and goat nations. Seek God for your assignment in the battle for your nation and become a tipping point within your career sphere of influence. Let God promote you to a place where supernatural gifting, wisdom, and favor can develop within you to bring your life into *career convergence*, the place where your gifts and passion combine in a role that pays you to do what you do best. Success in your career is something God wants to give you. It is a gift from God. Such a thing is not only possible, it is promised in the writing of Solomon.

> *"As for every man to whom God has given riches and wealth, and given him power to eat of it, to receive his heritage and rejoice in his labor—this is the gift of God."* (Ecclesiastes 5:19)

Be excited, but be watchful. In any new undertaking there are casualties. To minimize risk and maximize effectiveness, consider the following. Of all new businesses started in 2004, 80% will not be in existence by 2009. On the other hand 80% of new business started with a successful franchise will be in business and profitable in the same period. What does this tell us?

Every top performer from the realm of sports to the realm of business has a better chance of survival and success if they are following the application of an already proven system *and* have a relationship with someone who is committed to giving them step-by-step support, encouragement, and feedback. Those believers who work with a successful transformational coach are more likely to enter career convergence than those who insist on pioneering without a scout. Remember the rule for increase: relationship builds capacity. The quality of your relationships will determine the scope of your impact.

Real lasting skill development is the result of a process. You can become pregnant with an idea in an instant as a result of a powerful book or meeting, but in the natural it takes nine months of formation and a skilled midwife or doctor to deliver the baby. Relationship builds capacity, and a wise coach will be the kind of prayer partner and advisor you will need to help you form the idea, storm through the implementation, and deliver what God has placed on the inside of you. To attempt to do this alone, when your secular counterpart is climbing the same mountain with secular coaches by their side, is naïve. Remember the words of Solomon to the wise: "Two are better than one...For if they fall, one will lift up his companion" (Ecclesiastes 4:9, 10). Relationship builds capacity, and yours is multiplied by the quality of the guide you have climbing with you.

Reflection and Discussion Questions
Chapter Twelve: Transformational Coaching
for Sustained Motivation—
Unlocking the Advantage for Success

1. The key issue of trust building is described as wisdom's master key to influence others to align with God's assignment in you. What are some key behaviors that you look for in others in order to give them the gift of trust? What part of your life could most benefit from a transformational relationship to become more trustworthy with those you work with?

2. A primary result of EQ research is that relationship builds capacity; even exponentially. What evidences have you read or heard about regarding the capacity of a coaching relationship to bring a measurable Return-On-Investment (ROI)? What if you were trained as a coach to understand gifting/design differences in people and could match them on teams to complement their relational capacity for exponential impact?

3. The power of a true spiritual leadership has been described as the willingness of setting aside your own agenda in order to take up an agenda of service empowered by the Spirit of God. How does this differ from the standard coach conversations you may have heard about fulfilling your personal dreams and goals? What are

some of the Kingdom of God principles expressed in this statement; i.e. "seek first the kingdom of God and all these things shall be added unto you"? How has this been true in your life?

4. The illustrations from the lives of David and Joseph have reinforced the research presented on the role of wisdom and favor with God. To what would you attribute the fact that you have not heard this perspective before in other teachings or illustrations from the lives of these famous Bible characters? What does that say about the minimal emphasis on transformational coaching in the past generation, where we were simply told to find a mentor with all the answers rather than a coach who modeled all of these values and skills?

5. Which three of the twelve strategies to unlock the believer's advantage most challenged you? Which ones are you most ready to work on? How would a coach help you move forward in an accelerated manner as you begin?

Section Four:
Coaching That Builds Bridges to the Marketplace

Introduction

Within the next ten years, 10,000 transformational coaches will find ways to serve their co-workers in every culture and in every major mind molder. The home, church, education, government, arts and entertainment, media, and business and finance spheres will have an awareness of the benefits of coaching and will have an understanding as to what makes coaching transformational. One of the major transitions that is happening is that church and ministry leaders will be bridged in new supportive ways to marketplace leaders who want to make a Kingdom of God difference in the workplace. The wall of separation between church and stated career will come down.

This is nothing new. Once we clearly understand this principle, we begin to recognize it in our past history as well. John Woolman persuaded early Quakers to get rid of slave ownership by 1770. He did so by gently and persistently asking two powerful questions to slave owners over a thirty year period. His heart and methodology built a prototype bridge from the church to the community that others would travel on later. Here is what he asked:

> *"What does owning of slaves do to you as a moral person?"*

"What kind of institution are you binding over to your children?"

John Woolman's extraordinary conversations are an example of the dynamic way that transformational coaching spans paradigms, cultural strongholds, and generational prejudices. It is a wonderful example of how we can make a difference, one conversation at a time.

After twenty years of training pastors and missionaries for ministry, I have seen a significant percentage of them return to a secular career realizing that they were not really a good fit for a career in ministry.39 This is confirmed with the startling statistic that 55,000 pastors are in transition from their present role every year. I have a deep sense that a number of these outstanding men and women never had a transformational coach to help them discover their calling in the place where they were employed before coming to a ministry training school. As a result, they were in bondage to a limited perspective on what it meant to serve God with all their hearts.

In a recent PhD study of transformational leadership coaching and over one hundred executives, the conclusion was made that these executives had a higher view of their role and calling in their careers and a higher satisfaction level with what they were doing with their daily lives.40 Many of these had begun to see how their unique design and gifting was suited for their success and legacy in the marketplace.

Character is the foundation of every sustainable promotion from God. Contrary to the renowned "Peter Principle" that says a man or woman is promoted to their level of incompetence, those whom God promotes because of their integrity will be able to occupy that new territory with excellence. This has been the foundational teaching strategy of the Church to their marketplace members over the years. But something more is needed.

In the previous section we discovered that we need wisdom and favor to accomplish what is on the heart of God for the world and the leaders that He created and established. In this final section we will see that a servant's heart and attitude, coupled with the power of transformational coaching, will bridge the resources of God to the needs of those who realize their limitations on their own.

Much more will be written in the days ahead on the unique and critical role of transformational coaching in our culture. Perhaps your story will be part of that history as you avail yourself of a coach who cares enough to be sure you get more than a business transaction but a personal and business transformation.

CHAPTER THIRTEEN

Marketplace Parables—
A Personal Story of Servant
Success in the Marketplace

By Pam Johnson

W hen I contemplate the servant success that I have had over the past two decades, I am keenly aware that God has been preparing me for a unique purpose. The fact that you are reading this book suggests that God is preparing you for a unique adventure and purpose as well. I have experienced dynamic life lessons—lessons that have formed a bridge between my call to the marketplace and my call to be a person of character. In these next few pages I hope to relate to you some of the key principles that God has allowed me to learn through the opportunities that I have been given. Applying these principles will change your heart and your walk with God and bring you closer to realizing your desire to make a difference in your marketplace.

The Beginning of My Journey

Years ago, while praying about a new career, I knew in my heart that my purpose in life wasn't just about making money; it was about serving people. Ultimately, I wanted to make a difference in the lives of people. As I sought the Lord in prayer, He directed me to Psalm 119 in "The Book":

"Happy are people of integrity, who follow the law of the Lord. Happy are those who obey His decrees and search for Him with all their hearts. They do not compromise with evil, and they walk only in His paths. Oh, that my actions would consistently reflect your principles! Then I will not be disgraced when I compare my life with your command. When I learn your righteous laws, I will thank you by living as I should. I will obey your principles. Please don't give up on me. Blessed are you, oh Lord; teach me your principles. I have rejoiced in your decrees as much as in riches. I will study your commandments and reflect on your ways. I will delight in your principles and not forget your word. Be good to your servant that I may live and obey your word. Your decrees please me; they give me good advice. Give me an eagerness for your decrees; do not inflict me with love for money. Turn my eyes from worthless things and give me life through your word. Your principles have been the music of my life throughout the years of my pilgrimage. Now teach me good judgment and knowledge. "

To my seeking heart it, those words in Psalm 119 were a definite charge to follow Him and love His commandments. For me, it was a time for me to walk in a deeper surrender to His will and purposes and follow His lead. It was there that in that moment of reflection that a servant's heart was created in me, and I knew that whatever career I pursued, I would enter it as a servant, pleasing to Him.

Observing the Sabbath

The career choice that I decided on was real estate. My choice brought an immediate challenge to my commitment to please God. Even prior to obtaining my real estate license

I recognized that Sunday was a big day for realtors: open houses are held, out of town clients need to be served, and many other demands continually present themselves. I consulted with my husband and we made the decision to honor the Sabbath as we had always done.

Immediately there was an onslaught of negativity from those in the industry. In essence, they said: "You will never make it in real estate if you don't work Sundays! That is when everyone wants to see houses!" Being a bit conflicted, I began to wonder if I was being legalistic—or was it truly God's will for me to take this stand?

I prayed about this issue on my way to real estate class. One day, I saw a license tag with Proverbs 3:5 on it: "Trust in the Lord with all your heart and lean not unto your own understanding." It spoke to my heart, and I then knew that honoring the Sabbath was what God meant for me to do. Then I saw a license tag with Proverbs 3:6 on it which confirmed it: "Acknowledge Him in all your ways, and He will crown your efforts with success" (*The Living Bible*). I knew God was pleased with my obedience to honor Sunday, regardless of the cost.

Observing the Sabbath as a day of rest through the years, I have come to discover that there was no cost; it was a blessing—a gift from God. In our hectic, busy lives in the marketplace ministry we often take things too intensely. There is the feeling that if we don't do it, it won't get done, or at least not the way we think it should be done. This standard was the first principle the Lord taught me regarding marketplace ministry; it served well to allow my trust in Him to develop even stronger. If I could keep His commands regardless of how it affected my income, I could walk in a no-compromise position. I was surrendering the trust of my income and career completely to God.

The beautiful part of this is the blessing it brings. I understand there are many careers that would not allow a

Sunday Sabbath; however, one's heart attitude of honoring God's Word and taking a Sabbath rest is what is important to God. He created the rest for us; He knows that we are unable to continue functioning without a day of no demands—a day that gives us a "set-apart" time for Him and for ourselves. The principle is obedience—we are to do it because it's His Word—and because we trust Him that He *loves* us and knows we need to keep a day set apart to rest.

This Servant's Heart Journey

Before my career began, I knew I wanted to be His Servant in the marketplace. But what did that mean? I had always been bold regarding my relationship with Christ—not always in a loving way! God tempered me over the years so that I became less of me and more like Him. I stopped trying to "save the world" and began to understand His call to *be* His light, wherever I was, whatever I was doing. Often people avoid the implication of being a "servant." We don't mind "serving," but according to our will. We are not excited about being mistaken as a "servant."

The definitions of *servant* in Noah Webster's 1828 Dictionary include, *"one that waits; that is, stops, holds, attends or one that is bound"; "one in a state of subjection"; "one purchased for a price who was compelled to serve until the year of Jubilee"; "the subject of a king"; "a person who voluntarily serves another or acts as his minister, as Joshua was the servant of Moses and the apostles the servants of Christ"; "a person employed or used as an instrument in accomplishing God's purpose"; "one who yields obedience to another"; "one who makes painful sacrifices in compliance with the weakness or wants of others."*

All of these definitions aptly apply to the walk of a servant of Christ in the marketplace. As a servant of the Lord, it is not as much an outward doing as an inward attitude of heart; a willingness to conform our desires to His, to change our plans and agendas to His; to be willing to lay our lives down to honor and be used by Him, whatever the cost.

Being His servant does not mean we won't prosper in our careers. His promises are complete. As His servants we will want to be in His Word; it is our atlas for the journey. He continues to encourage us with His blessings promised for our lives through His Word.

Even though my heart attitude was changed to reflect being His servant, my flesh had to catch up! I had to go through many trials (and am still going through them) for God to enable me to become His servant in the marketplace. I am humbled that God allowed me to be set apart to learn and apply His principles in my day-to-day life in the marketplace. I have been blessed by His faithfulness and patience with me as I have made this journey.

In His mercy and grace God gave me an illustration in life that I will share with you here:

The Sand Dollar Story

There is a little isolated beach my husband and I love. I always walk the shore looking for shells and sand dollars. I walk the shore because I have a fear of the ocean. I don't fear people, business, or much else in life, but for some reason I was very frightened of the "unknown" of the ocean. It is so vast, and so much could be lurking in the deep.

Isn't that really how we are in life? For most people, the sure and safe will generally win over the vastness of the unknown.

On one particular visit, my husband and I were walking the shore as usual when a man strolling by asked what we were looking for. When we answered "sand dollars," he pointed out to a sandbar 300 to 400 yards out in the ocean and said, "If you go out to that sandbar you'll find all the sand dollars you'd ever want."

My husband, a tall, strong man and former deep-sea

diver, took my hand and said, "Let's go!" Immediately all of my "ocean fear alert beams" went off! Johnny knew, but just said, "Come on, you'll be fine."

On the journey to the sandbar, my heart and soul were gripped with fear. I began saying—in my heart only, not aloud—"Lord, please don't let me step in a hole. Please don't let a jellyfish sting me. Please don't let me cut my foot on a broken shell," and so on. Suddenly, just before reaching the sandbar, I heard the Lord whisper, "My people walk in such fear. They are afraid of everything." Then we stepped onto the sandbar and as the waves washed over it, we saw sand dollars everywhere! Like daisies in a field, everywhere we looked were sand dollars, complete and unbroken. Again I heard the Lord speak: "If my people could just overcome their fears, my supply is abundant! Whether it is sand dollars, finances, healing, relationships, whatever—My supply is abundant!"

I got so excited about what the Lord said and all those sand dollars. I told Johnny what God had spoken to my heart. He said that the Lord had spoken to his heart also, saying that 95% of His people walk up and down the shores of life and are never willing to step out into the deep of the unknown into God's best for their life. Only a few will step out and trust Him with their entire lives to overcome fear— the opposite of faith—and walk a life of abundance—the abundance of joy, peace and fruitfulness.

We took our treasures back to the cottage and placed them on the deck to dry. The next morning was our last day at the beach. Johnny suggested we get some more before leaving. Arriving at the shore, we saw the most amazing thing had taken place: the sandbar with all the sand dollars had shifted during the night. It was now at the edge of the shore. There was no need to walk out into the deep to find the treasure; it was right there at our feet. As we giggled and enjoyed picking up our treasures, the Lord again spoke to my heart: "It just gets easier and easier to trust Me. The more you step out, the easier it becomes to see my constant faithfulness in every area of your life."

Overcoming the fear of the unknown is the beginning of an incredible journey in finding and being in your purpose in life. Only without fear are you able to walk into a life of His perfect love. God's perfect love, indeed, casts out all fear.

We had to leave our glorious days at the beach and return home that afternoon. A storm was coming and we had a short boat trip across the sound. As Johnny was packing, I began gathering sand dollars off the deck. I was able to get only a small bag of them when he called that the storm was imminent and we should leave now; we could get the rest of them next weekend. I reluctantly left them and got into the boat.

The next weekend we came in the evening to the cottage. On the way over I said to Johnny, "The sand dollars will not be there." He was sure they would be, but I knew in my heart that they would not. When we arrived at the cottage, we found only a couple of broken ones on the ground. Johnny said, "We'll go out in the morning and find more." He did; he went to three sandbars and came back with nothing. As I walked to meet him, I found one small perfect sand dollar. Immediately the Lord spoke to Johnny and me at the same time: "When I give you a treasure, don't let the fear of the storms and winds of life rob you of my treasures! When I give you a blessing, hold onto it. Make it yours—regardless of the obstacles that come up in life!"

This has been an incredible lesson in life that has deeply impacted Johnny and me. Do you see how important that occurrence was in my life? Even today I thank God for revealing to us the incredible knowledge of "fear not" through this experience. I began to understand better how I could trust God and His Word. Suddenly things became clearer to me regarding the blessings of keeping His commands and staying the course to follow His Word.

Be Love Motivated

As Christians in the marketplace we have an awesome responsibility to shine with the principles of God. The Bible is our light. It illuminates our paths. The first step in our journey toward bringing His light to the marketplace is to discover the noble truth: "I [Jesus] am the Way, the Truth and the Life. No one comes to the Father except through Me [Jesus]" (John 14:6).

What is His noble truth for us as marketplace ministers? In a daily environment of business activities we have multiple opportunities to influence those around us. A deposit of good can change the course of another person's journey by our response in any given situation. We need to be motivated by agape love. This is the kind of love that God gives; it is unselfish. This agape love abandons our own agenda, our motives, and our priorities. Agape love extends a hand to any person in need. Even to the most seemingly insignificant person in our sphere of influence—or the most prominent. We all have needs!

Being marketplace ministers does not mean wearing a big cross or carrying a Bible to work. It is a call to influence the world around us with the love of Christ and the principles of His Word in action.

The key thread that flows from Genesis to Revelation is one noble truth: *Love*. God so *loved* the world that He sent His Son. It has become clear to me that *love* is the noble truth of the heart of our Father. When we are walking in love, we are doing the one thing that will always cause our Father to smile. Walking in love sounds simple, but it is a continuous growing, a continuous journey, a continuous lying down of our desires and will to support others and help them grow.

We are created to be victorious in Christ, to be able to do all things through Him, yet somehow we get caught up in being victorious in ourselves—doing things through our will and power and knowledge and skill. We move from the journey in life to the race for *our* success, *our* goals, *and our* blessings.

As marketplace ministers we will be called to lay our endeavors down in order to bless others and do the will of our Father. The Word says we are blessed so that we might be a blessing.

With the growing knowledge of this truth, the servant's heart begins to take shape. As we grow in this truth of love, we will be able to shape and transform the lives of those around us. We begin to have an understanding that God's greatest commandment, in Matthew 22:37-39, "...love the LORD your God with all your heart, with all your soul, and with all your mind...[and] your neighbor as yourself," is liberating! His truth brings freedom. There is a release from the pain of fear. Perfect love indeed casts out *all* fear. As we are perfected in His love, we become more effective as marketplace ministers.

Being love-motivated and allowing God to fill us with *His* agape love allows a new level of relationships. We learn how to "Leave Them Whole."

Leave Them Whole

As His servants in the marketplace, we are entrusted by God with the lives of those we come into contact with, whether employees, clients, customers, or those supporting our businesses. The command is to "Love your neighbor as yourself," and "Do unto others...." The principle is the love-motivated life. Putting others' needs before your own. It must be from a motivation of pure love with which we support, encourage, and hold accountable.

There is more to holding people accountable than just "holding them." It is a responsibility we have to direct and keep them from continuing in a pattern of sin that could change the course of their lives. It is our responsibility to motivate them to engage God for themselves by hearing the lessons that God gives us in life. Hopefully, we will keep others from having to make so many trips around the same mountain. We must first learn and submit ourselves.

To support is the act of upholding or sustaining. This is not just referring to money. As servants in the marketplace, God will surround you with broken, wounded people. We are *all* broken and wounded in some way; except for the grace and mercy of our Lord, we would all be hopeless.

One definition of support is "to endure without being overcome." That is what we are to do through Christ when supporting those that God puts in our path. Another definition is "to sustain; to keep from sinking." We have the power through influence and the example of our walk to help sustain those in need.

Everyone needs to be encouraged. There is an innate desire in all of us to do well, to please, to succeed, to create and do our best at what we are called to do.

God has put seeds of creativity in each of us. Like small children dreaming of all they can do and be, we have dreams. Too often life takes unexpected turns and our dreams and hopes seem to crumble.

Just getting by on a daily basis is sometimes more than we can handle. Our confidence takes a dive and we need to be encouraged. The word encourage is defined as, *"to give courage to; to give or increase confidence of success; to inspire with courage, spirit, or strength of mind."*41 That is a strong call—to support and encourage others.

Often in the marketplace the zeal to win and the burdens of our own path become so magnified that it is hard to stop and think about supporting and encouraging others. As servants in the marketplace, we must recognize how important this is.

In the Bible Jesus says that "My yoke is easy and My burden is light" (Matthew 11:30). With a pure love-motivated walk growing in us, it becomes a joy to allow the Lord to use us to lighten the load of those around us. The Holy Spirit gives us grace to move on His behalf; a simple smile instead of rushing to our task, a note of encouragement, taking a few minutes to guide or instruct a new person uncertain of their responsibilities, coaching someone in areas where you have strengths. Can you see how easily a love-motivated life can begin to sow joy wherever one is? It becomes a lifestyle of scattering love, joy, peace, patience, and all the fruit of the Holy Spirit.

Can you see how blessed a servant's walk is? Like Paul's tent making, our careers furnish the avenue to carry God's love into a dying world. It is a matter of simply becoming His servants where we are. Supporting and encouraging others becomes a lifestyle. You begin filling the holes in the hearts of people around you. You begin leaving them whole! Once again, the command is to love.

In accountability we must still remember the command, "Love your neighbor as yourself." There is more to holding people accountable than just accountability. It includes the responsibility to hold up a mirror to them to see the destructive patterns of behavior that could negatively change the course of their lives.

The definition of accountability is "the state of being liable to answer for one's conduct; the liability to give account and to receive reward or punishment for actions."42 It is our responsibility to pour into lives, with love, the lessons that God has given us to keep them from making so many "trips around the mountain."

When walking in love, it is sometimes hard to embrace holding others accountable. Supporting and encouraging comes more easily.

Some will find it difficult to require accountability in a gentle way. The fear motivation will cause pride to rise up and correct with a harsh or condescending attitude. Thank

God for His example of righteousness and mercy in our lives as He corrects us with gentleness and patience.

You can picture the effect our response or reaction will have on people's lives. We respond by being love-motivated. We react by being fear-motivated.

To leave a person whole, there must be a love-motivated balance of support, encouragement, and accountability.

God's example is that He always supports us, but not by just giving us everything that we ask. He encourages us with the confidence we have in Him and find in His Word and that, in His infinite love, wisdom and righteousness will always hold us accountable so that we continue to grow in love and learn His ways.

Part of leaving people whole is to lay down the attitude too often exhibited in the marketplace—being a respecter of persons or posturing ourselves around those who can give us a boost in our careers.

I feel that because this attitude is so pride-driven. It will keep us from the favor of God. But, once again, fear drives every attitude that is not love-motivated. It reeks of a "what can you do for me" mentality. As servants in the marketplace we must allow the Holy Spirit to work in our lives so that we do not fall into that pit. The scripture that comes to mind is Hebrews 12:1-2: "Let love for your fellow believer continue and be a fixed practice with you [never let it fail]. Do not forget or neglect or refuse to extend hospitality to strangers...for through it some have entertained angels without knowing it" (Amplified Bible).

For some, this comes naturally. For some it will require work. Who are the strangers? Anyone you come into contact with that you have an opportunity to bless, make them feel they are of some importance—to shine for the Lord in their life, whether by a kind word or smile. Anyone you have the opportunity to encourage: they are all strangers—but not to God!

Too often when we are busily doing things and racing through our daily lives, we forget that every person carries their own bundle of burdens. Allow God to use you to not add to their load, but to lighten it just a little. That is part of being a servant in the marketplace.

Reflection and Discussion Questions
Chapter Thirteen: Marketplace Parables—
A Personal Story of Servant Success
in the Marketplace

1. The story of a personal conviction to "keep the Sabbath" for a realtor that does most of her business on Sunday seems to go against the standard definition of success. It is similar to the famous example of Eric Liddell whose decision not to compete in the Olympic races scheduled on Sunday was immortalized in the movie "Chariots of Fire". Where have you discovered that honoring your conscience in an area that others would not understand, even mock, was the most successful thing you could have done?

2. The story of the sand dollars illustrates the necessity to step into our fears and find that God has already prepared an abundant table for us "in the presence of our enemies" (fears). Where is God nudging you to step out in your ministry and career in a way that causes you to face an inhibiting fear? How could a coach be the difference that would allow you to make that step? Where have you learned a key lesson in the past that could be used to encourage another in making their "fear busting" step?

3. To be a "servant in the marketplace" may sound like a foreign language to those who are inundated by the self-help and self-promotion books and magazines of our day. Yet, any marketplace transformation begins with a radical approach to serving others to help them be successful. How might you proactively seek out ways to do this in your career calling? What needs to happen in you first to be able to do this with the right heart, motive and attitude?

CHAPTER FOURTEEN

Workplace Relationships by Design—Signature Coaching That Transforms

By Charlene Fike

I remember the first time my husband Doug and I took a personality test, some twenty years ago. After reviewing our profiles, the test administrator said with a grin, "I'd like to be a fly on the wall in your house, to hear how you two work things out!" This seemed like a strange statement at the time, but he got our attention. We're both intense, opinionated people, on a quest to live lives radically abandoned to God. We knew that in order to grow in our relationship without killing one another, we needed help in understanding each other better. However, after showing us the test results and giving us a paper explaining our tendencies, he disappeared.

Sadly, our experience was not unusual. Many of us have taken some form of personality test, gaining a measure of understanding but lacking handles in how to convert our new insights into life-changing patterns. This is particularly true in the workplace. I have coached countless persons through the years who knew bits and pieces about their God-given design, but were at a loss as to how to implement those understandings in ways that make a difference. They didn't know how to develop their individual strengths, guard against their weaknesses, or leverage the strengths of those around them. Their valuable new insights did not become useful assets in their ongoing journey of personal growth and transformation.

Elements of Personal Transformation

Personal transformation occurs when several basic elements are in place, beginning with a solid commitment to the Lordship of Christ. This foundation is essential if we are to commit to the hard work involved in personal transformation, and open ourselves to the perspectives of those He will bring alongside. Another element is a willingness to grow in self-knowledge, and to apply our cumulative insights in developing new behavior and life-patterns. Lack of self-knowledge will otherwise become a tremendous hindrance in our personal journey. We urgently need accurate self-perception, which God in His wisdom intends for us to find in the context of our faith community.

The Holy Spirit leads us on the journey of fully embracing Christ's Lordship. We choose daily whether we will grow in self-knowledge, and develop increasingly fruitful and transformational patterns. This process is fueled by key relationships which provide the "relational mirrors"43 we need along the way. When these three elements are in place, growth happens exponentially.

The more accurately we see ourselves, in the context of safe, supportive relationships, the easier it is to let go of our old debilitating patterns and more fully embrace the diversity of those around us. Paradoxically, we cannot really know others until we know ourselves, and we cannot really know ourselves until we know others, in light of how God sees us both. Understanding ourselves and understanding others are actually two sides of the same coin.

The Language of Personalities

In theory, most Christians embrace the fact that we are all part of the same family, and members of the same body. Thus, in principle we are committed to celebrating our similarities and our differences. However, in practice we often have not fundamentally understood and embraced God's unique design in our own lives, and frequently misunderstand—or even condemn—the other guy's basic wiring.

It should come as no surprise that other people's minds don't work the same as ours. They do not reason as we reason, make decisions the way we do, communicate like us, or value the things we value. We know this cognitively, but burn up a surprising amount of emotional energy and relational capital dealing with this reality in everyday life. We bump into each others' differences every which way we turn, but often experience suspicion or stagnation rather than synergy as a result.

If you can't confidently:

- Identify the gifts and personalities of others in most situations,
- Recognize the key characteristics and functions of each,
- "Speak the language" of the different gifts and personalities,
- Know how to place people in the roles that best suit them, and
- Troubleshoot conflicts from the perspective of God's design....

...then you should consider having a coach work with you to develop a growth plan designed to equip you for greater effectiveness in this critical area.

If you are unfamiliar with personality theory and types, find someone who can introduce you to one or more of the systems in widespread use. DiSC, Meyers-Briggs Type Indicator (MBTI®), and StrengthFinders® are all good starting points. Written materials and specialists are widely available for each of these systems. You can also go to the TLC website to locate a coach who will come alongside you on a journey of discovering and activating your God-given gifts, and help you celebrate and unleash the gifts of those around you.

Each personality and gift assessment system has strengths and weaknesses. Each has its own "language." Familiarity with more than one system can be helpful, as each has different ways of identifying the complexities of human personality and communication. In time you will notice some overlap among the different approaches. On the other hand, one system may be more adept than another at describing particular aspects of human personality. But a good working knowledge of at least one approach to identifying, describing, and working with the diversity of God's design in those you relate to on a day-to-day basis will be invaluable.

Communication by Design

Each personality type and gift combination has characteristic patterns, preferences, vocabulary, and trigger points. Understanding these will make it substantially easier to avoid or resolve conflict, strengthen communication, and work effectively with others. Doing so will enable you to recognize and address your own idiosyncrasies as well. Regardless of your own personality type, you will be able to connect with others more effectively, and empower them toward greater effectiveness and fulfillment in their own journey. You might even develop empathy for persons you never thought you could tolerate!

Several years ago I was serving on an executive board of a Fortune 500 company. As the board interacted with the corporate officers over the course of several months, we became aware of a situation with the potential to damage the credibility of the company. The appearance of impropriety on the part of one of the officers prompted a barrage of questions. The officer responsible responded by storming out of the room.

During the awkward break that ensued, I asked the Holy Spirit to help me see beneath the surface and understand what was really going on. At first glance, the officer who walked out of the room appeared intentionally dishonest. What I began to see, however, was that his behavior was fed by a pattern of attempting to please people, saying what he thought others wanted to hear until he worked himself into an impossible situation. I knew him well enough to have a sense of how he was wired, but had been so focused on my own frustrations—and genuine concern for the potential damage to the company—that I hadn't stopped to reflect on how his personality type was contributing to the problem.

His personality is all about connecting with and influencing people, and tends to place a high value on being well liked. But the flip side—his Achilles heel—was that he could easily become paralyzed by his need to please and be liked by others. (In the DiSC profile he is a high *"I."*) Given my personality type (high *"D"* in the DiSC), I tend to dig in my heels when I feel taken advantage of, or don't feel like I'm getting a straight answer. I get off-kilter when I think someone is massaging the facts in an attempt to manipulate me. Our personality and communication styles were on a direct collision course.

The officer walked back into the room knowing that his behavior had been inappropriate. In the meantime, I had had a chance to step back and gain some perspective on the impasse. I was able to reframe my questions in a way that honored how God had designed him, which gave him the room to respond less defensively. This new pattern of communication allowed us to collaborate in pinpointing the problem and devising a workable solution. I experienced and recognized how important it is to honor gifting and personality in team situations. Through this experience I gleaned a key insight:

> **Relating to others on the basis of *their* personality type**
> **rather than through your own filter,**
> **encourages personal transformation**
> **and yields creative solutions.**

As I learned when working with this corporate officer, it's too easy to jump to conclusions, make judgments about someone's character, and miss critical personality clues that might otherwise unlock the situation.

Gift-Given or Gift-Driven?

As my husband and I have walked alongside leaders and organizations over the past 20+ years, we've seen many breakdowns rooted in lack of self-understanding in key leaders. The founder of a missionary organization comes to mind, who was spread far too thin. He was over-committing and over-promising, to the point that his staff didn't take his pronouncements seriously anymore. The pattern was actually rooted in a desire to "do the right thing" for his staff in each situation, but created increasingly unrealistic expectations. The situation played right into the weak side of his gifting, feeding on his need to maintain harmony and get along with everyone.

Unbeknownst to him, some of his key staff were making plans to leave the organization. They had finally come to the conclusion that the leader was simply lacking in integrity. What began simply as a gift-pattern in need of some discipline had mushroomed into a life-threatening organizational crisis. His natural response—to smooth the situation over and once again inspire the troops to greatness—was indeed beginning to compromise his integrity. But it didn't start that way, and needn't have deteriorated to that point.

Rather than acknowledge the fact that we are overextended and can't deliver, some of us tend to deal with overload by ignoring the problem as if somehow it will go away. Meanwhile, unanswered phone messages pile up and people begin making character judgments. "Avoid her; she is lacking in integrity." The truly sad thing is, an integrity deficit may not initially have been at the heart of the matter, but lack of self-awareness, compounded by avoidance patterns, can eventually spawn cover-up patterns that are indeed dishonest.

Sometimes leaders develop self-defeating habits—and are even embarrassed by them—but are stuck and don't know how to break the cycle. Sometimes they operate out of the assumption that they just need to keep trying harder, doing what they have been doing only harder, louder or longer. This takes the place of surrounding themselves with people who complement their personalities and can relieve the strain, freeing them to focus their energies elsewhere.

Such leaders are what we have come to call "gift-driven." Their God-given gifts are driving them rather than empowering them. Their relational patterns are governed by distinct personality traits, but without self-awareness and therefore generally without discipline. In other words:

The behavior of gift-driven leaders is controlled by their gifts and personalities. Lack of self-awareness and self-discipline can cause traits that should be assets to become liabilities.

Thus, persons with a strong leadership gift may become

bossy or manipulative. Compassion-gifted persons can be particularly susceptible to co-dependency. High "C's" in the DiSC profile may become obsessively analytical or rigid—and so on. At points in our lives we are probably all gift-driven, but ideally as we mature we will grow in self-awareness and thus also in effectiveness.

Rather than drawing on people who can provide encouragement and accountability, gift-driven leaders become further isolated. They tap their available relational capital, and after a while have burned through their reserves and are simply going through the numbers, hoping someone will see the light and stick with them. As people exit through the revolving back door, they encourage themselves with the notion that people can be replaced, without stopping to reflect on how they might themselves be contributing to the problem. If someone points out how their patterns frustrate or are disempowering to others they shrug, "That's just the way I am!" They avoid facing the limitations or imbalances of their personality, perceiving this as disqualification or failure. Over time they are unable to build effective teams, because deep down they see others with different gifts as exposing—rather than complementing—their own.

Being a parent has provided lots of opportunities to learn about gift-drivenness, both in myself and in my children. As I was learning a new work-style in light of personality types, I realized I also needed to change my parenting style. I've learned some powerful lessons, and credit two very well-adjusted teenagers, in part, to discovery and application of these insights. With their permission, I'll share a bit of that journey.

It became evident at a young age that our daughter was gifted in the art of verbal persuasion. However, her mouth—which is a primary tool that God will use for His purposes throughout her life—repeatedly got her in trouble. As her parents, we were faced with a choice. Do we ignore her verbal excesses and hope she outgrows this? Do we react and discipline her out of irritation? Do we convey that her verbal tendencies are a "problem," or a strength that needs to be channeled and disciplined?

We set out to teach her that every day she had a choice. The path of least resistance, for her as for all of us, would be to function out of the weak side of her gifting. Articulateness run amuck morphs into manipulation. Persuasiveness can be developed into effective salesmanship, which can in turn be used for good or ill. Each of these, however, is a function of her God-given gifting, her special personality, her unique wiring. As her parents we are her greatest fans, but are therefore committed to providing feedback, perspective, and discipline that will enable her to grow into everything God created her to be. We will help her grow beyond being gift-driven, to help her truly maximize her God-given gifts.

Our son, on the other hand, is intense and analytical. Even as a youngster, unless his interactions with friends had purpose and significance they didn't seem worthwhile. One of his greatest strengths—and an asset God will use throughout his life—is his sense of focus, his laser-like conviction, and principled analysis. But, undisciplined and out of balance this gift-package can come across as overbearing and judgmental, with a tendency toward self-righteousness. He has had to work at learning to just "hang out," cultivating and enjoying more casual friendships, giving others room to be where they are even if they have not thought things through carefully or ended up where he has.

In other words, he has worked at celebrating and growing in his gifts, without being gift-driven. Both of the kids have gotten a life-impacting jump start as they have come to understand their unique design, while beginning to develop the discipline of not catering to the weak side of their gifting. These key tools will serve them well on their own life-long journey of growth and transformation.

In the nick of time and truly by the grace of God, their parents were enabled to come alongside and coach them through this critical transition. However, most of us were not so fortunate. As adults, many of us have not yet developed the necessary muscles to go there. And even then, it is a lifelong journey. We all need coaches and mentors that will walk with us along the way.

Celebrating God's Design

Transformation begins when you can move beyond simply identifying your strengths and tendencies, to understanding how your God-given design affects your work and home environment. Listen to your personality speak, find the key words that unlock your personal patterns—learn what's "normal" for you. For example, some personality types are naturally inclined to process their thoughts verbally, preferably with people they trust. Others naturally wrestle with questions and process issues internally and only then share their conclusions with others. Neither is "wrong" or "right"—but they are very different ways of processing and engaging the surrounding world. In the book *Work Types*,44 the authors explain the Meyers-Briggs Type Indicator (MBTI) system and the typical misinterpretations between these two different styles:

> *"**Extraversion** – Speak, listen, speak, speak, listen, speak, speak, speak – then perhaps reflect. This style may appear rude. The rapid speaking, the interruptions, and the building on each other's ideas may seem to exclude the more deliberate style of Introverts, and not to give an opening for their contributions.*

> ***Introversion** – Listen, reflect, listen, reflect, reflect, reflect – and then perhaps speak. This style of*

thinking it through inside before speaking can be very difficult for Extraverts to understand. They may interpret it as not being interested or involved, or they may assume that the Introvert is disapproving or judgmental, or worse yet, too stupid to respond."

Once we discern our God-given design and learn to celebrate it, the transformational journey kicks into high gear. We move beyond questions of "must" and "should," "right" and "wrong" styles, into the real issues: who God is, who He has created us to be, and how we are to interact with others in order to fulfill our destiny and empower them as well. We are enabled to go to the root of crippling feelings of guilt or inadequacy that emerge when we live our lives in comparison with others.

This has been a very personal process for me. A friend of mine played an important role in unknowingly serving as a "relational mirror" at a critical moment in my life. She made a passing observation that started me down the path of self-discovery. After watching the movie *Dances With Wolves*, Cate said: "Now I know what to call you Charlene—your real name is "woman who stands with fist!" I reeled a bit when she identified me with the movie's defiant heroine, but had to admit she was right. My posture before the Lord was one of supreme dissatisfaction with my design.

I wanted to be a "sweet tempered" woman, not one who was outspoken—even brash at times—in my search for reality and authenticity. Because I really didn't understand my wiring (and didn't have people who could helpfully interpret both the positive and negative aspects of who I was), I focused on who I was not. I had few role models and mentors who could give me needed perspective. I struggled to see my uniqueness as strength, my style as useful, and my perceptions as assets to the Body of Christ. I became fixated on the inherent weaknesses of my God-given design, and thus raised my fist in disgust.

My friend's comment came as a wake-up call. It helped me see that I was wasting a lot of emotional energy fighting God's design, not taking the time to understand His unique purpose for me, finding little to celebrate. It finally dawned on me that complaining about my design would never propel me toward a life of significance and purpose, which is what I really hungered for. If I was to mature in Christ, I needed to stop fighting and start growing.

Looking in the Mirror

Relational mirrors are vital if we are serious about personal transformation. If our goal is to be conformed to the image of Christ, we must practice speaking the truth in love. Ephesians 4:15-16 encourages us to "grow up in all things into Him, who is the head ... from whom the whole body, joined and knit together by what every joint supplies, according to the effective working by which every part does its share, *causes growth of the body for the edifying of itself in love*" (emphasis added). Love compels us to be mirrors for each other, both sharing encouraging perspective and identifying blind spots that hold us back. Some of the things we would prefer not to hear can, in the end, produce the greatest growth.

Several years ago I had an employee who I discovered was on the verge of quitting. Although she didn't directly report to me, our paths crossed several times throughout the day. Unbeknownst to me she had been gathering "evidence" that I didn't like her. I was so task-oriented that I would walk in to the room—literally not seeing her—and would keep right on going, without stopping to see how she was doing personally. She interpreted this pattern as thinly veiled disapproval and judgment. I don't tend to look for relational reassurances on a regular basis, so it didn't occur to me that she would need it. I wasn't sending subtle messages—I was just focused on my endless "to-do" list. I came to work to get the job done, not to "hang out."

I met with her to try to get to the bottom of the situation. As we talked, she provided a "mirror" which gave me a different perspective on myself. When she shared how she interpreted my actions, I had a choice to make. I could have just looked at the facts from my perspective, and secretly muttered, "Oh, grow up!" I could then have ignored her feedback and thought of this simply as her problem.

However, deep down I knew something more fundamental was going on. I talked with a mentor who knew us both, who helped me step back from the situation and take an honest look. I was functioning in ways that worked for me, but not for her. I realized that if I wanted to grow in Christlikeness and effectiveness, I no longer had that luxury. I needed to get better at identifying and adapting to the gifts and personalities of others. I needed to have this become second nature to me, not an afterthought.

Mentors and coaches in my life have provided some of the relational mirrors and key, helpful tools that have fueled my growth. This comes at a price, and can be intimidating if we are still uncertain about letting anyone see us as we really are. But I have become convinced that, if we are hungry for real transformation as followers of Jesus, opening our life to others is not an option.

One of the strengths of my gift mix is generosity. However, my mentors have helped me see that once I feel taken advantage of, my generosity quickly turns into stinginess—a complete pendulum swing in the other direction. I used to be so ashamed of myself when I reacted that way, because I generally thought of myself as a generous person. I truly needed the perspective of an outside party. My primary mentor helped me see what my trigger points are, and how the reaction is actually rooted in my gifting.

Rather than reacting, I can choose instead to manage my responses. On the strength of this insight, and with the support of my mentor, I developed a personal growth plan to work at this. These kinds of practical, real life situations are the areas in which we are often the most unaware of just how much we are being driven by our gifting, and it is in these kinds of situations that we most need trusted friends and mentors to provide the outside perspective we are unable to find on our own.

The Gift of Honor

Choosing to live this way forces us to listen deeply, and develop a culture of honor. I've come to define honor as proactively seeking to discover and bless the other person's unique design – attempting to see them through the eyes of Jesus—before seeking to be understood. Looking for what's *right* rather than what's *wrong* with the other person is a great starting point. For some of us, doing this is profoundly counter-intuitive, but it can be cultivated and practiced—to great benefit.

I once had an intern working for me who was really getting on my nerves. I found myself continually focusing on what was wrong with his job performance. It was all I could do to respond redemptively, looking for his God-given design. Some prodding from a coach helped me move in that direction. As his supervisor I had a choice. Do I take the time to serve him as a relational mirror, or do I let it slide and wait it out (he was leaving in a few months)? I chose to engage the situation.

James had a lot of raw leadership giftings. He reminded me of a garden filled with many weeds choking out future seeds of promise. He had lots of good intentions but was paying little attention to the cues he was getting from other people. He had a history of people being irritated by him and shutting him down. He knew there was a problem, but it

300

was illusive. I decided to help identify some of the weeds—or habits—he'd developed that were preventing his true potential from coming forth. It wasn't easy for me to take the risk to become a relational mirror, and it surely wasn't easy for him to hear! However, after recently seeing each other again this young man looked back on that day as a watershed event that transformed his future. Together we identified how to work from the strength of his gifting and developed a growth plan. I was uncertain how he would react to my perceptions and suggestions, but he felt honored as well as empowered to build the necessary muscles to bring about lasting change. It was well worth the risk!

We are each designed by God to see the world through our own unique lens, but He was wise enough not to make any one lens big enough to see the whole picture. We *need* other people, and the perspective they bring, if we are to fully understand our lives and callings. We in turn have a unique perspective to bring to the lives of our friends and co-workers. None of us will be able to handle every situation as well as we should. One man's strength will be another's weakness, and vice versa. We may know this is true, but we rarely live our lives this way. Coming to honor others' unique gifts and abilities, without reaction or comparison, is a key to accomplishing exponentially greater things in life.

This is especially true in the business world. While one person might be incredibly effective at handling the relational issues that arise in an office or business partnership, she might be terribly ineffective when it comes to administrative or financial management. The fiction of the modern world is that everyone should be competent in every area, and grow increasingly independent. But God did not design us to function independently—perhaps because He knew that, given the chance, we would do just that.

The Questions is...

Good questions help us discover how those around us are wired, and can provide handles on stubborn relational conflicts. The only way to know what's really going on, to understand what the other person needs, is to ask good questions—and then listen deeply. As an employer I continually made mistakes in this area. Much of my time was spent dealing with employees who misunderstood each other, resulting in conflict that I was somehow supposed to "solve." My natural tendency was to jump quickly into a problem-solving mode. Most of the time I really wasn't listening for underlying messages, because I was so focused on finding a "fix" for the problem. In hindsight, the outcome usually involved simply putting a Band-aid on the blister.

Several years ago, I intentionally hired two employees who had completely different personality types. I needed the strengths that each of them brought to the team. Once they got to work, Margaret constantly complained that Sandy was lazy—she was "shirking her responsibilities." Margaret had become convinced that Sandy would leave certain menial jobs unfinished, intending for Margaret to be saddled with the task. Margaret became fixated on the issue, as she perceived it, and Sandy wasn't even aware there was a problem.

Initially I came up with various plans, attempting to solve the problem through structural adjustments or new patterns of accountability. This would work for a while, and Sandy would *try* to change. But the cycle would repeat itself sooner or later. I'd hear Margaret's complaint, suggest a solution, and in a few weeks we'd be back at the same spot. As the cycle continued I grew weary of the conflict and was getting ready to fire someone.

Then, one day, I realized that I was defaulting to my personality style without first taking the time to *understand* Margaret and Sandy. My assessment of the situation was that we weren't dealing with fundamental character flaws, but my efforts at resolution still weren't getting anywhere. I wasn't asking enough questions—or the right ones—to unlock the situation and lead to a different outcome. "Insanity," Albert Einstein once said, "is doing the same thing over and over again while hoping to achieve a different result." Ouch!

One of my coaches likes to remind me, "Charlene, nothing can be sliced so thin that there aren't two sides." Taking her advice to heart, I began experimenting with a new way to handle the conflict. I had to listen in a new way, to get to the other side of the story. I shifted my focus away from Margaret's complaints, and began looking for Sandy's core design. What was going on in Sandy that triggered Margaret's reaction? I tried to help Margaret understand Sandy: to "stand-under" Sandy's perspective. I encouraged Margaret to think about her own personality type—how her strengths could contribute to a lasting solution. In time she began to reflect on a whole new set of questions about Sandy, about their relationship, and about their workplace tensions.

As Margaret came to understand Sandy's wiring, real change began to occur. She began to recognize Sandy's strengths and limitations, within the context of her God-given design. She stopped attributing motives to Sandy's behavior. Instead of asking herself, "What would it mean if *I* did that?" Margaret began looking for Sandy's strengths, and asking herself how they could complement each other. New questions lead to new insights, and in time they developed a healthy, effective workplace rhythm. They discovered that they actually liked each other, and came to enjoy working together.

A great story illustrating the power of questions involves Barbara Bush. When George Bush was first running for president, she had to choose a personal platform should she become First Lady of the United States. She describes in her autobiography how, after much thought, she finally decided that her issue would be literacy—that everything would be better "if more people could read, write, and comprehend."

"So the campaign was told that literacy was my interest—but we forgot to mention that I knew absolutely nothing about the subject, at least not yet." One day, on a campaign stop, she was led into a meeting where the host said, "We are so excited about your visit. I have collected literary experts from all around Milwaukee, some forty-five of the most informed people…. We can't wait to hear what you have to say.'"

"I was lucky," writes Mrs. Bush, "for suddenly it came to me what to do. After saying a very few words, I asked them a question: 'If you were married to the President and had the opportunity to really make a dent in the field of illiteracy, what one thing would you do? How would you go about it?'" Needless to say the room came alive with excellent suggestions.

"I certainly did learn something there," she concludes. "People would rather hear themselves talk than someone else. So when in doubt, keep quiet, listen and let others talk. They'll be happy, and you might learn something."45

Every time you open your mouth you have two options: make a statement or ask a question. I don't mean "Why can't you ever get it right?" or "Why do you always do this to me?" kind of questions. It is virtually impossible to provide rational, positive answers to these questions. It's not so much who, what, when, and where we should be looking for, but the how and the why. "Why did you make the decision you made?" "How did you get from here to there?" Better questions provide better answers, and better answers lead to better solutions. Improve your questions and you will improve your relationships, at home and at work.

For example, I've found it helpful to ask "Tell me what you like and don't like about the outcome?" or "Compare your current reality with your hopes and dreams, and describe the difference?" Lately, I've been asking the following coaching question with incredible results. "Knowing that Satan hates you and his goal is to discourage your heart *and* separate you from God... what strategy would you devise against yourself if you were him?"

Our Challenge

The world is waiting for leaders who are interested in their own transformational learning as well as for those interested in supporting the transformational learning of others. Leading inevitably involves trying to effect significant changes. However, it is very hard to lead others without first considering the possibility that we ourselves must also change. This requires both intention and attention. *Intention* as we develop the necessary muscles for personal transformation as we in turn give *attention* to the relationships entrusted to us. Learning to coach by design provides fertile soil and a rich learning environment for those we are privileged to have worked with us and for us!

Reflection and Discussion Questions
Chapter Fourteen: Workplace Relationships by
Design—Signature Coaching
that Transforms

1. Many readers can relate to the author's experience of taking an assessment and then being left in the dark as to how to maximize its value. In what areas of your life or career would you most like help in assessing your unique design? Where has this inability in the past held you back from reaching the potential that was available in that project or relationship? How might a coach bring transformation to and through you in the future?

2. In the story of the team leader storming out of a board meeting how often do you relate to others only on the basis of your design rather than on their unique personality type? What situations could you have diffused in the past if you had this flexibility? What value would be added to your company or team if that was part if their training? Check out the TLC website for the specialized workshop on gifting/designs that can be offered in your organization.

3. Gift-driven behavior is readily seen in the parenting example. How did your parents enable you to live by your gifts rather than be driven by your gifts? What would happen to our culture's parenting success if parents were coached on how to respond to their children in a more creative way in this area? What if you were one of those coaches?

4. Honor has been described here as proactively seeking to discover and bless another person's unique design. Who has bestowed that gift on you in your career development? What organization are you part of that seems to excel in this gift giving? What if transformational coaches were used to impact an organizational culture by modeling this and by multiply these in key leaders?

5. How did the story of Barbara Bush illustrate for you the power of asking questions? How can you practice more asking in the next month and note the different responses than the ones you are getting now? If you are not sure of the value of this heart and skill find a coach to model this to you and see the impact on your life.

CHAPTER FIFTEEN

Case Studies of Salt and Light Coaching

By Jerry Graham

Introduction

The leaders of today's organizations are facing unparal-leled challenges. The leadership environment continues to intensify as life now moves at the speed of light. One of the few unchanging realities in today's organizations is that "change" is here to stay. Those people who have God's call on their lives to lead (in the church or in the marketplace) must remain teachable as they continue to embrace God's preferred future. Business, organization, and church leaders agree—leadership development will not look the same in the future.

As leaders continue to move away from the "command and control" management style of yesteryear, interpersonal skills, passion, and unselfishness have become the new currency to become rich in the leadership world. While much has been written about both Christian leaders and busi-ness leadership, many who follow Christ as Lord have strug-gled to bridge the gap. Now God is using Christian leaders to reach, impact, and bless the gatekeepers of other important segments of society (business, journalism, the arts, et al.).

What is the catalyst for this new form of outreach? ...Transformational Coaching.

In this chapter, I review some ways in which Christians are applying this coaching methodology. First, I will review how coaching is being used to quickly move to "heart-level" conversations with people in the marketplace. Next, as the culture of caring is established, discover how leaders are helping others to discover passion and purpose. Finally, as inner transformations are addressed, the relational friendship is a comfortable context to talk about spiritual issues and ultimately spiritual needs. It all begins with caring... and understanding how to apply the best coaching techniques in the appropriate situations.

Coaching has become a very important tool for individuals and businesses to increase their productivity. As the previous chapters of this book have suggested, the art and discipline of coaching has invaded the organized church and is producing the same great benefits there that it has previously demonstrated in the marketplace. A significant difference that this book seeks to highlight is that transformational coaching is not just coaching techniques applied to Christians, but it has the potential to be an incredibly effective tool to touch the hearts of the leaders and gatekeepers of other important segments of society, e.g., business, the arts, journalism, et al.

As Gary Collins discusses in his book, *Christian Coaching*, a coach is utilized to get you from where you are to where you want to go. This is true whether the coach is a motor coach transporting individuals from one geographic location to another, or if the coach is an athletic coach helping a team move from mediocrity to excellence in a competitive endeavor. It is no less true for a personal coach helping an individual do a better job in their chosen field or even at home with their family.

While coaching is widely promoted as a vehicle for

self-improvement, there has not been much attention given it as a tool to assist the transformational believer or their ministry organization to be more attractive to others, i.e., be salt and light. Acts 1:7, 8 makes it clear that the power to witness the gospel to others by life and words has been delegated by God to us, the disciples of Jesus, and is therefore not something that we can just passively pray that God will do for us. We must recognize that we have a major part to play in modeling and spreading the truth of the gospel and learning how to use wisdom as we carry out our mandate.

Coaching skills allow an individual to quickly develop significant relationships with another person. This is the first step in what has come to be known as "relationship equity." The major difference is that in the case of coaching, the client is usually the one seeking a coach, which puts the transformational coach in the enviable position of the one being pursued rather than being the pursuer.

Another, often overlooked, feature of coaching is that those who are open to being coached are often the leaders, the "shakers and movers" of society. They are those who are already successfully accomplishing significant things in their chosen fields, but who are frustrated due to a burning desire to do even more. Yet they recognize that "something" is holding them back. By and large, this segment of the population is already hungrily consuming those things that will make them even more productive. Often, these people are the aforementioned "gatekeepers" to reach even larger segments of society. How much more desirable it is for their coach to have a biblical worldview instead of being "blind leaders of the blind" (Matthew 15:14).

As an interesting but very relevant aside, Dave Buck, president of CoachVille.com, recently wrote in a newsletter that no matter what the reason that a client hires a coach, within a very few sessions (usually no more than three), the discussion begins to open to personal issues, e.g., life balance, marriage/relationship, etc. This is a particularly exciting observation as it clearly demonstrates a significant level of trust and opens the door for the transformational coach to bring a biblical perspective into the dialogue.

It is important at this point to interject that this is not a duplicitous strategy designed to "trick" the client into a relationship with a Christian for purposes of carving another notch on their gun handle. Ethical coaching requires that the coach have the best interests of the client in mind through the entire coach/client relationship. The coach must truly be delivering the sought after improvements in the client's life. The coach must truly believe in the God-given ability of the client to accomplish whatever it is that they are seeking to do. However, how much better for a client to develop a deep, interpersonal relationship with a coach that has the Father's heart, the mind of Christ, and is being led by the Spirit than is the alternative. The transformational coach must be content with simply building bridges and allowing people to cross over at their own time and pace.

Transformational Leadership Coaching is a proven discipline of building bridges which has already demonstrated its effectiveness both inside and outside the walls of the traditional church. What follows are a number of "stories" of the successful application of these coaching techniques by TLC trained coaches, all of which demonstrate the power of this paradigm to invade the marketplace.

Staff Development at a Junior College

Wyatt Fisher is a Ph.D. candidate who is just beginning his internship as the final requirement for his degree in psychology from Regent University in Virginia Beach, Virginia. Since his TLC training, Wyatt has been aggressively pursuing opportunities to develop a coaching business. While living in North Carolina and teaching a couple of courses at a nearby junior college, the opportunity presented itself to pioneer a coaching-based staff development program for the college. At the time of this writing, Wyatt is a little over halfway through the program and the feedback has been extremely positive.

As an overview, Wyatt begins his coaching relationship with a one-hour session with about half being spent in sharing life experiences as he begins to develop a relationship. During this time together the client names a team of five to eight individuals who will participate in a 360-degree feedback process regarding the client. Wyatt sends out both a quantitative and a qualitative survey to the team to establish a baseline from which to measure the client's progress. When the surveys have been returned, Wyatt consolidates the results into one report and then he and his client review the results looking for overarching themes and obvious areas of concern. The client takes a week to process the results and determine which areas he/she would be motivated to work on for improvement. Once the improvement opportunities are identified, the client and the coach define SMART goals, list the resources and obstacles surrounding those goals, and then collaboratively develop an eight-week growth plan to achieve the desired results.

At this point, the client begins an eight-week, weekly series of half-hour sessions in which he/she reports progress on growth assignments and makes process goals for the coming week. At the end of the eight weeks, Wyatt will send the quantitative feedback survey back out to the team so as to provide a quantitative measure of the client's progress. As a wrap-up, Wyatt will also have the client fill out a Wheel of Life chart to facilitate a meaningful discussion of other areas where life coaching might be of benefit. At that time, the client will be offered the opportunity to receive additional coaching at his or her own expense.

As a pilot of this cutting edge leadership development

system, Wyatt has five highly motivated clients all from the operations side of running the college campus, e.g., the Director of Administration and Counseling, the Director of Library Services, the Director of Facility Services, one of the staff training facilitators, and one of the key IT personnel. The five clients are working on a range of improvement goals such as organization strategies, decision-making skills, and articulation of departmental values, anger management, and improving their social skills. Initial feedback has been extremely positive to this coaching approach to staff development.

It is interesting to note that this entire process is done via telephone—Wyatt has not personally met any of his five clients. Both the coach and the clients are finding this approach to be highly convenient, allowing the clients to maintain their coaching appointments even when away from their offices. Also, since the coach is anonymous, Wyatt feels there is a certain amount of additional openness in what the client is willing to share.

Since this is a secular institution, Wyatt does not feel at liberty to openly share his Christian perspective on issues, but is free to go there if the client takes the conversation in that direction—and several have. Three of the five clients have openly discussed Christian themes or topics and about 15% of the conversations with those three have had Christian overtones. Wyatt feels that this is a great opportunity for a Christian coach who has a heart and desire to bridge the secular world to Christ in whatever way possible—a consistent byproduct of a transformational focus.

Wyatt verifies the hypothesis proposed by CoachVille's Dave Buck (mentioned earlier) that all coaching ultimately leads to life coaching. The weekly process of reviewing action items from previous sessions frequently opens the door for stories from the clients about how they are applying what they are learning in their home/personal lives.

However, Wyatt has chosen not to entertain too much discussion about a client's personal life in his attempt to stay focused on producing quantitative and significant results to the college, especially during this pioneering effort.

Finally, Wyatt compares coaching to his Christian counseling training with the following observation: "I definitely still really enjoy counseling, but coaching is very liberating because I'm able to be more honest and say, 'Hey, I think that is an awesome idea,' or 'One thing that I would caution you about here is....' There is just a liberty to be free and use myself in the process more. With counseling, at least based on my training, you feel far more restricted."

Wyatt is also providing life coaching to a local real estate agent who hired him to help him grow his real estate business. Over the course of their relationship, they have worked on a number of issues including weight management, organizational skills, and gaining a better perspective on the client's identity and life purpose. This young man does not share Wyatt's faith, yet the TLC exercise in which the client was challenged to identify and articulate his values led to a discussion wherein the client acknowledged his recognition and belief in a supreme being that is watching and coordinating the events in his life. This allowed Wyatt to plant some seeds that, by faith, will bear fruit for spiritual transformation at some point in the future.

A Fresh Approach to Bridging People to God
There are several incidents of coaches who have allowed their TLC training to completely revamp their approach to sharing Christ. For example, Rob McCleland is the Dean of the Washington, D.C. branch of Nyack College. At the time of this writing, Rob is finishing up his dissertation on the subject of executive coaching. This is the final requirement to earn his Ph.D. in Organizational Leadership from Regent University. He completed the TLC coach training about two

years ago and has been using his coaching skills in a number of settings, but most notably in the area of personal evangelism. Obviously, his role with Nyack means that he is around Christians a good share of the time, but when he is intentional about it, his role also gives him the opportunity to frequently interact with vendors and other marketplace representatives.

Rob reports that since his TLC training, he takes a much more "coaching" approach to personal evangelism while talking to marketplace people. He finds that when he listens carefully and asks powerful questions such as "What are some of the dreams you want to fulfill?" or "What are some of the things that are holding you back?" that the conversation soon turns inward and easily leads to spiritual issues.

Rob reports finding that people are much more receptive using this approach rather than the eternal destiny approach that he had led with for so many years. He admits that he has an agenda and a "hoped for" line of conversation, but his use of the coaching skills makes this much easier and more natural. In other words, Rob's new approach is just to engage his friend as a holistic person rather than just as a spiritually needy one. Ironically, his new friend often discovers for himself that he is indeed spiritually needy. He finds that often the best places to conduct this type of conversation are over a meal or in a golf cart.

While this example is obviously one that directly applies coaching skills to evangelism, it is also one that clearly demonstrates the power of coaching to reach persons of influence in the marketplace. Coaching opens the door to reach people that may never otherwise hear or listen to the gospel in a church service.

Rob also maintains a coaching relationship with one of his former employees in whom he has seen a radical transformation. Rob recalls that this individual was a "defeated believer" who had grown up in an inner-city environment that nurtured his "victim's mentality" and an overall attitude that the world was out to get him. Essentially, his client went through life feeling that every time something bad happened that it was someone else's fault.

Rob's client regularly attended church, but his victim's attitude had removed God's sovereignty totally out of the picture. Therefore, Rob worked on that sovereignty issue to help his client shift his perspective to see that God was using difficult circumstances to change him into the person He wanted him to be—God loved him too much to allow him to stay the person he was. As his client began to discover that he had been hampering God's plan to grow and mature him, he went through a period of tremendous shame and guilt, but eventually got to a place of repentance. Subsequently, he began to realize that some of the circumstances he faced were "holy" challenges and he needed to seek God's guidance in how he should react. In other words, he began to see things more from a Kingdom perspective. This shift resulted in an incredible change in his countenance. The client became much more patient, and his even his anger and bitterness began to dissipate. In short, he is now a much more pleasant person to be around as he walks around with a smile on his face, ready to face challenges with God's resources.

Rob's client had actually been out of work for several months, but after this amazing transition in his countenance, he actually found himself in the middle of a bidding war for his services. He ended up taking a job at a significant pay increase from what he had been earning. Rob continues to work with this client as they meet together a couple times each month, and Rob is now challenged to see God's sovereignty from a fresh new perspective.

Along those same lines of a shift in the approach to evangelism, Kevin Mahaffy, a youth pastor in the Hampton Roads region of Virginia reports that on a recent visit to his alma mater, Elim Bible Institute, he arranged to have dinner with an individual he had met several years ago while working at a factory in upstate New York. Kevin describes this young man as a person without any goals or purpose in life—just existing from day to day and admittedly very unhappy in virtually all aspects of his life. About three years ago, Kevin had dinner with his friend, and over the course of the meal clearly challenged his friend by sharing God's salvation story through the course of the meal. "This time," reports Kevin, "with the benefit of my coaching training, my approach was a lot different. This time, instead of the telling thing, I did a lot more asking questions and just listening. I asked him a lot of probing questions that got him to thinking about his life. I asked him questions that were designed to get him to think about his life and his future. I asked questions like, 'What do you think is the point of life?' 'Why are you here?' 'What's your purpose?' 'What's your passion?' 'What do you like doing?' It's not that he gave me a bunch of profound answers, but I know I bridged to a new place in his heart and got him thinking more about his life. It was so much more comfortable and natural to do. What I noticed most was the shift in the way I approached him. I know that this time I'm sure that I left him with more to think about than last time."

One last example along these lines comes from Rev. Gary Butler who lives in the eastern panhandle of West Virginia and oversees a denominational retreat center. Gary writes, "I have been building a relationship over the past couple of years with a computer programmer who works in Washington, DC. We met at a golf driving range and have played golf together a number of times. My approach has been to be an authentic friend and take an interest in him rather than be aggressive in pressing him for a spiritual decision. I have not hid the fact that I am both a Christian and a minister.

"I have used the coaching tool of asking questions, and have drawn him out to talk about his life, background, family, job, etc. This has opened the door for me to pray with him two or three times when he has found himself between jobs. He seems to have respect for me and appreciation for our friendship.

"We have invited him to our home and have gone out to eat a number of times. I have invited him to church, but so far, he has not accepted the invitation. I have not tried to tell him how to live his life, but he has asked me for advice concerning a number of personal problems. I believe some bridges have been built between us and our worlds, and that he would call on me in a crisis."

Master Carpenter and Master Coach

John Dorsch is a church planter living with his young family in Maryland. John is just at the midpoint of his TLC coaching training, but is already putting his new skills to good use. God has given John a special church planting vision that combines a new church with a new outreach focus directed at the marketplace. Financially, things are often pretty slow for church planters, and things are no different for the Dorsch family. Fortunately, John was a master carpenter before he came to Regent University to earn his M.A., and that marketplace skill is being utilized now in some very special ways.

Listen as John relates his story: "My family and I moved to the Baltimore Metro area to plant a church and to explore marketplace ministry as a means of reaching unchurched people. As I began my carpentry business here, I was hired by a woman to remodel a bathroom in her old house.

"In the planning and estimating stage, I began to ask the client a series of questions concerning her remodeling job (as usual). It was at this point that she asked me about my background and how I began my business. I was able to then share my testimony of how I came to Christ and how He has called me to ministry through serving people in the marketplace. She found my story interesting, and the job began. It was at that time that I realized that she and her roommate were same sex partners.

"Over the next five weeks, we had many conversations about the Bible, ethics, and Jesus. The clients initiated a good number of our talks. I was able to extend many of the conversations just by being a good listener, by not being judgmental, and by asking the right follow-up questions that were intended to draw conclusions from spiritual truths.

"The last night of the job, we sat down and they offered me a snack and the opportunity to share more about Jesus Christ. I shared the gospel clearly with them. At the end, one of the ladies told me that when I was ready to start my new church, she would like to become part of the first small group. I believe being a servant, being a good listener, and taking the time to ask the right questions to help people come to the truth planted many Kingdom seeds."

Coaching in a Half-way House

Rev. Jeff Sarine is a TLC certified coach who is the associate pastor of a large Methodist church in Maryland. Since completing his coach training, Jeff has been very actively applying the coaching paradigm within multiple venues in his church. At the time of this writing, Jeff is in the process of training a small number of men from his congregation in some of the simpler, more straightforward coaching techniques, e.g., asking powerful questions, listening skills, relationship building, et al. Each of these men will then be assigned a client in their recently established Harvest House, which is a state-approved halfway house for integrating paroled prisoners back into society. Harvest House is a separate not-for-profit entity that is not legally connected to the church in any way, but the visionary behind the project does attend the church that Jeff serves.

Harvest House is set up for no more than seven occupants due to zoning regulations, but plans already exist to purchase additional property to replicate what they are doing as well as to provide similar facilities for women. All of the parolees who are welcomed into the Harvest House facility are screened to ascertain their Christian beliefs and commitment as well as to judge the sincerity of their desire to reform versus just using this as an opportunity to receive parole.

The goal is to draw alongside these men for six months to a year, to establish a significant amount of relational capital, and to help the former inmates get back on their feet, spiritually and otherwise. The coach is there to help his client think through and answer the three basic questions, "Where are you now?" "Where do you want to go?" and "How are you going to get there?"

In addition to the Harvest House ministry, Jeff is currently halfway through a process of leading a number of members of the church who have acknowledged a calling on their life, but who don't know how to proceed, through a program to help them define more clearly what it is that God is calling them to and then develop the steps to move forward in that call. Essentially, Jeff is leading them through a slightly modified form of the TLC *Life Focus* track. Even at this early stage of this program, Jeff reports that great fruit is coming from this effort.

Conclusion

As Daniel Goleman writes in his now famous book, *Working with Emotional Intelligence*, "Unlike IQ [Intelligence Quotient], which changes little after our teen years, emotional intelligence seems to be largely learned, and it continues to develop as we go through life and learn from our experiences—our competence in it can keep growing."46 The author goes on to break down EI into two basic components:

personal competence (consisting of self-awareness, self-regulation, and motivation) and social competence (made up of empathy and social skills). Clearly, learning the fundamental coaching skills leads to a major increase in one's social competence, and likely also positively affects one's personal competence. Goleman continues, "More and more companies are seeing that encouraging emotional intelligence skills is a vital component of any organization's management philosophy."47

Imagine the exponential increase in the power of emotional intelligence if it is nurtured within a Christian worldview. Now, the motivation becomes one of love instead of lust. This is the awesome potential of Christian coaching. It is clearly a servant leadership style of influence...and what better way to be a witness for the power of the Gospel. So many today are Gospel resistant and will only hear through a relationship that either earns a hearing and/or exemplifies Christ.

Many feel that one of the next major moves of God will be a shift away from the traditional church and toward marketplace ministry. It is likely that more can be won to the Kingdom by taking the Gospel to the marketplace than by continuing to seek ways to get the marketplace to come to a church to get the Gospel. In summary, it will be much easier to get an audience with an unbeliever as a coach than it will be as a minister. Christian coaching is one of the major keys to the Kingdom in these last days.

**Reflection and Discussion Questions
Chapter Fifteen: Case Studies
of Salt and Light Coaching**

1. Many people are put off by religion or religious ways of people who communicate to them about significant life issues, even though they might mean well. How might the coaching paradigm break this perception and open up a whole new way of connecting to people? What if every church or ministry organization trained its people to relate in this manner to others, even if they were not actually coaching them?

2. Why might it be difficult for certain segments of the church to embrace the coaching approach to relationships? How does an approach to people as all being made "in the image of God" help to look for the pieces of that image that have been broken by the reality of sin? Where might transformation in your life change the way you look at life?

3. Which of the personal stories came closest to your life situations? What if you had someone like one of these coaches in the past in a significant relationship and conversation? What if you were that coach for some of

the people who have been treated as projects rather than as precious in the sight of God?

4. In the story of the rehabilitation of paroled prisoners what possibilities do you see for reducing the recidivism rate by having inmates coached on their values and purpose in life prior to being released back into the community? How might this enable them to say no to the old patterns by shouting YES to a transformed view of themselves and their future? What if you were playing a significant role as a coach to those who need someone to call forth the best in them?

CHAPTER SIXTEEN

Architects by Design—
Creating Coach Bridge Models
for Mobilizing Revolutionaries

By Dr. Joseph Umidi

In warfare there are a lot of bridges that are blown up. Commerce is ruined, supply lines are broken, and escape corridors are eliminated. Rapid advance of troops make the building of temporary bridges critical for surprise attacks and military maneuvering.

Political and social revolutionaries in most uprisings seek to overtake or destroy the bridge lines of communication by those in authority: media, oil and gas pipelines—whatever can halt the existing regime from supplying and reinforcing its ideology, methodology, or viability in the culture. Many idealistic young rebels with a cause have not thought through the rebuilding of their ruined societies with new bridges that will sustain and prosper a people where they had once been drained and poor.

Today's architects of accelerated learning, strategic and sustainable change, and transformational coaching are creating models for "people growing" that are replacing the worn out and overextended bridges of the past. Stand alone formal classes and lectures have become cost prohibitive, with decreasing connection to real world results. Informal workshops and seminars have sold millions of manuals, tapes, books, and methods without transforming the values participants need to face the inevitable challenges they encounter when they apply what they learned in their unique context. Today, the non-formal approach of coaching, added to the formal and informal approaches, is bridging the gap where the others alone fall short. Those who are traversing these bridges are the revolutionaries who are changing the way we transform people and organizations.

Here is a revolutionary agenda for radical change in the next ten years: bridges of transformation that will mobilize a new generation of life-long learners and transformational learning communities. The following models have been implemented by TLC or have been designed to be launched with the publication of this book:

Marketplace Mastery

Revolutionaries are building bridges from the church to the marketplace. Righteous men and women are finding that there is a Kingdom approach to life and business that will increase the bottom line while not decreasing the moral plumb line. Excellence can be the target without turning our backs on ethics. Integrity has become the key to appropriate the wealth of influence and access as well as finance. This is the day of the "Joseph Company," where promotion that lasts is coming from godly hearts and behavior defined by who we are and not from the political posturing behavior of who we know. Like Joseph in the Bible, there is a marketplace mastery that is saving the nations while serving the Lord of the nations.

TLC has formed strategic partnerships with Lance Learning Associates and other select world-class companies to enable men and women in business, education, government, media, and arts and entertainment to steward the favor they are experiencing with the wisdom necessary to be excellent in their careers. This partnership involves a creative combination of specialized learning resources, assessment instruments, seminar, web and tele-conference learning events, and high impact coaching that transforms the way we approach marketplace opportunities. Reports from participants in the international business community have exceeded expectations since the launch of this program in 2004.

One particular emphasis targets entrepreneurs who are designing and developing creative strategies to impact their target disciplines. Transformational coaching enables them to develop the ambassadorial level of emotional and relational intelligence to influence the gatekeepers in their careers. Core values and principles that give them an uncommon advantage are maximized to position themselves strategically to leverage those connections. Marketplace mastery requires a level of coaching that targets "tipping point" issues and relationships to bring true transformation. These will include the process of overcoming personal and corporate constraints to enhance the impact of these creative innovations and bring a level of mastery that goes beyond the competencies needed in the marketplace in past eras.

One hotel owner manager came to our seminar and signed up for the ongoing group coaching over the next three months. He recently reported that his staff and suppliers have noted a new level of connection and communication with him that they admire and appreciate. He attributes this to the assessment tools and ongoing coaching he has received in relational intelligence that he was able to immediately apply in his context. As a result, he is inviting the entire association of hotel owners and managers to our seminar when we return to his area. When transformation is real, it has its own way of marketing itself.

TLC is designing coaching tracks to help existing coaches understand the unique pressures and opportunities in the marketplace. These materials will be used both in

MBA schools and in coach training schools as the results are reported in field tests. One of our partners has received the leading international award in business coaching in his organization in bringing marketplace mastery to numerous companies.

Seminar Plus

The days of long-term results of stand-alone seminars are over. No longer will high power speakers defraud the high paying listeners into the delusion that they can simply apply the seminar success steps without a transformational change in their own paradigms, perspectives, or core values. A new model has been designed by the architects of the revolution: "Seminar Plus." Now the seminar content and impartation event is coupled with the relational capacity of a transformational coaching process, which makes the difference. This after-seminar "plus" is the key to walking out the principles behind the methods of the seminar manual so that there is a transformational process happening at the heart level after the seminar event. The plus is the support, encouragement, and accountability required for a movement from testimonial inspiration at the meeting to core value transformation after the meeting. Three to six months of coaching based on the key points from the seminar will integrate and inculcate the foundational principles necessary to insure that we will find a way through, around, over, or under the inevitable obstacles we will face in the gap between seminar and reality back home.

TLC has contracted with successful seminar presenters on various need-meeting topics to help them fulfill what they really designed their seminars for in the first place. Many successful people have a unique life message and want to leave a legacy behind of helping others achieve and become what they have in their own lives. Unfortunately, their best selling books, tapes, and seminars will only leave them a financial legacy, while over 90% of the participants will not be able to become or do what is needed on their own after the seminar event.

Now there is a better way; a way that brings sustainable change, a way that transforms a memorable moment into a meaningful movement. The following is one example of the seminar plus format:

A dozen coaches had already read the books, listened to the tapes, and gone over the seminar manual with the presenter the day before the public arrived to this popular one-day event. These coaches had been oriented to the options of assessment instruments they could utilize to meet the goals of that particular seminar's emphasis. They were ready to help participants develop tailor made growth plans to maximize any of the topics of the seminar that they wanted to incorporate into their lives and practice in the days ahead.

During the seminar the presenter kept noting that real change would only come to those who were willing to be part of a learning community for three to six months immediately following this high- powered event. Throughout the breaks participants were able to meet the coaches who were available to discuss how they could help and how they had already helped others. Participants could sign up for weekly group coaching of 6-12 participants by phone, or personal individual coaching sessions by phone. Both of these options would include a peer support partner over that time period. Carefully chosen assessments would be used to determine the specific return on the investment of these transformational coach services.

As a result of this "plus" factor the participants were not disappointed in their investment. The seminar presenter now could under-promise and over-deliver with integrity. The presenter had the satisfaction of adding more testimonials of those who replicated his or her success, including a passive income from those coaches who recruited clients for 3-6 months of coaching at the seminar. The coaches had the opportunity of working with highly motivated clients in which they both spoke the language of the seminar, opening up an opportunity to work with the client's circle of associates and friends to see transformational change in their lives.

Who is willing to pay for the Seminar-Plus model? Companies who want proven results from their training investment dollars are seeing the difference in the six months following a training event as a result of this bridge of transformational coaching. Individuals who are highly motivated for sustainable change are willing to do whatever it takes to move from being hearers only to doers. Those who have become seminar attendees only and who need to be convinced can join the weekly group phone coaching at nominal rates and witness the life changes as coach and a client model the accelerated progress right before their ears.

Transformational Leadership Coaching is partnering with select seminar presenters who have redefined success in terms of not how many seminar seats are filled, but how far others can reach their destiny by standing on their shoulders. Sending capacity is more important than seating capacity. These partnerships are win-win financial relationships that are designed for everyone, including the seminar participants, to receive maximum value for their investment. In addition, speakers find that a select group of these participants are rising to the top and are capable of becoming "associates" who can multiply these seminar presentations for the author. Finally, some who are so impacted by the plus of the coaching relationship will want to become transformational coaches themselves and increase the stable of coaches available to serve select seminar presenters in the years ahead.

Academic Coaching

The "education mountain" has continually been challenged to adjust their methodologies to match the highly competitive realities in today's world markets. The research we have conducted from our alumni has consistently confirmed that the number one issue that students wanted in their college and graduate level experience was a life giving mentoring/coaching relationship with the faculty that most only saw from a distance. That distance between the lectern and the desk is more than a few feet. It represents a generational gap between the hearts of emerging leaders for authentic dialogue and those professors whose own role models were hall of fame writers and heroic figures of inspired lectures.

Launched five years ago as a pilot class experience, TLC has now become the largest coach training organization, offering master's and doctoral level accredited hours in several disciplines: business, leadership, education, divinity, and psychology. The reason is simple but not simplistic. Transformational conversations are not limited to theories and philosophical discourses, but focus on how the life experiences of students, faculty, and administrators inform their values and principles in all of their "off platform" interchanges. Each semester we average 130 students in coach training classes that combine the formal, informal, and non-formal methodologies.

Students are now able to acquire both accredited degrees and coach certification at the same time, and this applies to both campus and distance education models. Utilizing only word of mouth advertising, the number of students taking these courses across the academic disciplines at Regent University in Virginia has been the largest in the history of the school from courses that are only considered electives and not part of a required core. With the increasingly high cost of tuition today, this says much about what is on the agenda for tomorrow's leaders and what they are willing to pay for it.

Recently, over two hundred business faculty professors from colleges across the United States gathered and were informed on how business and executive coaching from a transformational perspective would enhance their student recruitment, retention, and effective placement. As a result of this data, transformational coaching is now offered at Beacon University in Georgia from a distance model with several other schools seeking to incorporate coaching values and methodologies into their traditional delivery systems for education.

In addition to the introduction of transformational coaching into accredited universities, TLC has certified coaches who are providing coach services to high school students who want to find more compelling motivations and results for their pre-college preparation. The success of this three-year pilot program has opened up doors to the home school associations around the world to coach parents on the best ways to champion their children toward academic excellence. There are an increasing number of public school teachers who are taking coaching courses as in-service and continuing education training with several finding revolutionary approaches towards motivating and empowering plateued students into those who excel at the highest levels.

Extraordinary Conversations

Launched initially as the gateway to the TLC Accelerated Coach Training program for organizations, this seminar has become a stand alone introduction to experience the power of coaching conversations. Seminars for leaders of organizations in Canada, Brazil, USA, Korea, Singapore, and Indonesia revealed that those who came with their staff or leadership teams realized the greatest long-term relational impact upon returning to their offices or assignments. Humorously, many staff meetings began to practice these seminar exercises, resulting in a new level of enthusiasm and ownership for the success of these weekly meetings that had long become routine and predictable.

One of the unexpected outcomes of these seminars was the presence and interactions of parents with their teen age youth. To our surprise, we realized that we had created a uniquely safe and fruitful environment for first-time breakthroughs in the communication connections in the family. As a result, TLC is launching a parent/child and a husband/wife extraordinary conversations seminar and coach track to serve the families around the world who are struggling in these critical areas.

What is different from the standard skill training on listening and communicating is that these seminars prioritize the transformational approach to relationships. Certified coach trainers model the level of authenticity and heart for others that go beyond skill sets. When parents and students sense the heart of a coach rather than a skill or formula for coaching, they respond in tender and life-giving ways that have evaded them in the past. It is highly recommended that tissues are available at each setting because of the cleansing flow of tears that will come. Many families are finding a key to breaking and releasing the log jam in past patterns of conversations, and something new and fresh is released in their conversations. In fact, we believe that the conversation itself is the relationship and that the extraordinary conversations that result from this seminar have resulted in extraordinary relationships in the home.

Coach-based Leadership Training

The crying deficit in most organizations is not for certified coaches, but for transformed leaders. Now that TLC has prepared one of the largest pools of certified coaches from a transformational perspective, we have targeted the needs for leadership training as a place to introduce coaching into their tailor made training design. All TLC leadership training events for churches, non-profits, for-profits, and educational institutions begin with personal or organizational constraints that these organizations are targeting for leadership training. These constraints are either known through their own analysis or TLC has contracted with partnering organizations who bring world-class assessment processes to these leaders.

In addition to intensive seminars on these topics, the coach-based training design includes group and individual coaching, peer accountability, personal reflective exercises, and individual growth plans to measure both transformation and performance. A unique aspect of this leadership training is the parallel introduction of the Accelerated Coach Training (ACT) into the organization so that the unique coaching values and methodologies can be sustained by key in house leaders or supervisors responsible for training and development.

The ACT is a 21-week strategy that begins with the Extraordinary Conversations seminar that is open to the entire organization. This is followed by nine weeks of group tele-conferencing of 8-20 key people from the organization, utilizing a hundred-page interactive manual with CD-Rom input. A second one-day seminar prepares these leaders to coach others in the organization. The last eleven weeks brings a combination of tele-conferencing, group, and personal coaching of these leaders as they launch out to coach others. Leaders who complete this process receive an ACT qualified certificate and have two benefits. First, they can steward the coach-based aspect of their organization's leadership training, and second, they may use this qualification toward a professional transformational leadership coach certification that TLC offers for those who desire to utilize coaching as a career or as a key part of their portfolio in their present positions.

TLC has designed several thrusts for coach-based leadership training that are available through our team of certified coaches and coach trainers. These include gifting/designs workshops and training, conflict intervention workshops and training, cell leader coach training, church planting coach training, life purpose/focus workshop and training, marriage and parenting workshop and training, with more on the way. However, one of the values in the transformational process is the integration and activation of our core values integrated in every training event, as compared to a piece-meal approach towards training.

TLC will work with existing organizations to design a comprehensive strategy of leadership training that covers key areas of formation, leadership multiplication, and character and skill replication in an organization. This may involve the introduction of coach-based methods in the existing training programs or the creation of new additional training events that have the coaching methods already integrated within the process. In either case, the goal is measurable transformation, one leader at a time. Without this laser-like bottom line we will fall into the "feel good" training experience trap and see little growth due to the personal and organizational constraints that are the systemic causes to predictable mediocrity in the workplace.

One partnering organization is teaming with TLC to help churches move off the mediocrity plateau and into a healthy growth cycle. Since more than 80% of U.S churches are under 90 people, most will need an integrated process to reach and assimilate more members, workers, and leaders, and in today' culture, do so in a highly personalized one-on-one manner. This process will maximize the transformational aspects discussed in these chapters so that formal, informal, and non-formal approaches will each have its place in raising up the next generations of leaders who start and finish well.

Coaching Connection Centers

As the number of coaches continues to grow around the world, more and more people and organizations desire to know how to learn more about their services or their training. Standard of training, ethical integrity of practices, and quality of service will vary as there is more chaos than cohesion in the coaching industry. One volunteer organization, the International Coach Federation (ICF), has done a tremendous work in clarifying the foundational ethics and practices to make the coaching profession start at the highest levels. They have also developed a thorough methodology to insure that coach training produces results and have set standards of accrediting for coach training organizations to meet their seal of approval. TLC is in the process of applying to meet their standards. Progress on this can be seen by viewing our website atwww.transformationalcoaching.com. It is our full intention for our transformational coaches to meet or exceed these standards as we fulfill our mandate to launch a sustainable and effective coaching movement throughout the nations.

A number of our coach trainers have collaborated to design a replicating center for coaching services in various cities around the world. These centers are designed to expose people to coaches, coach training, and coaching methodologies for their personal or organizational needs. These centers will involve coaches from various companies and coach training schools as they partner together to serve their communities in tangible ways. Orientations on coaching, free coaching sessions, resources on coaching, and assessments on what kind of coaching and coaching leadership can best meet one's needs will be available at these centers.

Some of these centers, as the one in Kansas City, will emphasize the opportunity to understand life purpose by pursing this in a small group format led by trained coaches. Others, as is designed for Philadelphia, will emphasize the urgent needs of single parenting and family coaching issues in the underserved urban community context. South Africa's center will bring coach training to community workers who are seeking to stem the tide of the AIDS plague in their culture. Each center is designed to address the needs in their context and will meet certain standards to carry to promise of transformational change that is at the heart of the TLC mission.

Reflection and Discussion Questions
Chapter Sixteen: Architects by Design—Creating
Coach Bridge Models for Mobilizing Revolutionaries

1. How does the model of marketplace mastery mobilize you to see the role of coaching to accelerate your career calling in the workplace? What would it take for you to host such a seminar plus in your area? What role might you have in presenting this strategy to the nations?

2. Which high powered seminar have you attended this past year in which you initially raved about to others but now cannot see any real difference it made in your life? How does that reinforce the "plus" aspect of this coach model?

3. What would your academic training have been like if it included the academic coaching model discussed in this chapter? How might parents and educators become more effective in championing academic excellence through coaching? What role might you have in this arena?

4. Think of the last leadership training you received in a company or church. What role could coaching have played to enhance its effectiveness? How would you

design your organization's training strategy if you were a TLC certified coach trainer?

5. How might your organization utilize the accelerated coach training (ACT) described in this chapter? Would you be willing to bridge your organization's key people to a TLC representative to discuss how this may be a good fit for them at this time?

Endnotes

Section One Endnotes

1. See www.transformationalcoaching.com.
2. See *The 8th Habit*, Stephen R. Covey, Free Press, 2004, pgs. 93ff.
3. From conversations with Bob Biehl and video presentation called "Fourth Grade".
4. See discussion in author's article, "Lessons from the Coach", Ministries Today, March/April 2003.
5. A "coaching moment" is taking 5 to 10 minutes during a training appointment to formally coach a trainee through solving a particular problem or working on a personal issue.
6. "Lessons from the Coach", Ministries Today, March/April 2003.
7. Personal conversation with George Barna.
8. From seminar presenter Norm Wakefield, 2003.
9. See ACT website link from TLC website.
10. See author's article, "The Post-Modern Road Less Traveled", Envoy, Spring 2005 at www.vanguard-ministires.org.
11. John Eldredge, *Waking the Dead*, Thomas Nelson, 2003, pgs. 84ff.

Section Two Endnotes

12. See *Fierce Conversations*, Susan Scott, Viking Press, 2002.
13. My predictions of the Emerging Leader as Coach will have the following characteristics: more highly

relational, emotionally secure, empowers others well, listens and questions more, less formal in structures and titles, serves others more than being served.

14. This prejudice may come from the legitimate criticism of the wholesale embracing of the CEO style of leadership, borrowed from the business community that has been adopted by many megachurches, without an honoring of the biblical values and principles that this chapter is targeting.

15. One of our coaching partner church planting movements in Colombia, South America, first heard of coaching through one of their members who was a trained corporate coach in an international trading company based in the capital city of Bogotá. When they realized we could offer them a thoroughly biblical approach to coach training with the same degree of excellence, they brought us in to work with her. After the first six months, she said that nothing she experienced in coach training compared to the transformation that she experienced in this process.

16. Matthew 23 reveals the passionate righteous anger that Jesus expressed toward the toxic misuse of spiritual authority.

17. See Appendix for the present status of TLC certification and the International Coach Federation (ICF) accreditation.

18. See *Where are We Now*, William Beckham, Touch Glocal Publications, 2004.

19. See *Questioning Evangelism*, Randy Newman, Kregel Publications, 2004.

20. Williams, J. Rodman, *Renewal Theology.*

21. Greenleaf, Robert K., *Servant Leadership.*

22. Contact the TLC website for coaching packages

that include 360 degree assessments for you and your organization.

23. In a personal discussion with Dr. Ralph Neighbour of Touch Ministries International, Dr. Umidi was challenged to research his statement that it takes at least six experiences with relational debriefing feedback to add or change someone's core values.

24. See the powerful DVD series," Band of Brothers" by Stephen Spielberg and Tom Hanks.

25. "Finishing Well: The Challenge of a Lifetime," J Robert Clinton, Plenary address given to 1994 Leadership Forum, Estes Park, CO, 13-14. Clinton identifies 6 characteristics of leaders who "finish well:"

   • They maintain a personal vibrant relationship with God right up to the end
   • They maintain a learning posture, can learn from various kinds of sources
   • They evidence Christ-likeness in character as seen by the fruit of the Spirit
   • Truth is lived out in their lives so that convictions and promises of God are seen to be real.
   • They leave behind one or more "ultimate contributions"
   • They walk with a growing awareness of a sense of destiny and see some or all of it fulfilled.

26. Clinton, J Robert, FW 10-12.

27. "The Mantle of the Mentor: An Exhortation to Finish Well," J Robert Clinton plenary address given to the 1993 International Foursquare Convention, Louisville, Kentucky. This simple notion may seem self-evident at first sight, but contains a powerful key to enable leaders to get

"un-stuck" and move into new personal growth patterns. Rather than looking for the be-all and end-all master mentor, frustration yields to fruitfulness when we identify specific growth needs and areas, and cultivate an array of empowering relationships accordingly.

28. Clinton defines coaching as an intensive type of mentoring, one of several mentoring types which range from more intensive and deliberate to less so. Our use of the term overlaps with Clinton's, but draws also from the evolving coaching paradigm in the marketplace, which incorporates dimensions of formal and non-formal coach-training, certification, continuing education, professional coach-client relationships and organizational consultation. Clinton's mentoring resource material is highly recommended for further reading, beginning with *Connecting: The Mentoring Relationships You Need to Succeed in Life*, with Paul D. Stanley, NavPress, Colorado Springs, CO, 1992, and the manual-styled *The Mentoring Handbook: Detailed Guidelines and Helps for Christian Mentors and Mentorees*, with Richard W. Clinton, 1991, available through Barnabas Publishers, 2175 N. Holliston Ave., Altadena, CA 91001.

29. Related to the concept of "finishing well," Clinton identifies a late-life "convergence phase" in the lives of some Christian leaders, where God moves the leader into a role that matches gift-mix, experience, temperament, etc. During this phase, the leader is freed from ministry that doesn't match his or her gifting, and the best the leader has to offer is enhanced and put to use. "The major developmental task for [the convergence phase]," Clinton observes, "is the guidance of the leader into a role and place

where he can have maximum effectiveness. His response to God's guidance must be to trust, rest, and watch as God moves him toward a ministry that embodies all the development of preceding phases. Convergence manifests itself as he responds consistently to God's work in his life." *The Making of a Leader*, p. 47. While Clinton's research indicates that a minority of leaders actually experience convergence, our response to God and His processing is one of the major variables which determines the outcome. Mentors and coaches can be invaluable assets in helping us identify and respond well to developmental opportunities, and thus in staying on course toward our own "convergence phase." Convergence, then, is not simply a theoretical construct, but both a lifestyle and a destination.

Section Three Endnotes

30. C. Peter Wagner at his conference on Marketplace Ministry, 2004.
31. See Primal Leadership by Daniel Goleman, Richard Boyatzis, and Annie McKee, 2002, Harvard Business School Press
32. See www.lancelearning.com
33. http://www.icwm.net/articles.asp
34. "2005 A Season of Separation," an internet letter from Doug Fortune.
35. Strong's Concordance, 3498, yathar or yateer, "a primitive root; to jut over or exceed; by implication, to excel."
36. See Emotional Intelligence, Daniel Goleman, Bantam Books, 1997.
37. From *D.L. Moody*, by Daniel Day.
38. From *Maximized Manhood*, a book by the late Dr. Ed Cole.

Section Four Endnotes

39. See my book, *Confirming the Pastoral Call*, Kregel Publications, 2003 where I make a case for coming to grips with a ministry match in or out of the church.

40. See the 2003 PhD dissertation in the School of Leadership at Regent University, an important study on return on investment for coaching.

41. Webster's Dictionary

42. Ibid

43. Relational mirrors – those who first of all believe the best in us and covenant to walk with us as we discover God's purpose for our lives. They commit to providing support, encouragement and accountability. Not for the purposes of control but with the goal of lasting personal transformation.

44. See *Work Types*; by Jean M. Kummerow, Nancy J. Barger & Linda K. Kirby, Warner Books, 1997.

45. See *Barbara Bush: A Memoir*, New York: A Lisa Drew Book, Charles Scribner's Sons, 1994.

46. Goleman, Bantam Books, 1998, p. 7.

47. Ibid.

Contributing Author's Biographies

✦

Joseph Umidi, Senior Editor

Joseph received his Doctor of Ministry degree from Trinity Evangelical Divinity School and has taught at Regent University Divinity School for the past 20 years. His years of ministry experience include senior leadership positions in several churches, including his present position as senior overseer of six churches in the Tidewater, Virginia area. Dr. "J", as he is affectionately known by students, has received awards as outstanding teacher of the year, master mentor, and is well known as a leading coach and trainer. Dr. Umidi is the president and founder of Transformational Leadership Coaching (TLC, Inc.), and has been trained in the International Coach Federation (ICF) certified CTI school, accumulating the required hours to receive his PCC credentials with ICF in 2005. Dr. Umidi teams with his wife of thirty three years, Marie, with a passion to equip and release young men and women, in ministry and the marketplace, all over the world in their gifting and callings. Joseph and Marie have one married son and two grandchildren.

Andrew T. Arroyo

Andrew T. Arroyo began his ministry journey in 1993. Since that time, his diverse ministry tenure has included networking for regional stadium prayer, teaching in Christian and secular environments, pastoring an urban church, and participating in the house church movement. His three published books include /Seeds of Maturity/ (2002),

/Postured for Power/ (2003), and /Postured for Power Team Edition/ (2004). Andrew has also experienced success as a coach and manager in the corporate marketplace.

Charlene Fike

Charlene is a successful entrepreneur, creative problem-solver, and recent empty-nester. She met a youthful goal to own five businesses by the age of 40 as the ultimate entrepreneur, Jesus, taught her through trial and error principles of Kingdom inspired business. Charlene continues to work on business development and networks with others in business to mentor emerging marketplace leaders. She is passionate about networking artisans and creating an internet-based marketing platform which will empower disadvantaged women across cultures. Charlene is a gourmet cook, avid reader, and adventurous traveling companion for her husband Doug and children Justin and Janelle. For more information about Doug and Charlene Fike, access www.growthdynamics.org.

Doug Fike

Doug Fike serves as Executive Director of Growth Dynamics International, based in Warm Springs, Virginia. He and his wife Charlene operate a retreat center high in the Allegheny Mountains, where they walk with Kingdom leaders during times of transition, burnout, or retooling for a new season. The Fikes live in community and travel widely, encouraging leaders from a variety of spheres; wrestling with what it means to be the church unleashed in the new millennium. Previously Doug served as a church planter, pastor, and denominational renewal executive. He is a popular conference speaker, seasoned mentor, and passionate follower of Jesus. Doug is a founding partner of Transformational Leadership Coaching. For more information about Growth Dynamics International, access www.growthdynamics.org.

Jerry Graham

Jerry received an MS in Engineering from the University of Arkansas, M.Div. from Regent University and a D.Min. from Fuller Theological Seminary. His rich work experience includes 25 years with Eastman Kodak, Associate Pastor, and church growth consultant to over 150 churches. Jerry served Vanguard Ministries as its Executive Director during its formation and startup years, and has now transitioned into a marketplace ministry role as a lifestyle coach and home business consultant. Jerry is a certified Master Trainer with Transformational Leadership Coaching and is also serving Regent University's Master of Leadership Coaching program as an Adjunct Professor. For further information on Jerry Graham, log on to www.coachingpastors.com.

Bobby Hill

Bobby is the International Director of Vanguard Ministries, a global apostolic network of leaders and churches. Bobby has served the Lord for more than 30 years in ministry, as missionary and church planter; traveling extensively, preaching, teaching, consulting, and coaching domestically and abroad. His heart is to identify, train, and mobilize ministry leaders and to build and strengthen healthy churches. He is a recognized apostolic leader with strong teaching and prophetic gifts and a spiritual father to leaders across the globe. Bobby graduated from Regent University with an MA in Practical Theology, where he currently serves as an Adjunct Professor. For further information on Vanguard Ministries, access www.vanguardministries.org.

Pam Johnson

Pam's 18 years of successful real estate experience, her strong work ethic and dedication to a "servants-heart" attitude towards her customers has earned her the honor of being in the top 1% of the 3500 realtors in all of the greater Hampton Roads area in eastern Virginia. Pam is a certified Transformational Leadership Coach, and has coached and trained multiple award winning real estate teams, and mentored numerous community business leaders in the development of their unique marketplace ministry niche. Married to her best friend Johnny for 35 years, Pam has two grown children, daughter Amy and Son Chris and his wife Ana. Find out more information on Pam Johnson's award winning real estate team at www.servants-heart.com.

Tony Stoltzfus

Tony has 20 years experience in the business world, and 25 years in local and trans-local church leadership. He currently serves as Director of Training for Transformational Leadership Coaching, and was instrumental in developing the foundation for the transformational process of TLC. A full-time coach and coach trainer since 1999, Tony has a passion to help pastors and leaders discover their unique calling and destiny, create a balanced lifestyle, and navigate career transitions and wilderness seasons of life that leaders experience. Tony, his wife of 18 years and two children reside in Virginia Beach, Virginia. Discover more about Tony's passion to support pastors and leaders at www.coach-ingpastors.com.

Lance Wallnau

For twelve years Lance has been an advisor, consultant and coach for numerous CEO's, entrepreneurs, universities, corporations, nonprofit organizations and world leaders. Lance is engaged by organizations worldwide, including the United Nations, for executive team development. His perceptive consulting skills and captivating teaching style place him in high demand across America in conferences and seminars. Lance graduated at the top of his class from an elite U.S. military academy, and has an impressive background as an oil industry executive. Lance is Director of Pneuma Institute; and serves as President and CEO of the LanceLearning Group. Lance, his wife Annabelle and three children live in Rhode Island. Learn more about Lance's passion at www.lancelearning.com.

Bibliography

Brotman, L.E., Liberi, W.P., & Wasylyshyn, K.M. 1998. "Executive Coaching: The Need for Standards of Competence." *Consulting Psychology Journal: Practice and Research 50*(1), 40-46.

Collins, Gary. 2001. *Christian Coaching*. NavPress.

Elderdge, John. 2003. *Waking the Dead.* Thomas Nelson.

Goldsmith, Lyons, Freas. 2000. *Coaching for Leadership.* Jossey-Bass.

Goleman, D. 1998. *Working with Emotional Intelligence.* London: Bloomsbury Publishing

Hudson, F. M. 1999. *The Handbook of Coaching.* San Francisco: Jossey-Bass.

Katzenback, J.R. 1999. *Topgrading: How Companies Win by Hiring, coaching, and Keeping the Best People,* Prentice Hall, Englewood Cliffs, N.J.

Kiel, F., Rimmer, E., Williams, K., & Doyle, M. 1996. "Coaching at the Top." *Consulting Psychology Journal: Practice & Research, 48*(2), 67-77.

Kilburg, R. R. 1996. "Toward a Conceptual Understanding and Definition of Executive Coaching." *Consulting Psychology Journal: Practice & Research, 48*(2), 134-144.

Kilburg, R. R. 1997. "Coaching and Executive Character: Core Problems and Basic Approaches." *Consulting Psychology Journal: Practice & Research, 49*(4), 281-299.

Knowles, M. S. 1970. *The Modern Practice of Adult Education: Andragogy Versus Pedagogy.* New York, NY: Associated Press.

Lombardo, Michael and Robert Eichenger. 1996. *For Your Improvement: A Development and Coaching Guide.* Lominger Limited, Inc. ISBN: 0-9655712-0-3

Weisinger, Hendrie. *Emotional Intelligence at Work.* Jossey-Bass, 2000. ISBN: 0-7879-5198-6

Whitworth, Laura. 1998. *Co-Active Coaching: New Skill for Coaching People in Work and Life.* Davis-Black Pub.

Zeus, P., & Skiffington, S. (222). *The Complete Guide to Coaching at Work.* Sydney: McGraw Hill.

Transformational Leadership Coaching Tools

+==+

Transformational Leadership Coaching

Looking For Something

Leadership coaching is what today's Christian leaders are looking for—a coach to cheer them on, challenge them to a go deeper and reach higher, and help them stay focused on fulfilling their life purpose. Do you have the heart of a Christian coach? Many ministry leaders who've been through coach training say they've been coaching all their lives, they just never realized it. Coaches love to help others discover who they are and live out that destiny, and are energized by seeing people transformed at a deep level. Raising up leaders, building transparent relationships and seeing the potential in people are all a big part of Christian coaching.

Become a Coach

Does that sound like you? If so, becoming a certified leadership coach through TLC can take your effectiveness to a whole new level. Our professional coach training program gives you the tools to make every conversation transformational.

And if you're looking for an effective, systematic way to build and empower leaders throughout your organization, coaching could be the answer. TLC offers a complete program of services for bringing coaching to your organization, including:

- Full <u>professional certification</u> for key staff.
- The ability to become a TLC certified <u>coach trainer</u> for your organization and run TLC programs in-house.
- <u>Coaching workshops</u> and vision-raising events.
- An on-site, <u>accelerated training program</u> for groups.

What is Coaching Like?

What exactly is leadership coaching? In short, it's a one-on-one relationship where a coach helps you take the actions you want to take to reach a goal. Coaches are personal change experts who help others fulfill their destiny. Professionally trained in a unique set of leadership skills, coaches help others identify important goals and priorities, strategize about how to reach them, and overcome obstacles that crop up along the way.

Coaching appointments begin with a chance for you to report on your progress, and end with a clear set of action steps you choose to take in the week ahead. But what is that essential spark between you and your coach that makes the relationship so transformational? Below are four facets of the power of coaching:

- ***Coaching is a Transformational Conversation.*** The biggest surprise for first-time clients is realizing that the coach isn't there to give advice. Instead, powerful, incisive coaching questions stimulate you to examine the things in life that matter most from new angles. A coaching conver-

sation can transform the way you look at life.
- ***Coaching is a Transparent Relationship.***
A coach is a friend and confidant, your greatest supporter, someone who knows you well enough to recognize your greatness and then challenge you to rise to it. A transparent relationship with a coach frees you to go to places you've never gone before.
- ***Coaching is a Support System for Change.***
With support, encouragement and accountability from someone who believes in us, we can do far more than we'd ever accomplish alone. A coach helps you stay on track, overcome obstacles and convert your want-to into concrete steps that get in your date book and get done.
- ***Coaching is Continuous Leadership Development.***
Coaches don't give solutions: they help you solve your own problems. Coaching is helping you learn instead of telling you what to do. By leveraging every situation to build your capacity as a leader and a person, coaching prepares you to conquer much bigger challenges in the future.

The Distinctives of Transformational Leadership Coaching (TLC)

TLC coaching certification is a 40-week training experience designed to provide the practical skills and formation you need to succeed as a leader and a coach. It will probably be unlike any training you've ever experienced. Instead of simply reading or hearing about coaching skills, you'll meet every week with a personal coach or your peer to practice, role play, and get feedback on your progress. Whenever a new concept is presented, you'll get a chance to actually try it out, often in your own leadership sphere. Periodically, you'll meet with a larger group of fellow trainees for intensive practice in listening, asking questions, and other core coaching skills. Here are some other distinct characteristics of TLC training:

- **Values-Based**
  Designed from the ground up as a *Christian* coach training program by experienced ministry leaders. Starting from scratch with a solidly-grounded Christian value set and worldview has allowed us to adapt the best that the business world has to offer without compromising core Christian values.

- **Relational**
  Trainees get to meet biweekly throughout the program with a personal coach, and form a lasting, transparent relationship with a peer mentor. For many, the authentic relationships are the best part of the program!

- **Transformational**
  TLC training is based on the idea that "out of the abundance of the heart the mouth speaks". When you develop the heart of a coach, when you've really gotten coaching values down inside you, the right words will flow out natural. Great coaching is more than knowing coaching skills; it is *becoming* a coach from the inside out.

- **Real World**
  TLC uses an experiential training approach, rather than one that is classroom-centered.

For instance, you'll learn about healthy accountability by being accountable and holding others accountable on real issues, not simply by reading a book about it. Actually doing the things you are hearing and learning about vastly increases retention—and confidence!

The Transformational Leadership Coaching's Core Coaching Values

Transformation is Primarily Experiential, Not Informational

We fully grasp Kingdom principles when we see them in action and experience them at work in our own lives. Therefore, our focus will be on skills and formation becoming *actual practiced reality* in each coach's life, a reality they are equipped to pass on to others.

God Initiates Transformation Through Real, Everyday Life Experiences

God is the sovereign initiator of our growth, setting the agenda by getting our attention, motivating us to change and teaching His principles within the real events of our lives. Therefore, we will model, teach and discover together how 'all things work together for good' for those who are attuned to God's purposes and are learning from life.

Ministry Flows Out of Being

A coach can best impart to others what God has built into his or her life. Kingdom leadership ultimately rises or falls on character and formation, not skills or information. Therefore, we will learn to transform others through being transformed ourselves.

Each Person is a Uniquely Designed Individual Whom God has Entrusted With a Stewardship Over Their Own Life

Coaching deals with real lives, each one with a distinctive gift package, a different past, a unique call, and a God-given stewardship of the life He has given them. Therefore, we will respect God's design by building on a foundation of gifting, design and destiny.

Kingdom Success is Defined by Growth and Change

When God builds leaders, He is less interested in success and productivity than in forming who we are in Christ. Therefore, we will redefine Kingdom "success" in terms of growth, learning and formation as foundational to outward success and productivity.

We Will Invest Strategically in Leaders in a Way That Calls and Teaches Them to Impact Others

The investment of a coach or leader's time yields much greater returns when it activates and equips a person to pass on to others with what God has done for them. Therefore, our coaching will focus on helping clients become conscious competent so they can effectively pass on what God has given them to others.

Why Become a Coach

While some go on to become full-time coaches, most individuals who enter TLC coach training want coaching skills to use in their current position. Coaching is such a fast-growing profession precisely because it connects with the real needs of today's leaders. Here are some ways you might benefit from professional coach training:

- Improve skills in communication, conflict management and leadership development.

- Learn a proven, replicable way to build leadership character.
- Add an exciting new service to your counseling practice.
- Make a quantum leap in your ability to develop a team and keep it performing at a high level.
- Connect with post moderns, who love the focus on relationship, authenticity and experiential learning.

TLC offers training for individuals who wish to become coaches, as well as special services to organizations that want to begin an internal coaching or coach training program.

Training Overview

Here's a quick overview of the nuts and bolts of the certification process. TLC training is comprised of three segments, or "*tracks*", which you'll complete consecutively to become a coach. Each track includes approximately 60 training hours, for a total of 180 hours over the course of the 40 week training program.

New training cycles start three times a year on a semester schedule, beginning in January, May and August. The first track you'll take, <u>Formation</u>, focuses on the basic equipment of coaching: change tools, core coaching values, and on building coaching relationships. The second track is <u>Life Focus</u> dealing with destiny discovery and goal setting. The final track, <u>Implementation</u>, pulls together all you've learned and applies it to real coaching situations, with a focus on the coaching process, action steps, growth plans, and engaging growth issues.

You'll work from the TLC coaching manual, which includes over 300 pages of handouts, tools and exercises.

The manual is written in an exercise format, so you'll be completing exercises that you can turn around and give to clients as action steps when you start coaching. Many of the exercises are designed to be done as part of everyday leadership responsibilities, leveraging your time and helping you immediately apply what you are learning in real life.

The process is highly relational, including a peer coach you'll meet with every other week as well as biweekly meeting with your own personal coach (included in the training). In short, you'll learn coaching by being coached and coaching others, instead of by reading or hearing about coaching. There is also plenty of time for reflection, role-playing, practice, self-discovery, and feedback and debriefing.

What's Included

Here are some things you'll receive from TLC that are often extra-cost options or not available at all through competing programs:

- Regular appointments with your own ***personal coach*** throughout the training (Included!)
- Three individual day-long interactive workshops.
- A 300-page color-printed ***coaching manual*** with over 100 coaching exercises and dozens of tools, handouts and worksheets.
- All input is on 20 professionally-produced CD-ROMs you can also use with your clients.
- Access to promotional materials and outlines needed to put on several coaching-based training workshops using the materials in your coaching manual.
- A license to freely duplicate materials from the manual for your own one-on-one coaching.
- Twice the number of instructor contact hours as

in some competing programs.
* The option to get 9-15 hours of **graduate credit** or C.E.U.s for your coach training courses.

The Methodology

Celebrate the Difference!

While TLC training is based on patterns Jesus used with his own disciples, it will probably be completely different than any other course you've been through. For instance, there are almost no large-group sessions or classroom settings. Instead, one-on-one relationships are the key venue for the training, and most of your time will be spent actually *doing* things instead of hearing about how to do them. There are solid reasons for taking this approach. For instance, adult learning research at the National Testing Labs in Bethel, Maine found that the retention rate for lectures hovers around five percent. However, for discussion retention rises to 50 percent, for hands-on practice it reaches 70 percent, and when learners teach the material to others, retention hits 90 percent—nearly 20 times more than from a lecture! Clearly, interactive, relational training methods simply work better.

How Leaders Learn

The *Learning Circle* begins with a problem or challenge we face. The problem motivates us to go out and find a solution. Once we learn the new paradigm, skill or principle we need, we immediately apply it to the problem at hand. Because we're working at a real life situation, we then get some feedback—either our solution works, or it doesn't (or maybe it works but creates a whole new set of challenges!) Finally, our observations and reflections on what happened lead us to formulate new principles about how life works which we apply to the next challenge that comes along.

Life as a Classroom

Leaders grow best in real life situations and real relationships. Here are some concrete ways TLC training builds on how leaders actually learn:

- Training happens in the context of relationships with a coach and a peer.
- Weekly discussion times reinforce learning.
- Apprentices get regular feedback from their coach.
- 15% of training time is input; 85% is integration and application.
- Key skills are practiced repeatedly to build mastery.

Wherever possible, TLC training makes use of your existing relationships and leadership commitments, both to maximize impact and to minimize the time and energy training requires.

We encourage you to 'double up' on the interactive exercises wherever possible—do them with people you already need to meet with, as dates with your spouse, or with your leadership team. With the TLC way, what you learn will make a real difference in your life!

The Curriculum

Core Training Tracks

Certified coaches receive approximately 180 hours of training, divided into three tracks, each three months long. Training averages about four hours per week. The program is meant for those involved in ministry or leadership, and many exercises are designed to be done within current leadership responsibilities. The core TLC training tracks, with a brief synopsis of what the prospective coach learns in each, are as follows:

- **Formation:** Experiential learning of the bedrock values, techniques and relationships used to coach others through change. Apprentices develop personal accountability, authenticity, listening skills, a personal mentoring constellation, and patterns of reflection and receiving feedback.
- **Life Focus:** Apprentices discover their own calling and design while learning to coach others through the same discovery process. Covers dreaming, establishing a personal value set, goal-setting and a biblical life-planning process that systematically moves learners toward their dreams and calling.
- **Implementation:** Provides a framework for coaches to turn what they've learned in other tracks into concrete strategies ("growth plans") to coach virtually any life issue. This track also provides practical tools for identifying, discerning and engaging growth issues in others in a positive way.
- **Coach Trainer Track:** Walks a prospective trainer through the art of developing others as professional or non-professional coaches. This track also includes instruction in role-playing, coaching based-training, and how to set up and maintain an ongoing coaching and coach training program in your organization.
- **Gift-Based Ministry:** Focuses on the effective use of gifts in everyday leadership. Includes identifying your own gifts and those of others, then forming an in-depth understanding of each gift type. Learners practice communicating with, developing and deploying each gift for maximum team effectiveness.

Certified coaches complete the following three tracks: Formation, Life Focus and Implementation. Trainers are certified coaches who have gone on to complete the Coach Trainer track (for a total of four).

The Relationships

Your Trainer

Trainers are certified by TLC to train prospective coaches. They're seasoned leaders we've hand-picked, with a calling and proven ability in leadership development. Your trainer has completed every exercise you'll do during your training and is intimately familiar with the materials. The trainer is your guide during the certification process, modeling the skills and heart of a coach and providing feedback and perspective on your development. A life-giving relationship naturally develops between the two of you during the course of the training, as you meet every other week to review exercises, discuss what you are learning and troubleshoot any rough spots. The trainer also provides accountability for completing the weekly assignments.

Boundaries

Because coach training is a structured process culminating in certification, trainers will keep the relationship focused on the TLC curriculum. While they'll want to hear about what's going on in your life, the relationship with your trainer is not intended to be your primary source of support or perspective for your life. If you need counseling, extended prayer ministry, a buddy, or just someone to talk to regularly, the trainer will help you focus on developing other relationships to meet these needs.

Your Peer Coach

Authentic, growth-oriented relationships with peers are

vital to fulfilling the call of God on your life. TLC is committed to developing the skills and the habit of peer coaching in everyone we coach, so we've built in peer coaching as an essential part of coach training. You'll meet with your peer coach every other week for support, encouragement and accountability, and to discuss and apply what you're learning. Commitment to TLC training is also a commitment to your peer, because you'll walk through each step of the training process together. Your investment in your peer coaching relationship sets the stage for all that happens in TLC training.

TLC Certification

A TLC Trained Coach has completed our three core training tracks (Formation, Life Focus and Implementation—a total of 180 training hours) under the supervision of a trainer. TLC Trained Coaches are qualified to provide as-needed coaching to other leaders, and are licensed to use the TLC name and materials to coach others.

A TLC Trainer is a TLC coach who has also completed the TLC Coach Trainer track (a total of 240 training hours) and meets the higher continuing education requirements for trainers. Trainers are generally certified for a particular organization, and are qualified to train and certify new coaches, supervise coaches and run an ongoing coaching program within that organization. Trainers who function within the TLC coach-training system also complete one year of monthly supervision by a senior trainer. Contact TLC for additional information on the various levels of certification.

The Accelerated Coach Training Program (A.C.T.)

Many organizations want to provide coach training for leaders who will coach a few others or coach on a volunteer basis. TLC's new <u>Accelerated Coach Training Program</u> (A.C.T.) was designed for situations where serious coach training is needed but the time commitment to a full professional training program is not possible.

The ACT program uses the same exercises, role plays and coaching processes as our flagship professional certification program, but in a more accessible time frame. We'll come on-site to train a group of eight or more of your leaders (this program is only offered to groups), and have them coaching in only nine weeks. Each individual gets four sessions with a professional coach, a great relationship with a peer partner and a 100-page color coaching manual filled with useful resources. We even include 12 additional weeks of follow-up support while you coach, to make sure you get off to a great start.

Training Overview

The ACT program focuses on the change tools, values and relational skills needed for excellent coaching. Topics we'll cover include:

- Building authentic relationships
- Asking powerful questions
- Intuitive listening
- Providing healthy, empowering support and accountability
- The core coaching values and learning paradigm

The program kicks off with "Extra-Ordinary Conversations", a day-long interactive role-playing workshop (which can also be opened to the public), follows with 8 weeks of peer practice sessions, tele-classes, and life application exercises; then wraps up with a second interactive workshop. This first phase takes less than 3 hours per week. Phase II includes being coached and getting feedback on your own coaching from a professional coach, as well as 12 weeks of monthly training tele-classes and coaches' support meetings. This second phase is designed to minimize the impact on your schedule, and takes only an hour or so a week.

TLC even provides an upgrade path to our <u>professional program</u>, so if you decide you want professional coach training after finishing the ACT program, you'll still get credit for what you've completed. For more information on the ACT program, contact the TLC registrar at Coaching@Regent.edu, call 757-226-4884, or see our web site at www.ACTProgram.net

Workshops and Seminars

TLC offers a variety of workshops and coaching classes you can sponsor as leadership training events and to introduce coaching to your organization. Below are brief descriptions of several TLC workshops

Extraordinary Conversations

Most leaders spend a good portion of their time listening, asking questions, and talking things through. What would it be worth to you if you (and the leaders you serve with) could increase the effectiveness of your conversations? The Extraordinary Conversations workshop does just that, using proven coaching techniques to increasing the impact of your conversations. You'll take your listening to a new level, learn to ask powerful, incisive questions, and develop better relationships with those around you along the way.

Structure: One day workshop, two half-day workshops, or eight session tele-class.

Presenter: Varies
Marketing Resources: Promotional Flyer with session outlines available.

Discover Your Gifting

The Discover Your Gifting workshop uses interactive coaching techniques to help people discover—*and use*—their gifts. Innovative learning games are used to demonstrate the characteristics of each gift and train participants in how to understand and communicate more effectively with others. It's fun, engaging, and it will transform the way you relate to those with a different gift than yours.

Workshop sessions also cover gifts and conflict and developing gift-based teams. The workshop is based on the Motivational Gifts found in Romans 12. Participants receive a gift assessment and a set of fact sheets covering the characteristics of all seven gifts plus the gift combinations.

Structure: Workshop, one day plus an evening or other formats.
Presenter: Various
Marketing Resources: Brochure available (printed or e-flyer).
Materials: Additional gifting resources including books, gift assessments and CD-ROM input sessions are also available.

The Coaching Vision Seminar

The Coaching Vision Seminar gives you an overview of the exciting possibilities of leadership coaching. TLC's founder, Dr. Joseph Umidi, explores why coaching is becoming a worldwide movement and how it can transform your organization. The seminar also demonstrates key coaching techniques and expounds the values and learning philosophy that make coaching uniquely suited for today's leadership climate. This seminar is a great way to introduce coaching to your organization.

Structure: Seminar can be adapted to various time frames. Also available as one-hour tele-class session.
Presenter: Dr. Joseph Umidi

Seminar Plus

TLC has encouraged its top coach presenters to develop need-meeting seminars that have the double advantage of meeting the felt needs of churches and organizations while including the plus of on-site and after the seminar tele-coaching. Currently seminars are being offered for Marriage/Parenting Fulfillment, Life Purpose, Leadership Development and Marketplace Advantage with several others coming in 2005. Contact the TLC office for referral to those coaches and coach companies who will give you more details.

International Partnerships

TLC recognizes the strength and potential in having overseas partners committed to bringing coaching to their nation's leaders. Partners work with TLC to train and certify coaches, translate TLC materials for their culture, distribute TLC materials, and maintain coaching standards for their nation and culture.

TLC currently has partnerships in Korea, El Salvador, and Colombia and is developing partnerships in Brazil, Canada, Norway, Singapore, Indonesia, Russia, Jamaica, India, and several other nations. Materials are currently available in English, Spanish, and Korean with portions available in the languages of the above mentioned countries.

TLC partner organizations:
- Deeply grasp and live out core coaching values.

- Have a call to developing leaders in their nation or culture.
- Have access to their nation's leaders on a large scale and have a track record of resourcing leaders across organizational/denominational lines.
- Are well-respected for moral and financial integrity and Christian character within their nation and culture.
- Have the resources to translate materials and rework content where needed to fit their cultural context.
- Have a core group of established leaders who desire to become TLC coach trainers for that nation.
- Want to make a long-term commitment to coaching as a leadership training methodology and to relationship with TLC.

For information on existing partnerships in your region or developing a relationship with TLC, contact us at Coaching@regent.edu or call 757-226-4884.

For Credit Training

Graduate Level

Through a partnership between Transformational Leadership Coaching and Regent University, you can take coach training for masters and doctoral level credit in several of Regent's different schools. By taking three to four courses built around the core TLC coach training program, you'll receive nine to twelve credit hours plus a certification as a coach. For more information on the various courses offered and course requirements, contact the TLC registrar at Coaching@Regent.edu or call 757-226-4884.

Undergraduate and non-credit Level

TLC is designing courses for the church based non-credit certificate program at Beacon University in Columbus, Georgia. These courses are offered on line and will be available in the Fall of 2005. The Beacon University Web Address is http://www.beacon.edu/

TLC is in a partnership with Dr. Ralph Neighbor's Touch Glocal Academy which is a world wide on-line training school dedicated to the advancement of the cell church movement. The Touch Glocal address http://www.touchglocal.com

For more information on Transformational Leadership Coaching (TLC), check out our web site at http://www.transformationalcoaching.com/index.htm, or contact our office via email at Coaching@Regent.edu or call 757-226-4884.

TLC Relationship to the International Coach Federation

TLC adheres to the following ethical standards established by the industry leader, the International Coach Federation (ICF), in certification of coach programs and individual coaches. As of the publishing of this book, TLC is currently beginning the application process to ICF for Approved Coach Specific Training Hours (ACSTH) certification for our Coach Certification Program. Our desire is to be certified for the 60 Student Learning Hours (SCLH) that are required for an individual to apply to ICF at the Associate Certified Coach (ACC) portfolio level/

(Adapted, with permission from The International Coach Federation: www.coachfederation.org/ethics/code_ethics. asp)

Professional Conduct At Large

1) I will conduct myself in a manner that reflects well on coaching as a profession and I will refrain from doing anything that harms the public's understanding or acceptance of coaching as a profession.

2) I will honor agreements I make in my all of my relationships. I will construct clear agreements with my clients that may include confidentiality, progress reports, and other particulars.

3) I will respect and honor the efforts and contributions of others.

4) I will respect the creative and written work of others in developing my own materials and not misrepresent them as my own.

5) I will use TLC member contact information (email addresses, telephone numbers, etc.) only in the manner and to the extent authorized by TLC.

Professional Conduct with Clients

6) I will accurately identify my level of coaching competence and I will not overstate my qualifications, expertise or experience as a coach.

7) I will ensure that my coaching client understands the nature of coaching and the terms of the coaching agreement between us.

8) I will not intentionally mislead or make false claims about what my client will receive from the coaching process or from me as their coach.

9) I will not give my clients or any prospective clients information or advice I know to be misleading or beyond my competence.

10) I will be alert to noticing when my client is no longer benefiting from our coaching relationship and would be better served by another coach or by another resource and, at that time, I will encourage my client to make that change.

Confidentiality/Privacy

11) I will respect the confidentiality of my client's information, except as otherwise authorized by my client, or as required by law.

12) I will obtain agreement with my clients before releasing their names as clients or references or any other client identifying information.

13) I will obtain agreement with the person being coached before releasing information to another person compensating me.

Conflicts of Interest

14) I will seek to avoid conflicts between my interests and the interests of my clients.

15) Whenever any actual conflict of interest or the potential for a conflict of interest arises, I will openly disclose it and fully discuss with my client how to deal with it in whatever way best serves my client.

16) I will disclose to my client all anticipated compensation from third parties that I may receive for referrals or advice concerning that client.

The TLC Pledge of Ethics

As a professional coach, I acknowledge and agree to honor my ethical obligations to my coaching clients and colleagues and to the public at large. I pledge to comply with TLC Code of Ethics, to treat people with dignity as independent and equal human beings, and to model these standards with those whom I coach. If I breach this Pledge of Ethics or any part of the TLC Code of Ethics, I agree that the TLC in its sole discretion may hold me accountable for so doing. I further agree that my accountability to TLC for any breach may include loss of my TLC credentials.

APPENDIX B

Transformational Leadership Coaching Testimonies

The following quotes were taken from group debriefing sessions after the group had completed a TLC coaching track. They are all from experienced leaders – pastors, church planters, leadership consultants, cell group overseers, seminary professors, business executives and entrepreneurs.

"I've had these values [accountability, authenticity, relationship] for most of my life, but there is a relief to having actually lived them out; to have walked my talk and to feel the integrity of doing it." B.V.

"...it is so valuable to have material that is doable for the common person – it takes work, but it is simple. The exercises do a good job of breaking down a big concept into tangible, practical, bite-size steps... In fact, it's so practical and applicable to life, that people could easily miss how profound and life-changing it is." W.G.

"[Life Focus helped us] get a handle on the fact that we are doing too much for others and not giving our family its due...I think for the first time in our 41 plus years of marriage we will stick to the process and be able to get some more control over our lives." P.W.

"[learning to] ask powerful questions opened up entirely new doors to me. It made me look at people and try to draw answers out of them instead of just telling them – it was revolutionary." (Grad student)

"I am continually running into students and people who want to change life habits. Through a specific class assignment I read about their struggles and their plan for overcoming those struggles and I see that they will probably have little if any success in making the change, because of the method they are using to make the change. But it is the known method – 'I will do this...I will that...In the past I have done this, but this time I will...' Through the use of accountability - the NEW ACCOUNTABILITY, as taught in the formations track, I have been able to make several significant changes that I had previously been unsuccessful in making on my own." (Business School Dean)

"I like the whole idea of feedback, it really adjusts perspective. I wish I had done this earlier in the year. I will use this concept in more areas of my life when it is relevant that I know how things are really going (vs. thinking I know how things are going). When done well (right questions, right attitude), everyone benefits. My kids feel that they can speak about more than they could before. The lines of communication are more open. ... Thank you for changing my life. My family (wife and kids), school work, perspective and even my goals are the better for having gone through this process. Thank you." P.H.

"Prior to being in TLC I've never really had a peer coach or a coach. One of the things I've picked up is the incredible value of this..." (JN, fortune 500 VP)

"This had been life changing – its not that there has been a whole lot of new knowledge for me, but the whole experience has been like a real-time case study. [TLC training] doesn't just add a couple of tools, it spreads out into all the other tools I already had and adds another dimension to them." (Executive)

"I've probably gotten more out of this class than 98% of my other ones." (Grad student)

"I discovered the need to always be coached...That was a watershed for me...I don't want to ever stop being coached." (Grad student)

"I can't believe the way my husband engages me as a result of [TLC training]...he asks great questions." (Corporate executive)

"The whole potential of this for developing leaders just boggles my mind." (Consultant)

"This whole thing has opened my eyes to the deeper needs of people..." (Entrepreneur)

"Even though I went out and got a degree in violence prevention, through the TLC process I've seen that the real violence that needed to be eradicated was in me..." (Grad student)

"This has put words to a lot of what God has done in my life over the last ten years – and put feet to it." (Educator)

"The coaching method of learning puts the typical seminary educational method to shame. The coaching track has the advantage of being very focused, but I feel like I am

coming away with more practical knowledge than any other class." (Grad student)

"I was extremely skeptical [about working with an unfamiliar peer]...but I believe I grew more as a person by working with someone who didn't know me... It began to imbue me with the confidence to more aggressively pursue strong, spiritual, intimate relationship with other men, which doesn't happen in my culture." (African-American Consultant)

"The process I went through was more important to me then whether I got certified or not..." E.B.

"I brag about you all the time to my friends. I've been through counseling and all kinds of training in business and in church, but I've never had anything like this before, that combines the business world and the church and what is going on inside me...I'm just growing so much." (Entrepreneur, owner of 5 different companies)

"A pastor I'm coaching through life focus told me today that as part of his assignment he was coaching a member of his church from the business community (a banker who oversee 55 employees) through some of the life focus exercises. In their final appointment, the man made a comment about how much he cares for the people under him, wants to look out for them and help them in their careers and personal lives. The coach validated that in him, and highlighted how this businessman was really thinking like a shepherd for his employees in the marketplace. That touched something significant in this man, and he asked the coach if he would continue to meet with him regularly to help him flesh out what God would have for him to do in his job. This was the first person this coach had ever coached." J.E.

"Because the relational process [with the peer coach] is so intentional...within a short time we touched more areas in depth than I have with any of the other pastors I oversee." (Apostolic Leader after 7 weeks in TLC training)

"My productivity has gone up to a level it hasn't been at for 20 years...because I've focused on the goals I need to be working on." (Consultant)

"Sometimes I wonder if I'm making progress, but then I look back to where I was at 5 months ago and think, man, I've grown more in the last 5 months than in the previous 5 years." (Pastor)

"I have been in management with my law enforcement agency for almost 16 years and this has been one of the most successful tools I've encountered." (Executive)

"I've never come across anything like [TLC training]...Some other types of training programs cover these principles, but where else do you get to sit down and talk one-on-one with a coach on the phone?...This is having an immediate impact on my life and ministry – talk about getting a bang for the buck!" D.M.

"The SMART goal concept – I had taught it, I had just never done it." (Executive)

"This program is far beyond the [other coach training] I had. It isn't just good material, it's also well organized and will make it easy for me to do what I set out to do from the beginning: train lay leaders to become coaches without my having to reinvent the wheel for training purposes." (Pastoral Leader)

"The most significant learning experience has been developing authentic relationships with another person. Being accountable to someone else has showed me how important this is for assisting someone in reaching their goals and purpose in life. This whole experience made me feel lighter because I no longer felt I had to hide things. I guess the word is liberation." (Non-profit leader)

"My other coach training before TLC was not fundamentally an experiential learning process. It was more informational...in terms of things that personally impact you, that because they touched you then you can turn right around and do it with others...no, it was mostly head knowledge." (Manager)

"You bring some things [at TLC] in terms of professionally developed curriculum that nothing else I've seen comes close to." (Executive)

"Things that used to take twice as long to get through, because I would only communicate in my own gifting style, I now speak the other person's language and get through those communications right away!" L.D.

"In the future, people who are not coaches will not be promoted." Jack Welch (Longtime GE CEO)

"...it is so valuable to have material that is doable for the common person — it takes work, but it is simple. The exercises do a good job of breaking down a big concept into tangible, practical, bite size steps that anyone can do. In fact, it's so practical and applicable to life, that people could easily miss how profound and life changing it is." (Educator)

"I recommend TLC highly. Although I have only one other coach training program to compare it to, I think TLC is head and shoulders more effective and professional. The curriculum is much more interesting, user friendly and organized than that of the other nationally recognized program I took before, the trainer is authentic, there is no "tag team" approach to training, peer coaching is used much more effectively and is integral to the experience, role play in person is very effective, and the tools to implement the practice of coaching are outstanding. TLC is interested in promoting the practice of Christian coaching for the sake of the kingdom - not just in creating more money-making opportunities." (Church Leader)

"Because of her own life experiences my coach brings incredible insight to her role as a wellness and lifestyle coach. She brought me from drinking 8-10 diet cokes and 4-6 cups of coffee a day to someone who now regularly only drinks water (and lots of it) and I enjoy doing it. Beyond just making dietary changes (which I really needed) she has helped me to find balance and meaning in my life. She has helped me prioritize what is really important to me. A great listener and coach she has helped me to make significant progress in strengthening relationships with people, especially with my wife and children! I am truly gratefully for the changes she has helped me make in my life and I strongly recommend her." (Consultant referring to his TLC coach)

"Have you noticed that people are around here in the office are different? They really listen to you now!" (A staff member responding to the leader of his pastoral team, following two weeks of TLC coach training.)

"Honey, what's happened to you? You've really changed!" (A trainee's wife to her husband only 2 weeks into the training, Canada)

"When I started this coaching program, I thought of it as routine, just another thing to do for my job...but now that I've seen the power of it...if I had a coach like you when I was 20 or 30, my life would be so different, so I want to be a coach and do this for other people." (Korea)

"This is world class – this is state of the art! [TLC] is going to rapidly advance leadership development." (COO of an international non-profit)

"This is really rattling my world!" (District superintendent)

"I'm on fire! This is really helping me, and I can't thank you enough." (Manager)

"This material is immediately transferable and usable. Given opportunities to try out the coaching technique in the peer/coach context is very helpful. Being able to turn the learning experience over to someone else is immediately applicable. The coaching values are universal and stand true for everyone and that makes it immediately transferable." (Canadian Educator)

"The greatest thing I'm learning from this is how to work at change while keeping others responsible...After 22 years of pastoral experience giving people advice and providing answers, this is a whole different way of working with people...[and] I've gotten a taste now of what it can do." (Apostolic Leader)

"That workshop was like a landmine going off in our leadership — in a good way. It blew such a hole in our paradigm everybody is looking around and saying, 'Gosh, we've got to fill that hole!" (Denominational Executive)

"I looked at different coach training programs pretty extensively when I was researching this...and there is nothing out there that had this kind of detail on paper... This is top of the line, quality stuff. I wish we could start a church based around this." (Youth Pastor)

"I personally researched everything that I know with my staff world wide. I read more than 100 books about coaching, including Japanese coaching books, and contacted all the major coach training companies at ICF/IAC. I went to all the coaching workshops/conferences in Korea with my staff, including Samsung Co, Covey, Coaching U, etc. TLC is THE best for me. I am 100% committed to the TLC movement, not only because of the excellent process/content, but also the fruits of powerful transformation in lives.

This is my reality. I taught more than 40,000 pastors and leaders in the last 5 years. I believe that less than 10% experienced change. One year later, maybe one to three percent had experienced on-going transformation. But through [TLC coaching], more than 90% of those I work with experience transformation.

Before, I personally hated one-to-one stuff, but I loved a BIG show (big conferences and seminars). Now I am becoming much wiser after many pains, life lessons and teachable moments. I like TLC more than any other coaching program because it offers:

- *Christian worldview and integration with professional coaching resources.*
- *#1 strategy for NCD for empowering leadership.*
- *Outstanding academically. Doctoral/Masters credits available through Regent.*
- *TLC will have ICF credential capability.*
- *I think, there is only one (world class) Christian professional coaching process as far as I know...*

My wife now spends more time in coaching than any other hobby, job, or responsibility because she has experienced its power to transform her clients. It is very hard for me to stop her now and myself too." (President, NCD Korea)

Transformational Coaching Endorsements

"Transformational Coaching not only instructs the reader about what [coaching] is and shows us what it looks like but compellingly invites us all to become transformational coaches ourselves. What Joseph has to say rings with authenticity because he has gone to a deeper place to discover deeper answers."

(Luis Bush, International Facilitator,
Transform World)

"Joseph Umidi has distinguished himself around the world as a compassionate and capable expert in the field of coaching. We are honored to have his coaching pastor's course as a part of the Touch Glocal Training Center modules. Be sure you have a highlighter as you read this book! There is much to be reviewed after the first reading."

(Ralph Neighbour,
President, Touch Glocal)

"I highly recommend Transformational Coaching to anyone serious about making life count [in the ministry and the marketplace]."

(Larry Kreider, International Director,
Dove Christian International)

"Dr. Joseph Umidi has not only written a concise treatise on the subject of coaching, he has lived the principles he shares. I know first hand because he has greatly impacted my own life as a coach, mentor and apostolic leader. As you read <u>Transformational Coaching</u>, *you will be transformed in your coaching process and grow in your effectiveness as an influencer."*

(B. Courtney McBath, D. Min., Senior Founding Pastor, Calvary Revival Church)

"The Lord says over you Joseph, you will raise up a company of Josephs...you are going to mentor (coach) in leadership, in character, in ethics, in worship, this company of millionaires...and the Lord says write, write, write, write..."

(Cindy Jacobs, January 20, 2005)

Printed in the United States
95442LV00003B/187-219/A